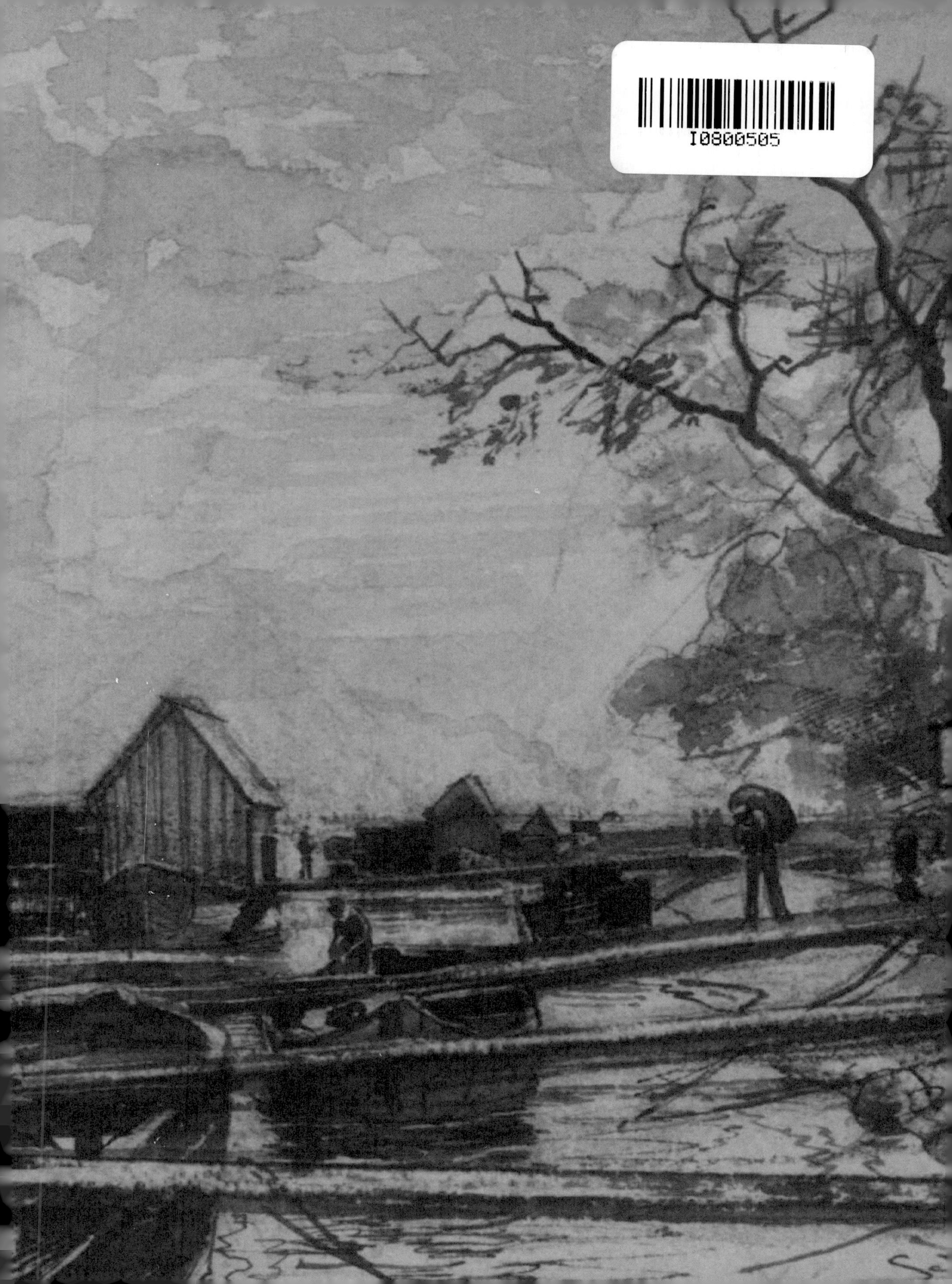

EMIL JAKOB SCHINDLER

Poetic Realism

Agnes Husslein-Arco

Foreword

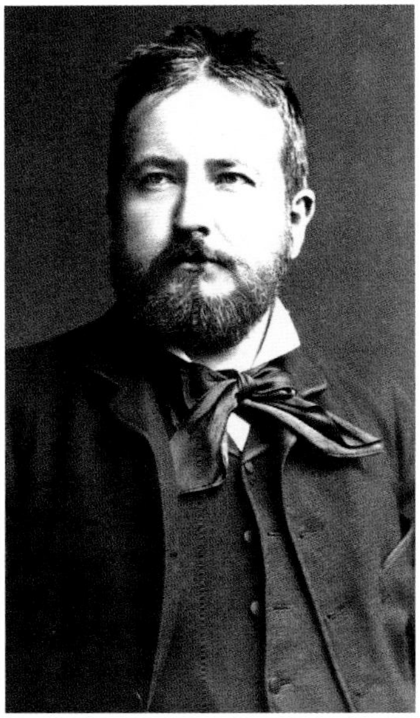

Fig. 1.
Otto Schmidt
Emil Jakob Schindler, c. 1875
ÖNB (Austrian National Library), Picture Archive, Vienna

The Belvedere's decision to show *Emil Jakob Schindler* in the series *Masterpieces in Focus* fulfils a desideratum that has been pending for a long time. It is now 70 years since Schindler's last solo presentation in a museum, and that too was organized by the Belvedere, on the occasion of his 100th anniversary. This year, Schindler, who was born in 1842, celebrates his 170th anniversary.

Schindler's work marks a radical change from the opulent art of the Ringstraßen era of an artist like Hans Makart towards a new view of nature. While Makart was painting *The Entry of Charles V into Antwerp*, his friend Schindler, who had found refuge with Makart during the cold winter months, dedicated himself to the painting *Moonrise in the Prater Meadows*. Rather than documenting the landscape realistically, he interpreted it by poetic transfiguration. In his painting he strove to capture the reconciliation of nature with the works of man, the harmony with nature and its rhythm.

Schindler himself chose the term *Poetic Realism* for his art, which was already used to describe a literary style of writings, for example, by Gottfried Keller, Theodor Storm, Wilhelm Raabe, Jeremias Gotthelf or Marie von Ebner-Eschenbach. Like Schindler, these writers were concerned with the observation of the sensually experiencable world in order to address universal questions of existence. As a result, their literature deals with the "relationship and the integration of the individual into the necessity of life, the environment [...] with deep and benevolent insight" and faces "the earthly conditions of existence rather critically, yet ultimately confidently, instead of embellishing them."

Schindler's generation renewed landscape painting, in which the simple landscape, the poetic moment, the special atmosphere of the everyday, be it a vegetable garden or the Danube meadows, are described and interpreted. Here the 1873 Vienna World Exhibition and the reception of the Barbizon School as well as the Viennese painting tradition of a Ferdinand Georg Waldmüller have left traces. Yet in Schindler's case it is not a withdrawal from the world in Rousseau's sense, who regards civilization as a disaster: thus manmade features, for example steamships and water mills, are interwoven in harmony with nature.

Even without a chair at an academy, Schindler influenced numerous artists, for example Carl Moll, Olga Wisinger-Florian, Marie Egner and Theodor von Hörmann. He conveyed new viewpoints to his students, which ultimately also facilitated the development towards an impressionistic outlook. The artist's new approach to landscape was formative for the painting of his time, while the main representatives of landscape painting, such as Rudolf Ribarz, Eugen Jettel or Carl Russ, stayed abroad for a long time and could thus not exert a decisive influence in Vienna. After Schindler's death, it was above all Carl Moll who represented Schindler's artistic oeuvre to the outside world by editing a publication on his

teacher and prompting and organizing exhibitions. Moll, who was already close to Schindler and his family during Schindler's lifetime, became his promoter and the administrator of his legacy after his death.
The exhibition *Emil Jakob Schindler – Poetic Realism* allows the visitor to go on a voyage of discovery through the eyes of a 19th century artist and to trace his experience of the natural world. Schindler's sensitive painting is still impressive today. The term nature protection had not yet been coined at the time. However, Schindler critically commented in his writings on the effects of industrialization, and his paintings convey a touchingly intimate relationship with nature.
At this point, I would like to thank Alexander Klee, the curator of this exhibition, for his passionate commitment and his convincing selection of works, as well as Markus Fellinger, who made an important contribution to the realization of this project.
My special thanks go to the authors who have written interesting contributions with profound expertise and enthusiasm – because this publication aims to draw attention to Emil Jakob Schindler's central significance for the beginning Austrian Modernism and to grant the artist his deserved position in art history.
Finally, I would like to cordially thank all the public and private loan givers for so generously entrusting us with their loans.

1 Carl Moll, *Mein Leben*, typescript, 1930, Wienbibliothek im Rathaus (Vienna City Library in the Vienna City Hall), Vienna, pp. 30f.
2 Gero von Wilpert, *Sachwörterbuch der Literatur*, 5th ed. Stuttgart 1969, p. 618.

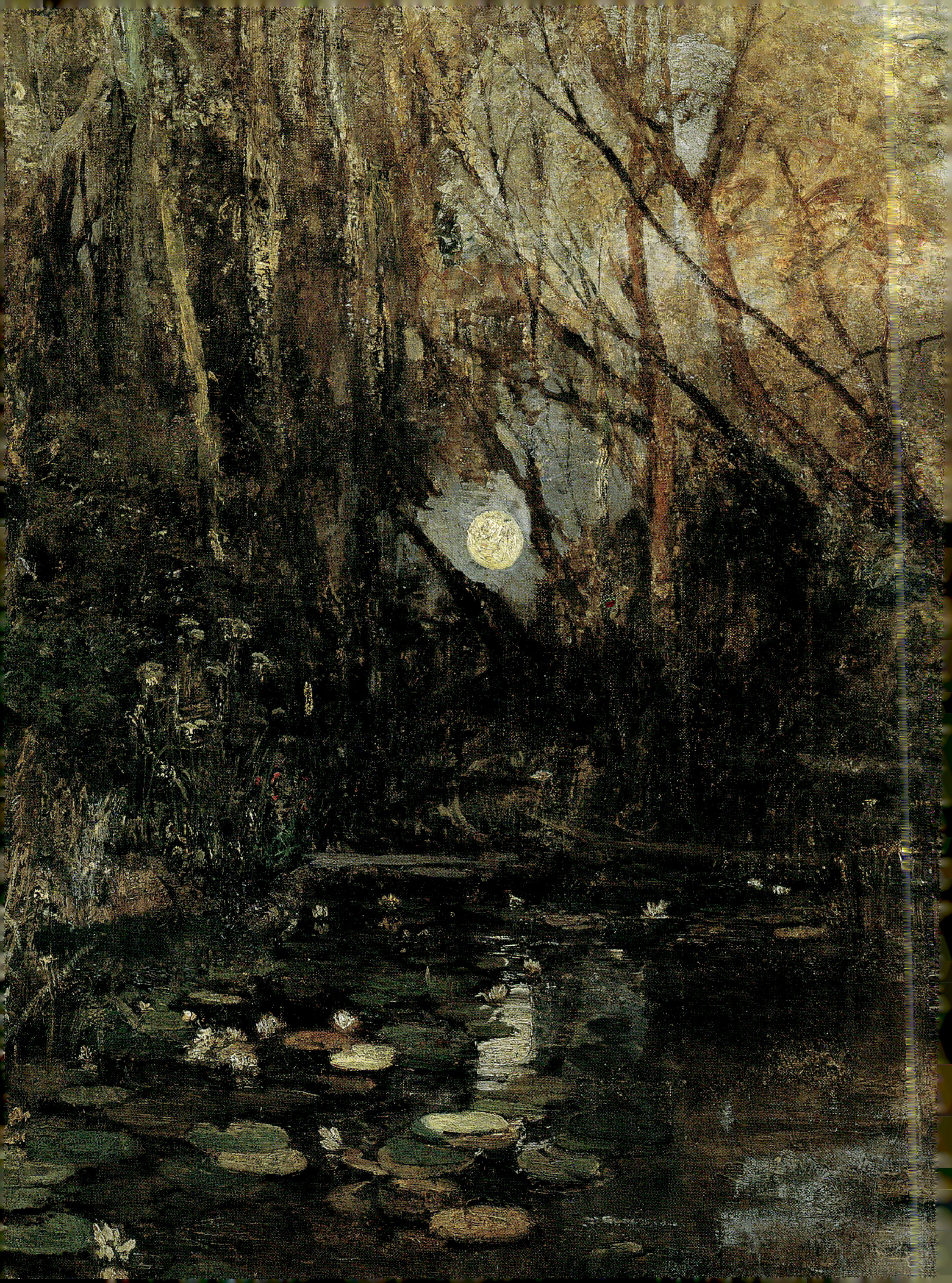

Alexander Klee

Paysage Intime – Atmosphere – Poetic Realism

Emil Jakob Schindler's understanding of landscape had a powerful influence on many younger Austrian landscape painters. He can be regarded as one of the main representatives of landscape painting in the second half of the 19th century – subsumed under the term Austrian "Atmospheric Impressionism". This article will examine the characteristics that distinguish Schindler as a typical representative of this genre and define it, as well as discussing his artistic development in its historical context and the art-historical formation of the concepts.

Schindler deliberately selected a landscape painter as his teacher when he chose Albert Zimmermann, who was called to the Viennese Academy in 1860.[1] Zimmermann had studied in Leipzig and Munich and afterwards had founded his own school for landscape painting in Munich. In 1857 he was called to the Academy of Milan by the Austrian government; in 1860, after Milan had fallen to the Kingdom of Sardinia-Piedmont in 1859, he followed a call to the Viennese Academy. In Vienna he replaced Franz Steinfeld as professor of landscape painting, who had lost his attraction for younger students.[2] By contrast, Zimmermann was at the height of his creative work when he was called to Vienna. Students such as Robert Russ, Eugen Jettel, Rudolf Ribarz and László Paál gathered around him. Similar to his predecessor Steinfeld, Zimmermann took his students on several-week study trips in the summer, which often took him to Salzburg, Berchtesgaden or Hintersee.[3] Here, the painters not only had the chance to study from nature but they could also discuss art developments with numerous colleagues from Vienna and Munich who worked there, for example about the Barbizon School, which was received in Munich as early as in the 1850s. Eduard von Schleich had made the start and was followed by Adolf Lier, Adolf Stäbli, Otto Frölicher and Anton Teichlein.[4] Later Teichlein's essays analyzed the art of the Barbizon School, for example Théodore Rousseau.

Zimmermann's heroic landscapes such as *Sunset in the High Mountains* (fig. 2) show references to Carl Rottmann, whose landscapes capture nature from the aspect of its geological development – less as a realistic rendition of elements of nature, but rather as naturalistic portrayals of landscapes.[5] The painting of Alpine landscapes – similar to seascapes – conveys God's infinity as symbol of nature in its immense size and power.[6] In the knowledge of nature and its true appearance, but also in the awareness of its natural-science contexts, landscape fits in as a poetic invention. Through its raised vantage point and the exact characterization of the landscape of the Alpine foothills, Schindler's *Old Mill at the Lake Chiemsee* (p. 71) suggests Carl Rottmann as a model.[7] Similar to Schindler's painting, his landscape in the foothills of the Alps *Staufen – Wals Heath*[8] (fig. 3) was seen from an elevated vantage point. In Schindler, small changes in the emphasis of the

Fig.1.
Emil Jakob Schindler
Moonrise in the Prater Meadows
(Mondaufgang in der Praterau), detail,
c. 1877/78
Belvedere, Vienna

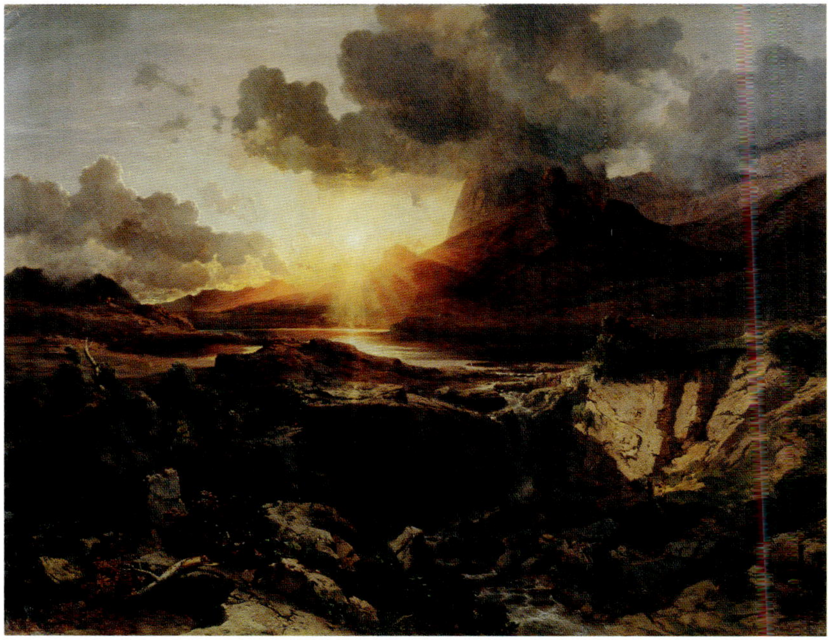

Fig.2.
Albert Zimmermann
Sunset in the High Mountains
(Sonnenuntergang im Hochgebirge), 1858
Belvedere, Vienna

composition suggest a transformed relationship to landscape, while Rottmann focuses his pictorial statement on the grandeur of the impression of nature and the tranquility of the untouched landscape.

Schindler, to the contrary, moves the lofty mountains to the right of the picture and breaks them compositionally by a young sapling in the foreground, which also rises above them. Underneath the sapling, the brook rushes leftwards to the mill, while down in the valley farmers are making hay. The detailed foreground gives evidence of a further decisive difference suggesting Schindler's appreciation of the close-up landscape views by Ferdinand Georg Waldmüller.[9] The arrangement of the landscape is a further aspect in this sense: it seems to open up, loses itself in the distance, while Zimmermann's landscape, like Rottmann's, takes the viewer to the monumental impression of the mountain realm. Schindler's transformation towards a more intimate view of landscape – he later adopted an ironic distance to the subject of mountain painting in his writings of 1879 – seems to be foreshadowed here.[10] Even though Schindler's work is marked by flooded mill weirs or foaming waves on the coast, unlike his teacher Zimmermann, he does not create heroic landscapes out of them.

Towards the end of the 1860s, works of the Barbizon School gradually reached Vienna via the art trade.[11] The collection of municipal architect Bösch with landscapes by Daubigny, Rousseau, Dupré and animal representations by Jacque and Troyon was on show in December 1868 in the Viennese Künstlerhaus (House of Artists),[12] as occasionally from 1869 were works for example by Troyon in the exhibitions of the Österreichische Kunstverein (Austrian Art Association). The collection of St. Stephen's music director, Peyer, also included French artists.[13] In April 1869 Friedrich Jakob Gsell's collection was put up for auction – it comprised landscapes by Jules Breton (1), Léon-Victor Dupré (1), Johan Barthold Jongkind (1), Jean-François Millet (2), Théodore Rousseau (2), Emile Diaz,

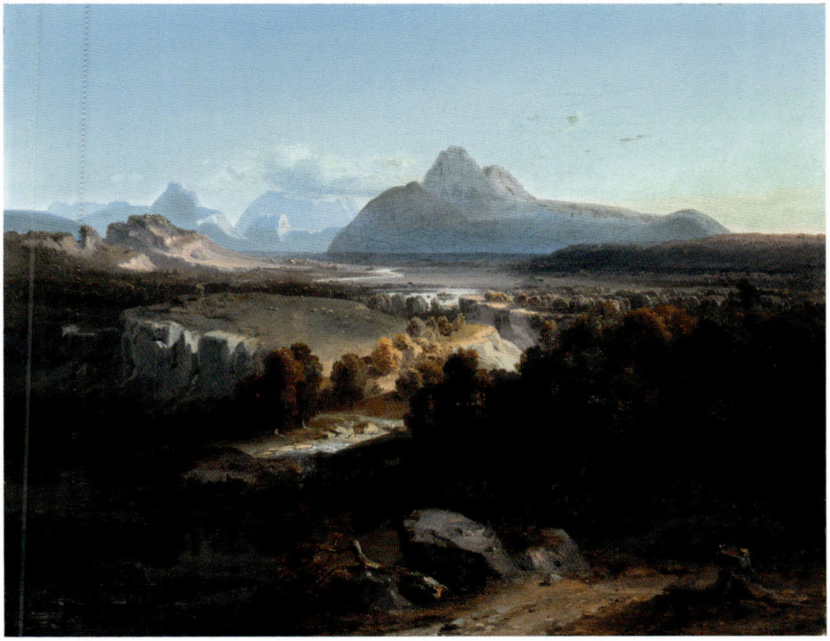

Fig.3.
Carl Rottmann
Staufen – Wals Heath
(Staufen – Walser Heide), 1833
Kunsthalle zu Kiel

a student of Rousseau (3), a large number of pictures (20) and almost the same number of drawings by Constant Troyon, but also works by Eugen Jettel (3) and Robert Russ (1). Even at this time, on the occasion of the annual exhibition in the Viennese Künstlerhaus, Schindler, Jettel, Russ and Ribarz were described as "decided followers of the French *Paysage intime*."[14]

Further works by Corot (4), Courbet (7), Daubigny (2), Diaz (5), Dupré, Harpignies (3), Jacque (4), Manet (2), Rousseau (1) and Troyon (4) were on show at the First International Art Exhibition in Munich from July to October 1869, while two landscapes by Troyon and one by Diaz came from the H. Lustig collection[15] in Vienna. At this time in Munich the art of the Barbizon School had been known for quite a while. For the young Viennese students, however, the exhibition provided the chance to analyze it, even though they might have already encountered some of the works. Yet this presentation could not convey the impression of a new school of landscape painting, since the number of works of the Barbizon School was too small, their selection was not formative. In return, the impressive painting *The Stonebreakers* by Courbet was on show. In comparison, the young Viennese of the Zimmermann class, such as Jettel (2), Ribarz (3), Russ (3) and Schindler (2[16]), were well represented. For them, this prominent exhibition was very significant so that presumably they could study in Munich besides the works of the Barbizon School also those of the Hague School[17], which was also exhibited. The brothers Andreas and Oswald Achenbach were also very popular and present; they were represented in almost every exhibition and earned Schindler's admiration.

At the 1873 World Exhibition in Vienna, France was represented with the biggest art selection – with 657 pictures by 317 artists. The paintings included Jean-Baptiste Camille Corot (11), Charles-François Daubigny (4), Narcisse Díaz de la Peña (6), Jules Dupré (1), Henri Harpignies (2), Jean-François Millet (2),

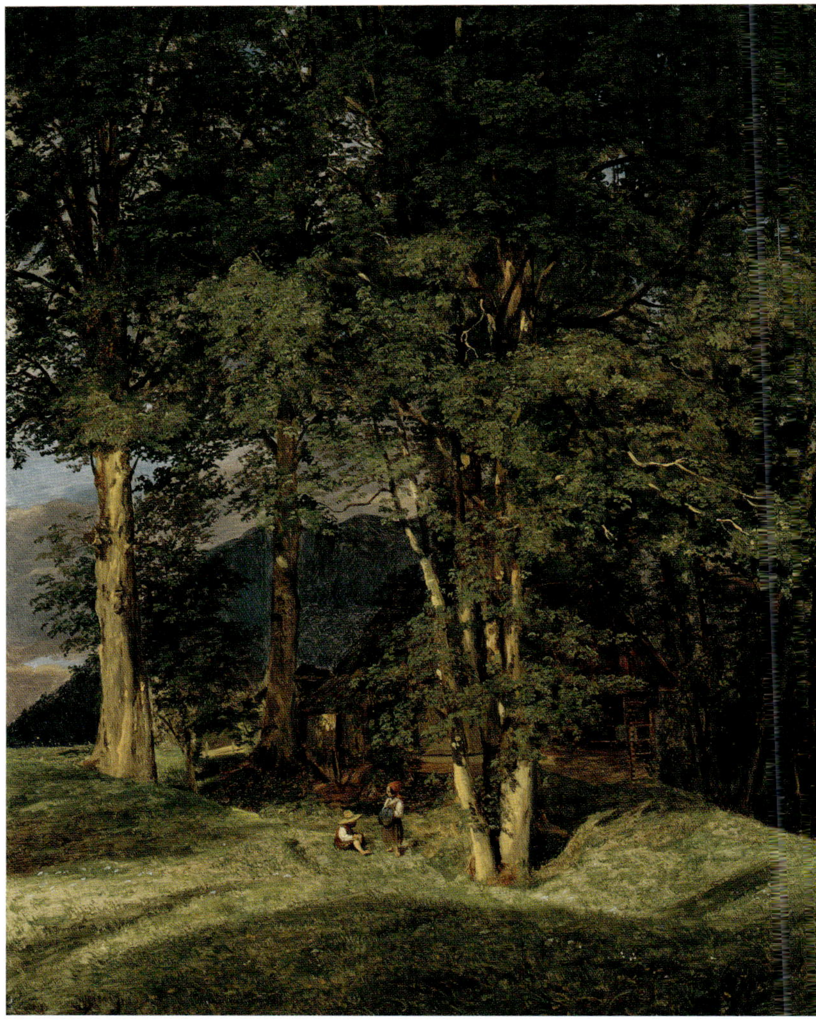

Fig.4.
Ferdinand Georg Waldmüller
Sycamore Trees near Ischl
(Ahornbäume bei Ischl), 1831
Belvedere, Vienna

Théodore Rousseau (9), Constant Troyon (12) and an entire show with works by Gustave Courbet in the Österreichische Kunstverein. It was possible for anyone interested in art to get an impression of the Barbizon School in this exhibition and specifically to analyze these trends. However, a formative influence could not be deduced, because the positions of official French art were still too strongly represented so that the Impressionists were not considered.[18] By contrast, new trends, for example Eugen Jettel (3), Rudolf Ribarz (3) and Emil Jakob Schindler (4[19]), were shown in the Austrian section. Yet the impression of the Barbizon School was so great that Jettel remained in Paris from 1875 to 1897 and Ribarz from 1876 to 1892. Ribarz searched for and made contact with the artists of the Hague School, with whom he exhibited in 1875 and 1876. Schindler visited Holland with Tina Blau in 1875, where he analyzed the Dutch landscape and the landscape painting of the Hague School. Most artists of the Hague School were only a little older than their Austrian colleagues so that contact with artists aiming at similar targets was obvious. By contrast, the great role models of the Barbizon School were already old at this point in time or, like Corot, Millet, Rousseau and

Troyon, had died. Only in 1881 did Schindler go to Paris, in order to see French art and above all the works of the Barbizon School. However, he returned disappointed with artistic life in Paris, where meanwhile the new direction of Impressionism had gained acceptance.[20]

The new painterly attitude of the Barbizon painters, their open brushstroke and the reevaluation of the sketch-like elements impressed Schindler and his colleagues.[21] Most of all the selection of the motif, but also the simple landscape of the *Paysage intime* met with the approval of the young Austrians such as Schindler. In contrast to the heroic landscape of his teacher Zimmermann, Schindler's landscapes allow the experience of seemingly familiar landscape details instead of wide views. Schindler traces the essential aspects of nature in these works. The unpretentious motif found in nature becomes the dominant feature in the picture. The studies are attributed a particular significance, they become authentic evidence of experienced nature.[22] Although Schindler finally composed his large-format works in the studio, acquisitions of sketches from his studio and his annoyance[23] about them testify to the great esteem and the increased significance of these works that were created directly from nature. The particularity of the painterly task as the individual mark of the artist increasingly came to the fore. The turn away from the ideal landscape or the heroic landscape and the orientation towards the simple landscape motif resulted in an interpretation of landscape as observed nature. The Barbizon painters were not interested in a detailed rendition of the section of the landscape. Rather they aimed to capture characteristic landscape situations that trigger associations of familiar landscapes in the viewer. Thus the Barbizon School's attitude towards landscape could be interpreted as experienced nature.

Schindler turned away from the wide-open prospects and to the details such as the rough screens and the wooden bridges leading over the small watercourses in the Prater meadows to the Kaisermühlen (p. 76), the boats on the Danube (p. 77) or the views from the Krieau (p. 72). Small-format works predominate, documenting the new relationship to the landscape through their sketch-like nature and seeming transience. This spontaneity and their small size differentiate Schindler's landscapes from the "true to reality" details by Waldmüller. Waldmüller, however, pushes "realism" so far that the paintings often seem to have been cut at the edges (fig. 4), while Schindler paints composed landscapes that approach the character of the landscape and look for its beauty in the detail. The everyday-familiar, such as the ruts of the carts in the clayey earth, is elevated into something special. Schindler does not imitate the lighting or the atmosphere in the Barbizon School landscape pictures, he rather transfers his own home environment into a new pictorial language – without national pathos or heroic-dramatic mountain landscapes. At the same time, he observes its ongoing change, which for example is obvious in the regulation of the Danube, and he documents it in oil sketches such as *Prater Study on the Deforestation for the Regulation of the Danube*[24]. Here, too, there are connections both to the Barbizon School and the Hague School. Thus in 1852, when he met Napoleon III, Théodore Rousseau expressed his concern about the beginnings of the deforestation of Fontainebleau forest. As a result 634 hectares of the forest were declared a *première réserve artistique*, a protection zone to be maintained in its original state.[25] Almost at the same time of the regulation of the Danube, in 1872 the *Nieuwe Waterweg* was built in Holland to take large steamships to Rotterdam, and in 1876 the North

Sea Canal was dug as direct connection from Amsterdam to the North Sea. Even in Holland, the heralds of industrialization became invisible in the form of steel bridges, railway lines or telegraph poles, which with few exceptions are left out, practically rejected or even fought against in landscape painting.[26] On the other hand, the courses of roads are endowed with a graphic beauty, and rusty paths reveal the tones of the layers of the earth, influencing with their different geological conditions the landscape's color. Thus Schindler also regarded the human being as the destroyer of the earth's natural beauty,[27] driving forward the industrialization and the urbanization of the surroundings of Vienna for example. "Certainly, nature is the most sacred thing that must bring a person directly to a certain religion, if he does not forcibly want to act against his conviction and so make himself unhappy; but I believe that I am more sensitive than many others, and this was the reason that destined me to become a painter."[28] Schindler regards himself as chronicler documenting the disintegrating community between man and nature, when he writes: "For me, everything in nature has to tell a story and everything does tell it, only the row of villas does not tell anything any longer, since in the shortest time this form of architecture in the greenery will be the only opposition we will be able to find, because the fanciful farmhouse, the mill the smithy will shortly cease to exist. So it is not only an easy and rewarding, but also a very important task to hand down these poetic remains, insofar as they are still at our disposal, in a true reproduction for posterity."[29] For Schindler, painting thus also meant an almost philosophical examination of metaphysics, i.e. the determination of that which has being against the backdrop of natural-science explanations and the rational-utilitarian application of new scientific findings. Schindler writes: "The good spirit [God] limited him [the human being] his mind in incredibly narrow confines and so he became the poor devil's friend, *homo sapicus* [sic! *sapiens*]. They now designate this good spirit with a word comprising not more than four letters in all languages. With the word that embraces everything in itself that they do not embrace, they are designating the one who knows everything or all that they would like to know themselves. They call Him 'God', they cling to Him, they tell Him marvelously much and they are convinced that He might be the master of the masters, yet that He had nothing else to do than being concerned about their wishes, their well-being and sorrows, but also about their future, so-to-say, about their life-long pension in all eternity [...] This after all implies the unconscious feeling of our globe swaying and floating in space and the desire for a nail that might yet fix it somewhere. Incidentally, this nail would be God, whom every people, even every individual establishes according to their own convenience."[30]

Schindler is aware of the dilemma that the painter's senses are no longer congruent with the reality of natural science and its orientation. Yet at the same time he recognizes the chance to poetically transfer the nature that reveals itself to him into pictorial works. The atmosphere replaces the view of the world that is disintegrating into individual, natural-science phenomena. He thus understands his atmosphere pictures metaphysically, as an outlook on the world and a definition of existence.[31] Schindler accordingly states: "Each work of art is something independent, a creation, and dependent on nature only insofar as it is impossible for the human spirit to go beyond the forms and appearances of nature, for the same reason, for example, as it will always and forever be impossible for the body to leave the atmosphere of the earth [...] May the artist direct his

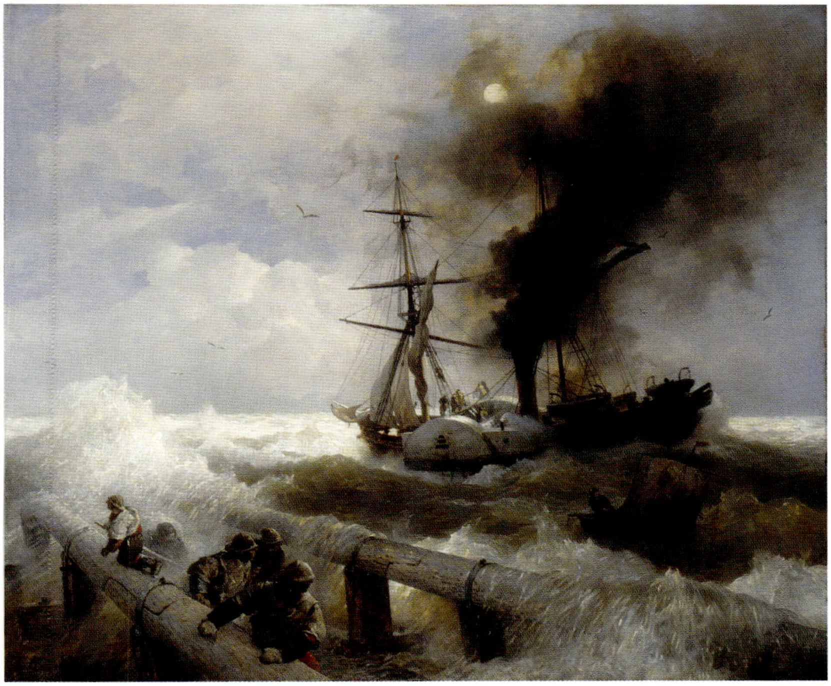

Fig.5.
ANDREAS ACHENBACH
Storm at Sea
(Seesturm), 1890
StadtMuseum Bonn

fantasy to all sorts of starry worlds, he can only design through the elements that he knows. So it is only the elements that can design. The young artist has to form within the given space, he has to go to the most extreme border in science and the arts, yes, he has to put his wishes even beyond it; but above all he has to ask himself: what is art? Visual [art] is the detachment of the appearance, the idea, the concept from that which has material being, in other words. He has to tell himself that from now on he no longer has to be a painter but an artist. He has to look for parallels of his own art in all the other arts, even in the sciences. He has to tell himself, while science dissects, analyses, he will make use of the natural forces, as far as they wish to allow themselves to be used. Art, however, forms, creates, and is thus on one level higher."[32]

In his article on Théodore Rousseau published as early as in 1868, Anton Teichlein refers to the significance of the correct, truthful empathy with nature which is necessary to produce a *Paysage intime*. A main precondition in this context is the "expression of a relationship of the human soul to nature comparable only to the intimate familiarity, the secrecy and the unconditional devotion of sincere friendship and true love."[33] While the meaning of the German word *intim* [Engl. intimate] describes the desirable relationship to nature. In this respect Schindler, too, admires Rousseau, who achieved for him the highest possible degree of truth of nature.[34]

Schindler associates the tonal general impression, the variation of the pictures in gray or brown shades[35] with the Barbizon School[36] as well as with the Hague School.[37] The *valeurs* connect the picture in itself and through their respective atmosphere endow it with a particular characteristic. Unlike the artists of the Barbizon School, who place special emphasis on the quality of the light, Schindler distinguishes the pictorial realization of the atmosphere perceived as sensual, of the air's ether,[38] i.e., from the 1880s he is concerned above all with the ephemeral atmosphere, entailing changes in the weather or the season. He differentiates the light situation, the misty air that wet und humid summer weather brings, a still wet street in the air clarified by rain, boggy paths in the wet and humid November with thawing snow and rainfall or the first green shoots of plants in a still wintery natural world that is just beginning to show signs of the approaching early spring. The artists of the Hague School pursue similar intentions: in their paintings they also depict transitory weather situations such as mist. Corresponding with the contemplative element of the *Paysage intime*, the artists avoid strong colors and mainly use muted hues. Accordingly, the compositions are subordinate to a generally gray tonality merging into brown. This earned the landscape painters the reputation of "gray painters". The restrained tones, however, allow a differentiated variation of the dark-bright color values and the contrasting or the coordination of colors with each other. Thus Schindler appreciates the dust covering everything on a country road: the trees, the ground, the people, animals and the air or the dark grayish-red of the streets in Holland paved with bricks, the silvery-gray band drawn by paths through sand dunes, the paths of the flat Hungarian plain that are covered by black to gray, velvety dust turned to mush by the rain, or the glittering silvery poplars.[39] Hartwig Fischel describes Schindler's *Country Road* as a symphony in gray, just as he describes his *Park Landscape*[40] as a symphony in green. Green, brown and gray are the dominant colors in most of Schindler's paintings. Gray as a mixture between black and white, green as the mixture between the brightest pure color yellow and a blue that tends towards darkness are close to one another as colors of a medium brightness. Green "is also the basis for our color perception, the comparative measurement. Since it is the middle wavelengths that trigger the sensation of green, they are the ones that balance the long-wave (active) and the short-wave (passive) radiation and thus become comparable to the gray (in the field of the achromatic)."[41] Green and gray are closer in this context than green and red. Like gray and carmine, green has a medium level of brightness, though it differs from red in its lesser chromatic intensity. Yet gray represents the totality of colors, their holistic and balanced color impression, since either the pair of complementary colors or three secondary and three tertiary colors or the totality of the purely chromatic colors can bring it about. In consonance with gray, green creates its complement, red, so that in the picture all colors are balanced again.[42] In many of his pictures Schindler gives green the greatest chromatic intensity, accompanied by the blue-gray tones of the sky and earth colors, above all olive and ochre tones. Compared to the French models, the chromatic intensity of the green in interplay with the olive-brown tones and the grayish colors marks the color characteristics of many paintings. Strong color contrasts that appropriate the emotion and the affect are avoided. Yet the atmosphere or mood extending the brief moment into a longer spell, a while, makes the viewer pause. However much Schindler appreciated Andreas Achenbach's works, he avoided his drama (fig. 5), which is opposed to this contemplative aspect of Schindler's works. Even in the unusual studies of the sea surf off Ragusa (p. 99) the drama of the natural forces threatening the human being is missing. The deep vantage point of the viewer conveys the sea's power, but the requisites and figures inherent in a dramatic situation are missing. Schindler's studies correspond to nature observations, the sensed atmosphere, the air heavy with salt and the rocks in

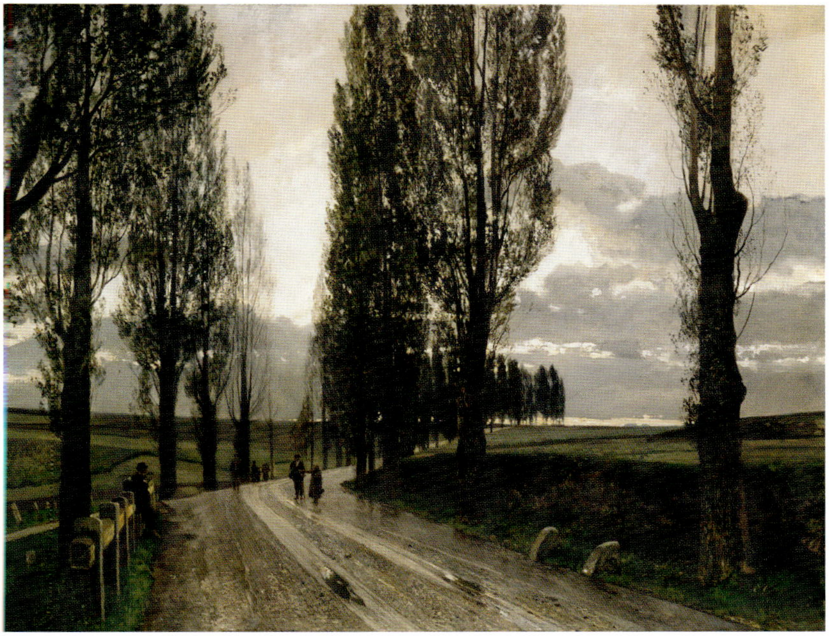

Fig.6.
Emil Jakob Schindler
Poplar-lined Road
after the Thunderstorm
(Pappelallee nach dem Gewitter), 1892
Landesmuseum Niederösterreich, St. Pölten

which the surf breaks. They are closely connected with the illustrations for the chapter "*Die klimatischen Verhältnisse*" (the climatic conditions) in the *Kronprinzenwerk* [i.e. the encyclopedia of the peoples, landscapes and regions of the Austrian-Hungarian monarchy, published from 1885–1902], in which he illustrates the moist Sirocco sea winds in a comparable coastal study.[43] And even his oil sketches (p. 98) are dominated by grayish-blue and brown tones. Schindler's particular interest in the fine nuances of dark and bright shades, in *Valeurmalerei* [i.e. painting in color harmony], is revealed in the study of Thomas Couture's *The Bird Catcher*[44] (fig. 7). The painting is part of Friedrich Jakob Gsell's collection in Vienna, where it was put up for auction in 1872.[45] Thus Schindler was familiar with this painting in its original and he possessed at least a copy of it, which stood for a time in his studio toward the end of the 1880s.[46] The painting has a tonality that Schindler appreciated and which possibly fascinated him. Restrained brown and gray tones dominate the pictorial impression, a break in the clouds briefly opens a view of the sky and lights up the bushes in green. The brightness of the illuminated wall is mutedly reflected in the bird-catcher's shirt, as the muted green of the bushes emerges again in the windowpanes of the house. Schindler often uses a comparable, calculated distribution of light in his works, which might have also interested him in this picture. In his writings, Schindler advises to consider the distribution of blue and green in studies, the main colors in landscape paintings, and like Waldmüller to complete the study gradually from nature.[47]

Yet in his paintings, Schindler did not strive for the exact reproduction of nature that can be found, for example, in Waldmüller. Because: "The closer the art draws to nature, the more it loses itself and finds itself again only with difficulty. It is a still unresolved question how many nature studies an artwork can bear at all. [...] If the student has clearly understood by then that he has to thoroughly

Fig.7.
Thomas Couture
The Bird Catcher (L'oiseleur), 1857
Szépmüvészeti Múzeum
(Museum of Fine Arts), Budapest

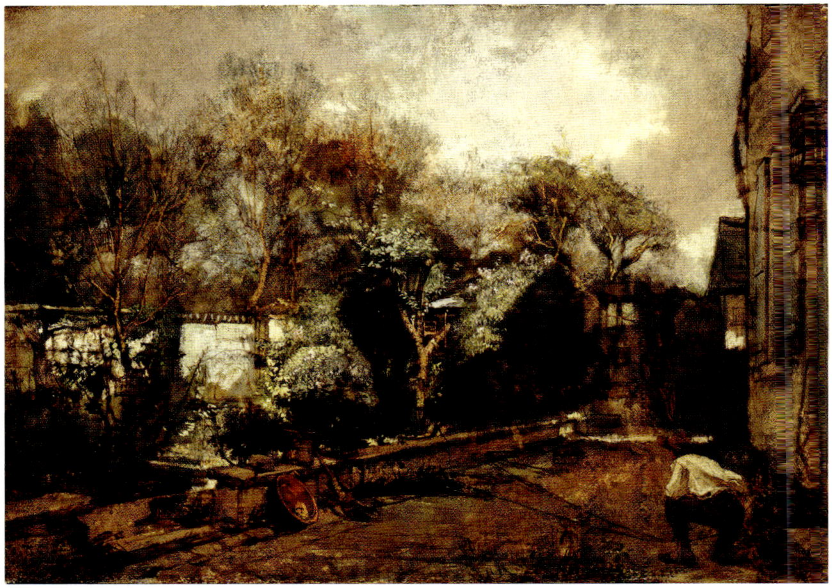

examine nature for it to shine through in the work of art, if he has understood that the artistic truth is not the real but a parallel one, if he has understood that the image is not a reflection but a newly created [...]"[48]
Schindler realized his large paintings in the studio from "plein-air" sketches. He only developed the final composition in the next steps in the studio. He himself described his artistic intention as "poetic realism"[49]. Schindler intended painting to be a poetic recreation and in this respect resembled the Barbizon School.[50] Hartwig Fischel writes of the typical features in Schindler's art: "Schindler's effort was aimed at the 'most perfect expressiveness in the poetic nature parallel'."[51]
With his painting *Pax* (p. 97) a circle closes for Schindler. The Romantic references that were recognizable in his early work *"Waldfräulein's" Birth*[52] (fig. 8), and even there were closely related to the portrayal of nature, come together again in *Pax* to become a symbolist depiction of nature. A monk stands in front of a freshly dug grave in a lonely cemetery. He is lighting another candle as a symbol of life, and the first rays of sunlight are falling through the clouds again, while puddles from the recent rain still cover the path. The cemetery surrounded by steep rocky walls is reminiscent of the *Isle of the Dead* by Arnold Böcklin, whom Schindler much admired.[53] At the same time, *Pax* conveys the connection to nature slowly re-taking possession of manmade monuments. Overgrown, covered in moss, decaying, the cemetery presents itself as an allegory of human transience and the works of man. The rising clouds breaking open and saturated by humidity, the light of the setting sun, the cool breeze, the flickering candlelight, the vertically rising cypresses in contrast to the graves turn Schindler's "atmosphere" into an experience for the viewer. Here, Schindler's particular affinity to watermills is revealed, which, mossy and overgrown, are often in a condition of permanent decay, allegorical of the symbiosis between man and nature. In this respect, the atmosphere represents a timely continuity, the "art activity that does not arise from an immediately excited feeling but from a compound atmosphere," an extended sensation.[54] On the other hand, the empirical sensation that appears

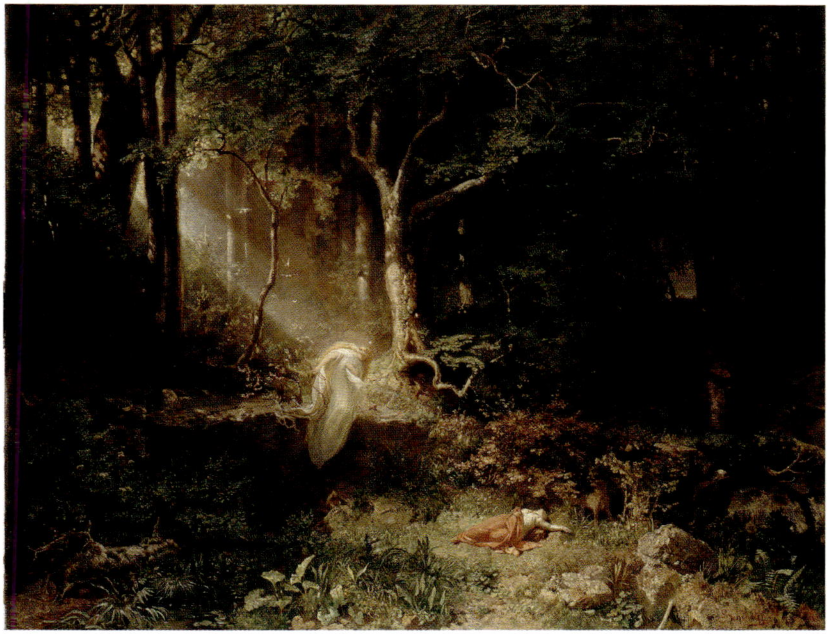

Fig.8.
Emil Jakob Schindler
Waldfräulein's Birth
(after a poem by Joseph Christian von Zedlitz)
(Waldfräuleins Geburt [nach einem Gedicht von Joseph Christian von Zedlitz]), 1868
Gemäldegalerie der Akademie der bildenden Künste Wien (The Paintings Gallery of the Academy of Fine Arts Vienna)

both to the artist and to the sensing viewer is decisive for the difference for example from pointillism, which drew on recent optical findings and pointed to a new form of perception. Schindler's characterization as a painter who romanticized the atmosphere poetically,[55] and the particular significance that *Pax* had for him as a painter, are thus understandable.

The intention of the Barbizon School artists, which eventually resulted in the *Paysage intime*, and Schindler's realization of his poetic realism are linked by various references and refer to the art of early Impressionism. The meaning of the "atmosphere" [in German *Stimmung*] proves here to be a connection while the translation of "atmosphere" into the French term "impression" has led to the unfortunate pleonasm Austrian "Atmospheric Impressionism" [in German *Österreichischer Stimmungsimpressionismus*]. This term, which was introduced as late as in the 1950s,[56] has become standard as a result of the popularity of French Impressionism. Its use detached from art historical contexts may be irritating, and may even be seen as misleading. The constant criticism, however, has revealed its dubiousness as a "label" and resulted in a more detailed examination and characterization of the respective artist's individualities.

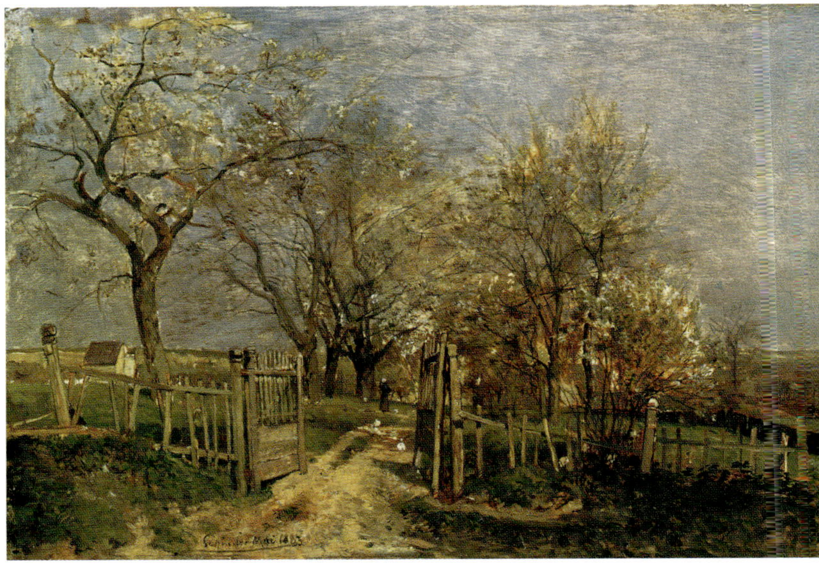

Fig. 9.
Emil Jakob Schindler
Spring in Hacking
(Frühling in Hacking), 1883
Belvedere, Vienna

1 Andrea Winklbauer, "Vom Berg in die Au – Albert Zimmermann und seine Wiener Schüler", in: Gerbert Frodl/Verena Traeger (eds.), *Stimmungsimpressionismus* (exh.-cat. Österreichische Galerie Belvedere, Vienna 2004), Vienna 2004, p. 45.
2 Carl von Vincenti, *Wiener Kunst-Renaissance. Studien und Charakteristiken*, Vienna 1876, pp. 366, 372.
3 Winklbauer 2004, p. 44.
4 Richard Muther, *Geschichte der Malerei. 18. und 19. Jahrhundert*, vol. 3, Leipzig 1909, p. [illegible]9.
5 Above all the *Neun Briefe über Landschaftsmalerei* by Carl Gustav Carus were influential in this connection. Cf. Barbara Eschenburg, "Die historische Landschaft. Überlegungen zu Form und Inhalt der Landschaftsmalerei im späten 18. und frühen 19. Jahrhundert", in: Christoph Heilmann/Erika Rödiger-Diruf (eds.), *Landschaft als Geschichte – Carl Rottmann 1797–1850. Hofmaler König Ludwigs I.* (exh. cat. Kurpfälzisches Museum der Stadt Heidelberg, Heidelberg 1997/98), Munich 1998, pp. 66–74.
6 Eschenburg 1998, p 71.
7 Schindler appreciated Rottmann and devoted a whole chapter to him in his own writings. Elisabeth Edith Kamenicek, *Emil Jakob Schindler (1842–1892). Sein schriftliches Werk im Kontext von Kunsthandel, Mäzenatentum und Kunstkritik seiner Zeit*, doct. thesis, Salzburg 2002, vol. 2, p. 311.
8 Carl Rottmann, *Staufen – Walser Heide*, 1833, oil on canvas, 37 x 47,5 cm, Kunsthalle zu Kiel.
9 Hartwig Fischel, "Emil Jakob Schindler", in: *Zeitschrift für bildende Kunst*, vol. 33, NF 9, 1897/98, p. 103.
10 Kamenicek 2002, vol. 2, pp. 297–302.
11 Hartwig Fischel, "Jacob Emil Schindler", in: *Die Graphische Kunst*, 16. yr., 1893a, p. 47. – Cf. also Carl Moll, *Emil Jakob Schindler (1842–1892). Eine Bildnisstudie*, Vienna 1930, p. 15.
12 Martina Haja, "Der österreichische Stimmungsimpressionismus", in: Götz Czymmek (ed.), *Landschaft im Licht. Impressionistische Malerei in Europa und Nordamerika 1860–1910* (exh. cat. Wallraf-Richartz-Museum, Cologne 1990, Kunsthaus Zürich, Zurich 1990), Cologne/Zurich 1990, p. 158.
13 Moll 1930, p. 15.
14 Peter Peer, *Die österreichische Landschaftsmalerei in der zweiten Hälfte des 19. Jahrhunderts. Stilkritische Untersuchungen zu ihren künstlerischen Einflüssen*, doct. thesis, Graz 2002, vol. 1, p. 78.
15 The titles of these two works by Troyon are *Cows Grazing and a Bull* and *Cows on the Isle of the Seine* (German titles: Weidende Kühe und ein Stier and Kühe auf der Seine-Insel), that of Diaz' painting *Bathing Orientalist* (German title: Badende Orientalin).

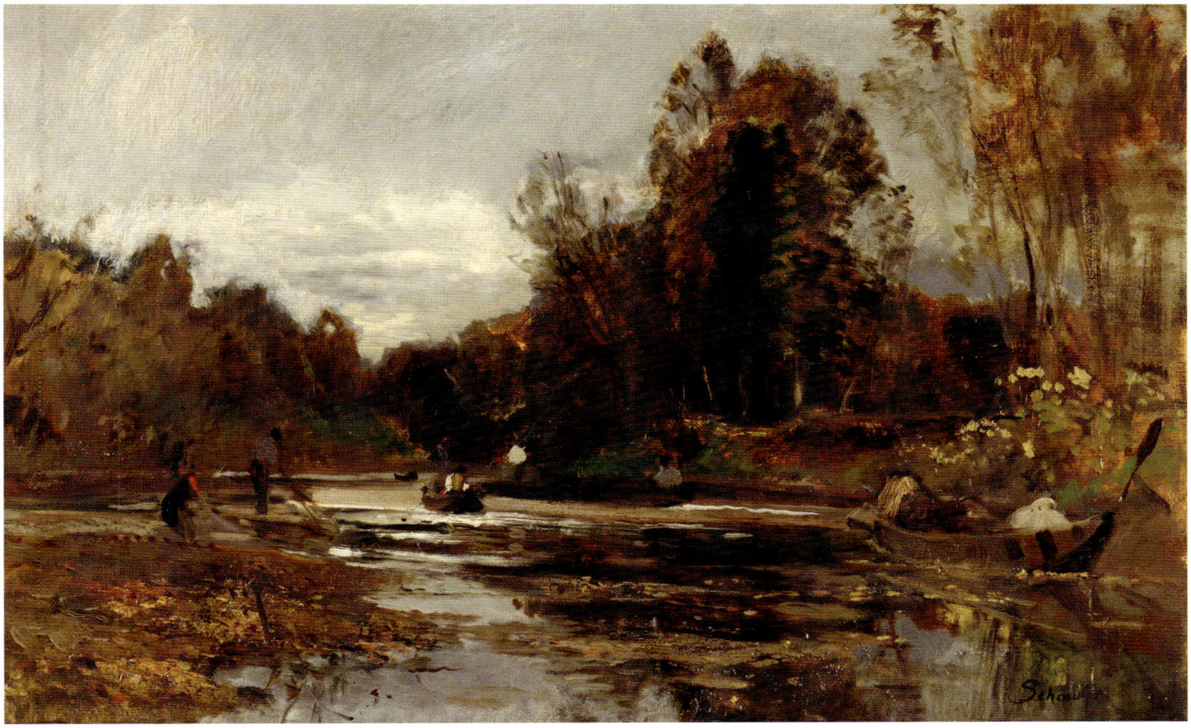

Fig.10.
Emil Jakob Schindler
The Heustadlwasser in the Prater
(Das Heustadlwasser im Prater), 1876/79
Eisenberger collection, Vienna

16 *Wood Scene* and *Alp* (Waldpartie and Alpe).
17 Andrea Winklbauer, "Kunst für Künstler. Wien und die Haager Schule", in: Roland Dorn (ed.), *Van Gogh und die Haager Schule* (exh.cat. Bank Austria Kunstforum, Vienna 1996), Vienna 1996, p. 327.
18 With the exception of a single picture by Manet. *Weltausstellung Wien. Officieller Kunst-Catalog*, Vienna 1873, No. 472.
19 *Bathing Boys*, *Tree Felling Goods*, *In the Kaiserwasser* and *At the Landing Place* (Badende Buben, Holzschlägerwaren, Im Kaiserwasser and Am Landungsplatze).
20 Moll 1930, p. 27.
21 Vera Huber, *Die Entwicklung der Paysage intime in der schweizerischen Landschaftsmalerei des 19. Jahrhunderts*, Zurich 1946, p. 15.
22 Schindler noted on one of the paintings: "Schindler April 1880 after Nature" (*Pond in Atzgersdorf* [Weiher in Atzgersdorf], 1880, oil on canvas, 42 x 56 cm, Eisenberger collection, Vienna).
23 Kamenicek 2002, vol. 2, pp. 81–83.
24 Emil Jakob Schindler, *Praterstudie von der Abholzung für die Donauregulierung*, 1873, oil on wood, 25 x 42,5 cm, fig. in Heinrich Fuchs, *Emil Jakob Schindler. Zeugnisse eines ungewöhnlichen Künstlerlebens. Werkkatalog*, Vienna 1970, p. 164, No. 133.
25 On Rousseau as protector of the threatened wood of Fontainebleau cf. Günter Busch, "Barbizon", in: *Zurück zur Natur. Die Künstlerkolonie von Barbizon. Ihre Vorgeschichte und ihre Auswirkung* (exh.cat. Kunsthalle Bremen 1977/78), Bremen 1977, n.p.
26 Jenny Reynaerts, "Die Ästhetik der Polderlandschaft", in: *Der weite Blick. Landschaften der Haager Schule aus dem Rijksmuseum* (exh.cat. Neue Pinakothek, Munich 2008/09), Ostfildern 2008, pp. 47f.
27 Moll 1930, pp. 32f.
28 Fischel 1893a, p. 43.
29 As cited in: Kamenicek 2002, vol. 2, p. 263. In these statements, Schindler takes up the motif of the mermaid at the water, which Corot often used in his pictures and which is why he was criticized. Meaning that Schindler knew Corot's oeuvre very well. Kamenicek 2002, vol. 2, pp. 264, 322.
30 As cited in Kamenicek 2002, vol. 2, p. 228. – Cf. Moll 1930, p. 33.

31 Cf. Joachim Ritter/Karlfried Gründer (eds.), *Historisches Wörterbuch der Philosophie*, Darmstadt Basel 1998, vol. 10, col. 173f. s. v. the German term *Stimmung* [in English 'atmosphere'] "*Stimmungen* are more than mere conditions of the emotion, they are comprehensive relations to the world, in which light and the reality appear in a different way. They do not establish the references to single objects but to the whole of my world, which might pertain from the near horizon of my surroundings to the distant horizon of the starry sky. *Grundstimmungen* often remain hidden and subtle, they are immaterial-general, mostly instable, swaying [...] '*Lebensstimmungen*', the numerous facets of the position to the world, constitute the lowest layer for the formation of world views'. Even if the philosophical systems may perish, the *Stimmungen* at their basis remain in existence: 'metaphysical science is a historically restricted phenomenon the meta-physical awareness of the person is eternal'."

32 As cited in Kamenicek 2002, vol. 2, pp. 286f. – Cf. also Hartwig Fischel, "J. E. Schindler über die Landschaftsmalerei (Aus seinen hinterlassenen Schriften)", in: *Ausserordentliche Beilage zu den Monatsblättern des Wissenschaftlichen Club in Wien*, IV on No. 6, XIV. yr., 1893b, pp. 103–105 – Alois Riegl occupies a comparable position in his text published in 1899 "Die Stimmung in der Modernen Kunst": Alois Riegl, "Die Stimmung in der Modernen Kunst", in: *Alois Riegl Gesammelte Aufsätze*, with an afterword on the new edition by Wolfgang Kemp, Berlin 1995 pp. 38f.

33 Anton Teichlein, "Theodor Rousseau und der Paysage intime", in: *Zeitschrift für bildende Kunst* vol. 3, 1868, pp. 284f.

34 Schindler on Théodore Rousseau: "Rousseau was the first pure naturalist and so far the greatest [...] He did not go into nature in order to master it, but to serve it. This technique was so complete that it became completely invisible, in order to totally dissolve in the process of nature. He looked for and found with the paintbrush the structure of a cloud, of a stone, of the tree. He wanted to paint light, shining, radiating, true daylight. Everything animated under his hand. Eventually, he painted no paint strokes any longer, but he painted elements, he painted space." As cited in Kamenicek 2002, vol. 2, p. 326. – Cf. Fischel 1893b, p. 102.

35 In a contemporary essay, Jakob von Falke, director of the k. k. Österreichisches Museum für Kunst und Industrie (Imperial Austrian Museum for Art and Industry), examined the predominant gray tone. Falke here pursues a cultural history argumentation, according to which social changes follow fashions influencing art. Jakob von Falke, "Grau", in: the same, *Aus alter und neuer Zeit. Neue Studien zu Kultur und Kunst*, Berlin 1895, 2. ed., pp. 241–251.

36 "Rousseau had eavesdropped on all the effects of nature, painted all the atmospheric nuances, but the atmosphere itself was for him only an object of representation, one more means to vary the great theme of painting. The effect had to have form, the attitude was more important for him than the atmosphere as such. Each one of his paintings has also, like a well rounded music piece, its own tonality (*sa tenacité à lui*), which he captures in the light, in the shadow as in the half-tones through all planes near and distant, [...] But alas '*le grand neutre*', as Rousseau expressed himself, or '*la masse du ton*' as Dupré says, that general atmosphere without which the most tasteful color bouquet is nowhere near a coloristic work that pleases the taste of the *paysage intime* masters, something like that does not arise out of nothing." (Teichlein 1868, p. 289.)

37 Reynaerts 2008, p. 41.

38 In his theoretical writings, Schindler dedicates a whole chapter to this theme. Cf. Kamenicek 2002, vol. 2, pp. 236–243. – Fischel 1893a, p. 50. – Fischel 1893b, p. 100.

39 Kamenicek 2002, vol. 2, p. 267. – Cf. also Fischel 1893b, p. 107.

40 Fischel 1893a, p. 59. [Landstraße and Parklandschaft]

41 Johannes Pawlik, *Theorie der Farbe*, 2. ed., Cologne 1971, p. 63.

42 Pawlik 1971, pp. 81f.

43 Emil Jakob Schindler, *The Scirocco at the Dalmatian Coast* (Der Scirocco an der Küste Dalmatiens), fig. in: *Die österreichisch-ungarische Monarchie in Wort und Bild*, summary vol., 1. sect., *Naturgeschichtlicher Teil*, Vienna 1887, p. 179.

44 Thomas Couture, *The Bird Catcher*, 1857, oil on canvas, 42 x 61 cm, Szépművészeti Múzeum (Museum of Fine Arts), Budapest, inv.no. 253 B.

45 *Versteigerung der Grossen Gallerie und der übrigen Kunst-Sammlungen des am 20. September 1871 verstorbenen Herrn F. J. Gsell zu Wien in den Sälen des Künstlerhauses am 14. März 1872, durch den Kunsthändler und Auktionator Georg Plach*, Vienna 1872, in this No. 244, Thomas Couture, *The Country Estate with the Artist's Studio, in the Garden a Man Catching Birds* (German title: Der Landsitz mit dem Atelier des Künstlers, im Garten ein Mann, Vögel fangend), 1857, 43 x 61 cm.

46 "For a long time, he had Couture's '*The Bird Catcher*' in his studio in front of him in order to use this picture as a 'tuning fork', in order to train his eye in the resonating and merging of the colorful appearances. During these studies, sometimes strange elements may have come into his

paintbrush, even though he tried to see honestly with his own eyes." Fischel 1893a, p. 48. – Cf. also Moll 1930, p. 15.

47 Kamenicek 2002, vol. 2, pp. 262, 284.

48 As cited in Kamenicek 2002, vol. 2, p. 288. Schindler's quote here resembles the famous statement by Cézanne: "Art has a harmony which parallels that of nature."

49 Fischel 1897/98, p. 102. Today the poetic realism or else the middle-class realism embraces above all in the field of literary history the period between 1848 and 1890. During the restrictive time after the German March Revolution of 1848, the authors of the poetic realism addressed themes such as the depiction of the home country, its landscape and its people. The representatives of poetic realism are among others Ludwig Anzengruber, Marie von Ebner-Eschenbach, Gottfried Keller, Theodor Fontane, Theodor Storm and Peter Rosegger. Cf. Martina Haja, "Emil Jakob Schindlers Zyklus 'Die Monate'. Zum 160. Geburtstag und 110. Todestag des Künstlers (1842–1892)", in: *Belvedere. Zeitschrift für bildende Kunst*, no. 2, 2002, pp. 15f.

50 "What he [Rousseau] admired most of all in nature, where it seemed as an unattainable model for him, that was the complete ability to live, the '*ça-y-est*' of their organisms. And he, the storming colorist, whom his friend Thoré shouts to: *Tu ne cherchais pas le fini dans la peinture mais l'infini dans la poesie* [...]" (Teichlein 1868, p. 289.)

51 Fischel 1897/98, p. 108.

52 Emil Jakob Schindler, *Waldfräuleins Geburt (nach einem Gedicht von Joseph Christian von Zedlitz)*, 1868, oil on canvas, 95 x 119 cm, Gemäldegalerie der Akademie der bildenden Künste Wien (Picture Gallery of the Academy of Fine Arts, Vienna).

53 Kamenicek 2002, vol. 2, pp. 327–329.

54 Thomas Lehnerer, *Die Kunsttheorie Friedrich Schleiermachers*, Stuttgart 1987, p. 255.

55 "As in figurative painting, single elements stand out through a deeper, spiritual content and ask us to pause for longer, so this time in the landscape, too, we encounter some pictures that in their artistic physiognomy say more than mere nature extracts are able to do; on top here is E. Schindler's landscape poetry which is designated 'PAX' [...] Schindler has [...] achieved something truly significant with this first bigger work and has shown that he is able to design the nature motif in an artistic manner and that he also has the necessary technical means at his disposal to poetically romanticize a landscape picture through the atmosphere." (*Kunst-Chronik*, supplement to the Zeitschrift für Bildende Kunst, NF, 1. yr., No. 25, August 5,1890, col. 339f, as cited in Kamenicek 2002, vol. 1, p. 89.)

56 Bärbel Holaus describes the genesis of the term in detail: Bärbel Holaus, *Studien zu Emil Jakob Schindler*, dipl. thesis, Vienna 1994, vol.1, pp. 157–173.

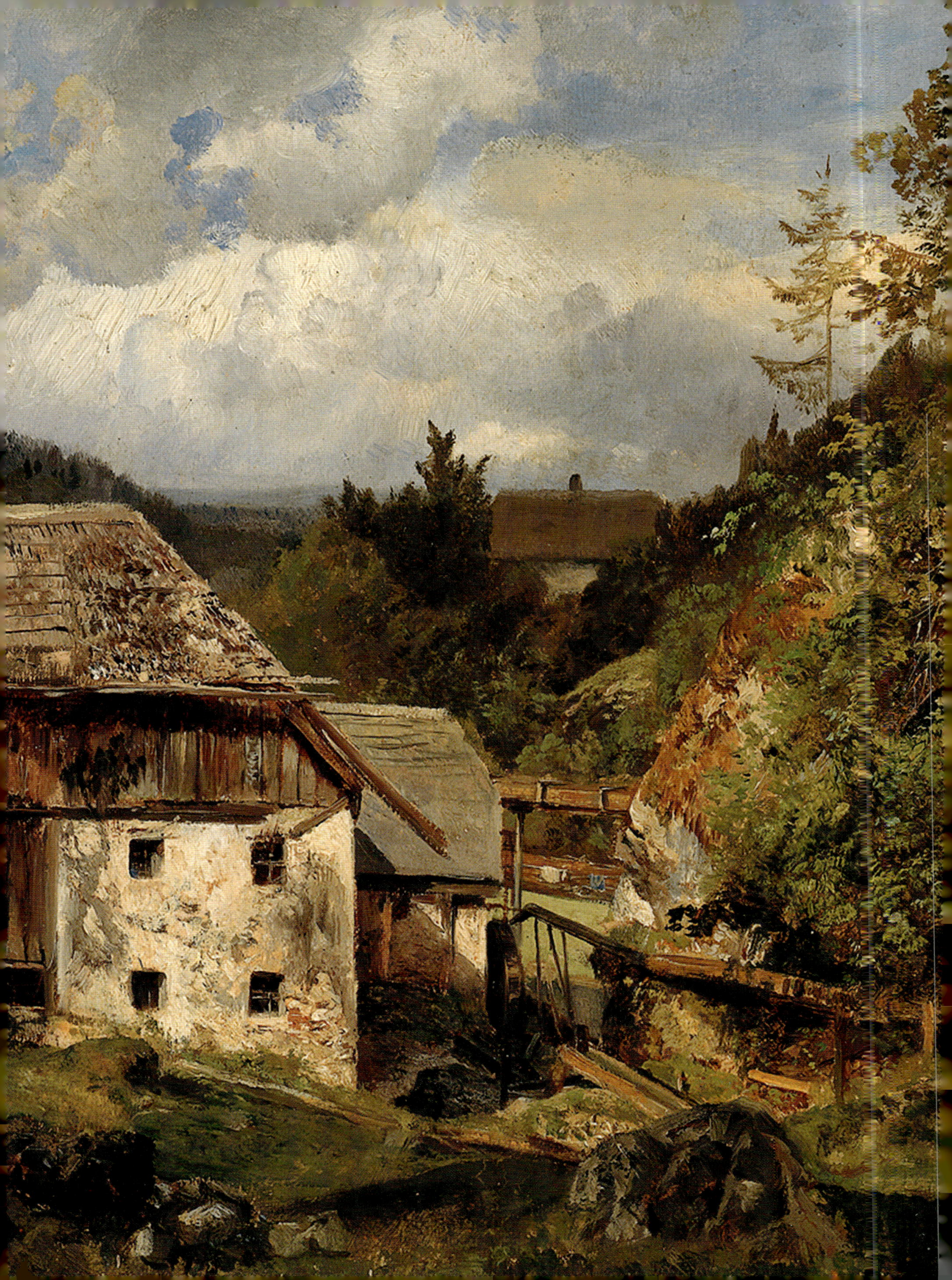

Andrea Winklbauer

"He sees his picture inside" Emil Jakob Schindler and the Photographic View

So-called "Austrian Atmospheric Impressionism"[1] is one of the realistic movements in European landscape painting of the second half of the 19th century.[2] Emil Jakob Schindler is regarded as its most important representative. It has long been clear that Schindler's landscape painting is indeed related with the *Paysage intime* of the Barbizon School, but not with French Impressionism. Schindler places his emphasis on something other than the purely exterior appearance of the world. So he writes in one of his art historical texts that are preserved as a typescript:[3] "Self-evidently, the pure landscapist has more than any other artist to be the master of the controlled art form, but more than anybody else he must also be entirely subordinate to the appearance of nature. The absolute landscapist will never be in the position to copy nature, but he certainly has to discern it. He needs an unfathomable knowledge, and in this context, the real sciences support him only very little. His plant cannot be found in any botanical work, his stone is not part of any mineralogy. In all things, he only has to deal with the extract that his eye may see in their existence. This eye must be emotionally enhanced through the soul, so that it becomes a second soul."[4] This very romantic attitude may have been conveyed to Schindler by his teacher at the Viennese Academy, the Saxon mountain specialist Albert Zimmermann, who was educated in Dresden. "It is not the true depiction of air, water, rocks and trees that is the creator's task, but his soul, his sensation should reflect in them,"[5] writes Caspar David Friedrich, or also in short in the well-known saying: "The painter should not merely paint what he sees in front of him, but also what he sees in himself. But if he sees nothing inside him, then he should stop painting what he sees in front of him."[6]

On viewing Schindler's landscape pictures it becomes clear what he means. The projection of the inward to the outside takes place poetically. Schindler shows nature in its very particular moments, ordinary but also atmospheric. But how did these pictures come into being, what did he see "in front of him" – and which other ingredients must he then have seen "in himself"? Ultimately, this is also a question about Schindler's modernity. The research on this leads deep into Schindler's working process. We know that, as was generally common at his time, he made both drawings and colorful sketches outside, but that his pictures were generally only painted in the studio. Existing study material on completed paintings reveals that Schindler often planned these sketches, too, as paintings and did not only capture the exterior reality in them, but already connected a composition, an idea for a picture with their extracts.[7] He then further processed the pictorial idea in the work and completed what was often only vaguely laid out in the sketch: atmospheric condition, day- and night-time as well as the character and mood of a landscape (cf. the study *Mill Weir in Plankenberg*, p. 92, and

Fig. 1.
Emil Jakob Schindler
The Woodmill (Die Waldmühle), detail, 1869
Private collection

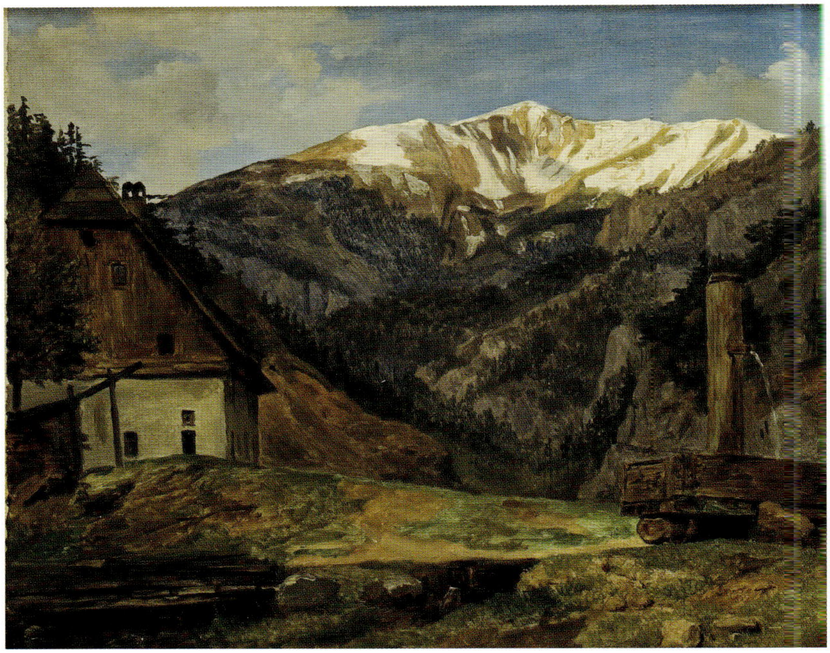

Fig.2.
Ferdinand Georg Waldmüller
Entrance to the Höllental
(Eingang in das Höllental), after 1840
Landesmuseum Niederösterreich, St. Pölten

Mill near Plankenberg, p. 93). In this context, a preserved diary from the year 1879 betrays how much Schindler was artistically at odds with himself and how often he seemingly abandoned pictures as "spoiled" in the working process and started again.[8]

"[...] **dependent on nature** [...]"

It is self-evident that in Schindler's case the seen was allowed, yes, even had to be reformed according to the requirements of the artistic. Carl Moll writes about Schindler's working method: "Again I watched Schindler's painting from nature [...] He paints the 'bridge', the silvery water with bridge and willow grove [...] Schindler paints, the bush becomes trees, the Saarstein mountain clouds. He sees his picture inside; he only takes from the outside whatever fits into this picture."[9] Schindler's thoughts on Ferdinand Georg Waldmüller also fit into this "view". As is generally known, Waldmüller advocated completely the opposite artistic position, namely that the painter was to paint without fail what he saw in front of him. In his theoretical writing Schindler comments on Waldmüller mostly dismissively. To his mind, Waldmüller had been "as a very small talent dependent on nature as no one else," and only, when "nature [was] so kind as to present a complete mood to him, was the picture then also quite coincidentally a very complete one."[10] Schindler's arrogant attitude towards Waldmüller is only marginally softened by his recommendation to obtain information about nature studies from him.[11]

Schindler either did not know or was indifferent to the fact that Waldmüller's truth to nature was accomplished according to a formulated artistic concept.[12] But it is a fact that Waldmüller's picture findings arrived in Schindler's oeuvre after all. As Bärbel Holaus stated, Schindler oriented himself on various models depending on the respective motif: "So the analysis of the Barbizon School

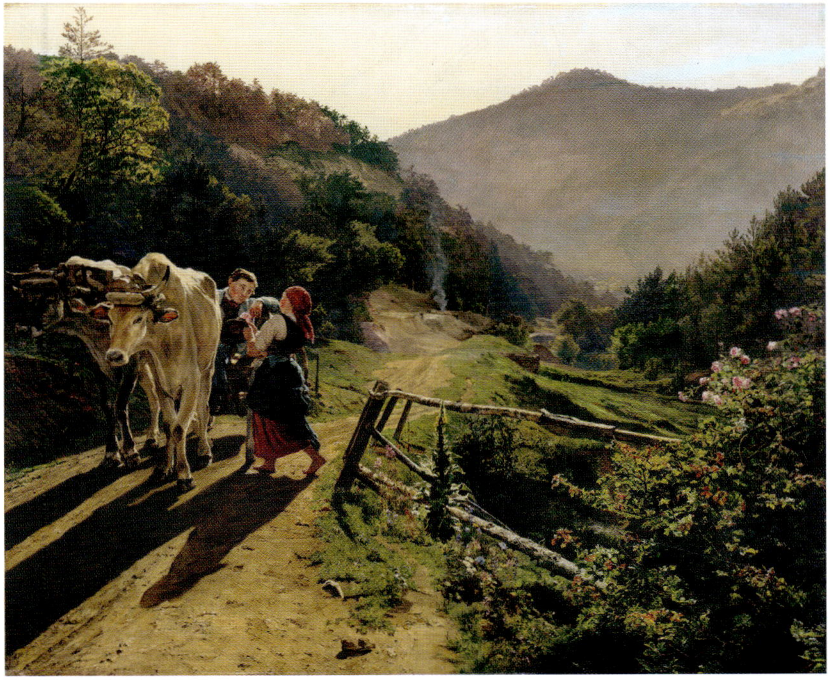

Fig.3.
Ferdinand Georg Waldmüller
The Rose Season (Die Rosenzeit), 1862-1865
Wien Museum

representatives always seeps into the meadow and pond landscapes. The mills show allusions to the Dutch landscape painting of the 17th century and the concern with the Düsseldorf School. The seascapes are marked by the almost pathetic character of Andreas Achenbach (see fig. p. 15), and the coastal landscapes are reminiscent of the lyrical sounds of Oswald Achenbach's motifs. In the gardens and park landscapes, however, the artist continues the Austrian realism based on Waldmüller."[13] For an entire series of themes for landscape pictures by Waldmüller, Schindler had no use at all: he is neither interested in depictions of mountains, nor in topographically recognizable motifs nor in anecdotal figure compositions. There is an astonishing consonance of motif and composition, however, between the early Schindler painting *The Woodmill* (fig. 1) and Waldmüller's *Entrance to the Höllental* (fig. 2). In both paintings, a farm building on the far left of the picture is set in a mountain landscape, and both pictures are even dominated by similar colors: under a slightly cloudy sky we see landscapes in olive-green, brown and a touch of grey. Their realism is unusual. Schindler paints light and shadow on the bright wall of the mill. Landscapes in bright sunlight with sharp shadows, as known in Waldmüller's work, were not really Schindler's concern. For him, either through its warmth or through a slightly misty air, a sunlit landscape had to preserve the necessary painterly unity that is called atmosphere. (cf. *Park Landscape in Plankenberg [Lilac]*, p. 105, or *Flower Garden in Weißenkirchen*, p. 87). But especially Waldmüller's late work already contains the precursors for this tendency, be it the wonderfully damp *The Rose Season* (fig. 3) or the *Mountain Landscape with Vineyard* (fig. 4). Both pictures already anticipate much of Schindler's garden and park pictures of the late 1870s and 1880s.

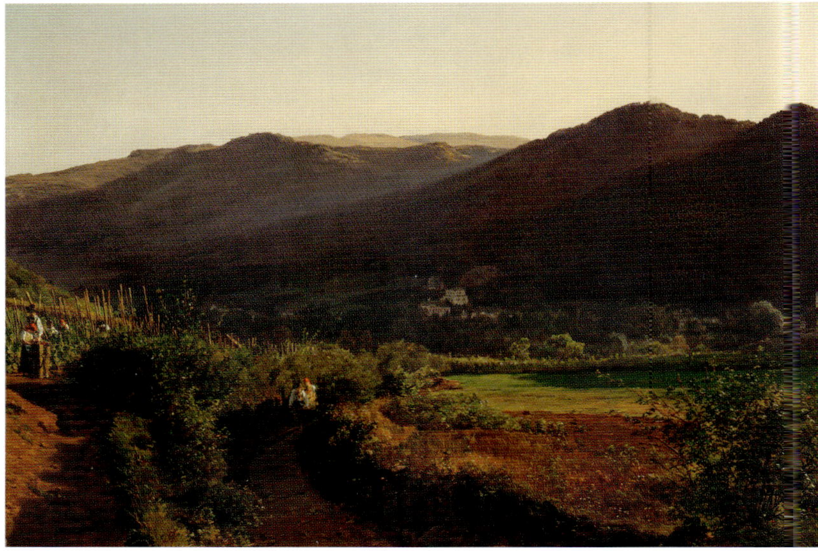

Fig.4.
Ferdinand Georg Waldmüller
Mountain Landscape with Vineyard
(Berglandschaft mit Weingarten), 1862
Národní galerie v Praze
(National Gallery in Prague), Prague

Photography

Ferdinand Georg Waldmüller is one of those artists in whose work Heinrich Schwarz sees the anticipation of the photographic view even before the invention of photography or its announcement in 1839.[14] Waldmüller also made use of technical aids such as the camera obscura or the Claude glass (black mirror).[15] According to Schwarz, like a photo camera Waldmüller not only indiscriminately recorded the richness in detail in landscape paintings of the 1830s but would also have "restricted the design of the extract [...] to the mere, unchanged rendition of a picture that had not been arranged [...]"[16]. But it is exactly this aspect that Schindler criticized in Waldmüller: the "unedited" rendition of the seen, in the course of which, to Schindler's mind, the general impression would suffer from the depiction of a wealth of details. Interesting in connection with the "photographic view" of Waldmüller is the fact that Schindler himself did indeed avail himself to photography. This is no contradiction: from Schindler's preserved theoretical writings we know that he regarded photography as a means of the painter to "facilitate the assembly of materials" or to capture rapidly moving objects, even though he also warned of an all too easy treatment of photographic models.[17] With his criticism of Waldmüller's realistic painting, while also appreciating photography (as study material), Schindler is close to the conservative French art critic Maxime du Camp, who damned Courbet's realism as "servile imitation" as early as in 1866 and preferred photography to him, which "[is] by far more precise, and can never go astray."[18]

It is not known when Emil Jakob Schindler first employed photography as a technical aid. In his diary of 1879 already referred to, it is repeatedly mentioned with the utmost naturalness. Schindler writes about the pictures he is working on. We learn things such as: "Done a few strokes of charcoal from a photographic study." Or a few lines further: "Towards the evening started the little picture from the photograph. So far it is still nothing. Daubigni must have painted in this way, after all."[19] Some days later he writes: "I took the French photographic image still on the table and put it into the right atmosphere. I have to start it all over again.

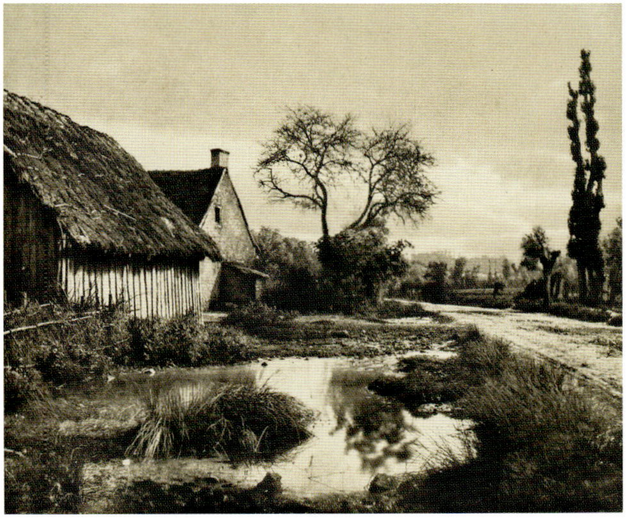

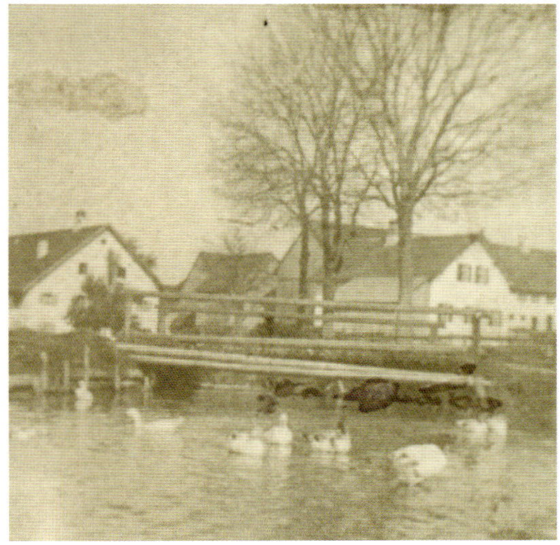

Fig.5.
André Giroux
Farmstead near Barbizon
(Gehöft bei Barbizon), c. 1855
Wallraff-Richartz-Museum/Museum Ludwig, Cologne

Fig.6.
Emil Jakob Schindler
Village Pond with Geese
(Dorfweiher mit Gänsen), c. 1891
Letter to Anna Schindler
of November 11, 1891
ÖNB (Austrian National Library), Department of Manuscripts and Rare Books, Vienna

But draw it all through, then glaze it like that. It is a charming motif."[20] In the few months this diary covers (the beginning of February to the end of May 1879) Schindler reports on this and another "French" photograph, an English and a Dutch one that served him as a model for pictures. Furthermore, the diary contains a list of works in which a whole series of pictures after photographs are mentioned, starting with a mountain landscape exhibited in 1869 after a photographic study,[21] via the paintings already mentioned up to several pictures from photographs from Munich, one from Rattenburg, three from Weißenkirchen, one from Regelsbrunn as well as one painted "photographed from a motif moment."[22]

We learn that Schindler bought photographs,[23] which might have been common among painters at the time. Many of them favored photography as an aid, as did landscape painters such as Jean-Baptiste Camille Corot. In 1849 for the first time, the photographer Gustave Le Gray took his camera on the trail of the painters of the Barbizon School in Fontainebleau forest; others followed him. From 1851, series of artistic photographic models were published in France as works in folders that were addressed directly to painters as studies from nature.[24] The photos by Le Gray, Charles Nègre, Charles Marville, André Giroux and others are artfully ambitious and show nature with a view that was prepared by the painting of the Barbizon School artists (fig. 5). There is much to suggest that Schindler, too, availed himself of such or similar photographs. He writes about the "French photo", from which he is painting at the moment: "[It] must become a fine evening. The photograph's atmosphere is of a nameless charm."[25] Or about some new acquisitions: "Yesterday I bought photographs – among them some very charming winter pictures."[26] Schindler thus thought that the photographs already contained what constituted for him the essence of landscape painting.

The Painter as Hobby Photographer

In the literature it has long been known that Schindler painted from photographs.[27] But the hints that he took photographs himself, too, have been almost disregarded for a long time, and it is only recently that photos by Emil Jakob Schindler have

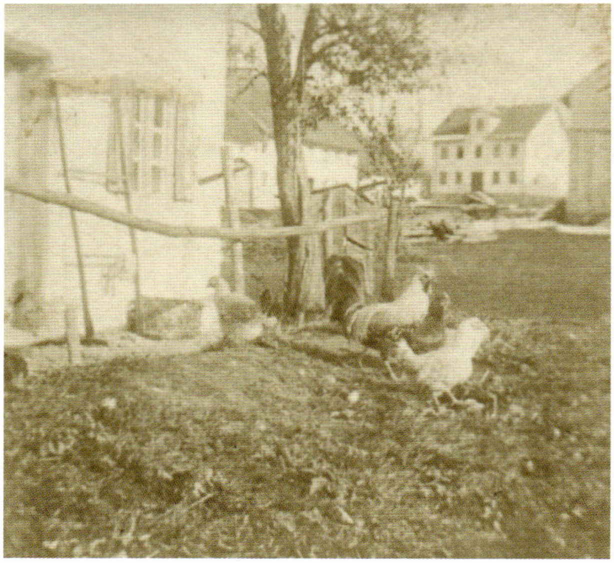

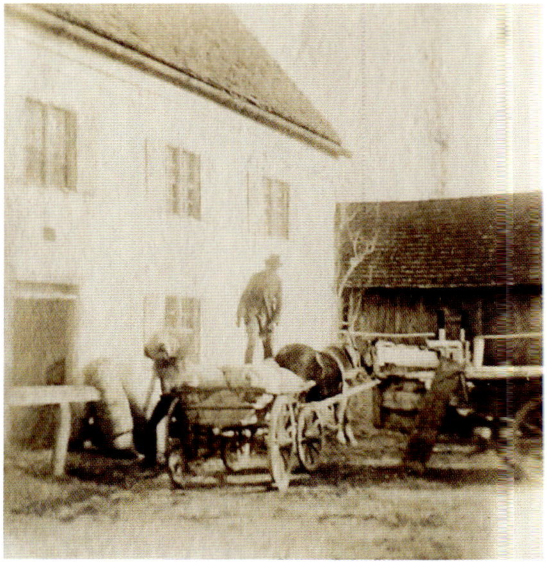

Fig.7.
Emil Jakob Schindler
Chicken in Front of a House
(Hühner vor einem Haus), c. 1891
Letter to Anna Schindler of November 11, 1891
ÖNB (Austrian National Library), Department of Manuscripts and Rare Books, Vienna

Fig.8.
Emil Jakob Schindler
Man Loading a One-Horse Dray
(Mann beim Beladen eines Einspänners), undated
Undated letter to Carl Moll
Wienbibliothek im Rathaus (Vienna City Library in the Vienna City Hall), Vienna

been published for the first time.[28] It is not known when Schindler himself started taking photographs, but this practice might have been relevant to him as early as in 1879.[29] The few preserved photos, pasted into letters to Schindler's wife Anna and his student Carl Moll, each one not more than 4 x 4 cm in size, are surprising.[30] The small, pale pictures, developed and cropped by Schindler himself, have little in common with the art photography of the Barbizon School surroundings, even though they show rural motifs. In a letter, dated November 11, 1891 to Anna Schindler, for example, there are four photos by Schindler showing a village landscape and its surroundings: women hanging out the laundry, a farmer with horse and cart on a country lane, chicken in front of a farmhouse (fig. 7) and a village pond with geese, a wooden jetty, trees and houses in the background (fig. 6). The "atmosphere" is completely different, the people, the animals, the houses, the farm implements and landscape details are marked by a down-to-earthness (fig. 8), which Schindler's escapist paintings never convey. Even though exclusively rural (fig. 9, 10), the photographed world of Schindler accommodates us much more than the painted one. It is this "certificate of presence"[31] which makes these "snapshots" by Schindler so exciting. They have less in common with the art photography of the time than with the already existing amateur snapshot photography.[32]

Even though it can be assumed that Schindler took these "preservations of motifs" with regard to paintings to be composed later, he probably at most took individual motifs from them, but presumably not compositions. That would have been difficult, in any case, since the majority of the photos preserved were cropped by Schindler in an almost square format. He never used this format for his paintings even though it played an important role in connection with the artistic secessions[33] and the art of the turn of the century. In this context, it should be mentioned, however, that in his text on the art education Schindler recommends square sketch books, because he regards the square format as an aid to perception.[34]

What is thus Schindler's personal contribution, alongside the ingredients from a world that surrounded him? What makes an artwork out of the things seen?

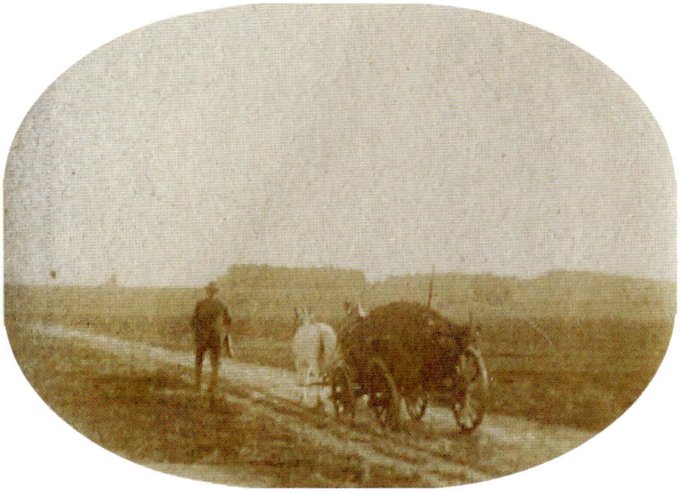

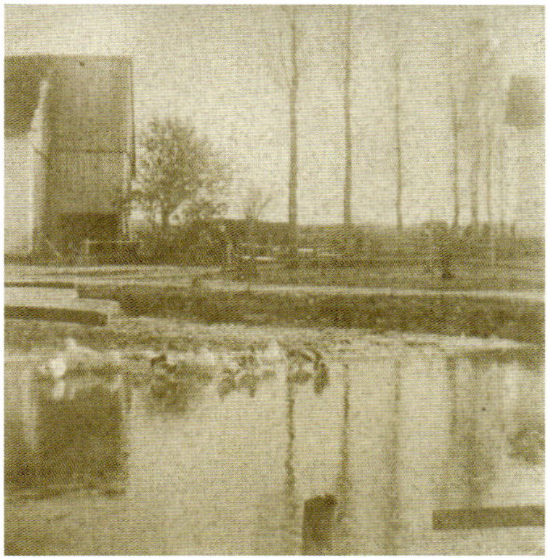

Presumably, it is the synthesis between seen nature and a sentimental, painterly poetry which, despite their realism, often allows his landscape paintings to appear slightly lost in reverie. This attitude might have still been appropriate in the 1870s and 1880s, but in view of the simultaneous developments around Impressionism and Post-Impressionism it was never really pioneering.

Fig.9.
Emil Jakob Schindler
Man with Horse and Cart
(Mann mit Pferdewagen), undated
Undated letter to Carl Moll
Wienbibliothek im Rathaus (Vienna City Library in the Vienna City Hall), Vienna

Fig.10.
Emil Jakob Schindler
Village Pond with Poplars
(Dorfweiher mit Pappeln), undated
Undated letter to Anna Schindler
ÖNB (Austrian National Library), Department of Manuscripts and Rare Books, Vienna

1 Fritz Novotny used the expression for the first time; Fritz Novotny, *Hundert Jahre österreichischer Landschaftsmalerei*, Vienna 1948, p. 11. – As far more correct designation, the term "Austrian Atmospheric Realism" was suggested quite a while ago; cf. Otmar Rychlik, "Zum Begriff des Stimmungsrealismus", in: *Natürlichere Natur. Österreichische Malerei des Stimmungsrealismus* (exh. cat. Kunsthaus Mürzzuschlag, Mürzzuschlag 1994), Mürzzuschlag 1994, pp. 7f.

2 A good overview over parallel movements in many European countries was provided in the exhibition *Landschaft im Licht* in 1990, which was again of all things only promoted under the label of "Impressionism"; cf. Götz Czymmek (ed.), *Landschaft im Licht. Impressionistische Malerei in Europa und Nordamerika 1860–1910* (exh.cat. Wallraf-Richartz-Museum, Cologne 1990, Kunsthaus Zürich, Zurich 1990), Cologne/Zurich 1990.

3 Österreichische Nationalbibliothek, Sammlung von Handschriften und alten Drucken (Austrian National Library, Department of Manuscripts and Rare Books), cod. ser. n. 20731 Han to cod. ser. n. 20751 Han.

4 Emil Jakob Schindler, "Menschenwerk", typescript, Österreichische Nationalbibliothek, Sammlung von Handschriften und alten Drucken (Austrian National Library, Department of Manuscripts and Rare Books), cod. ser. n. 20739 Han; as cited in Elisabeth Edith Kamenicek, *Emil Jakob Schindler (1842–1892). Sein schriftliches Werk im Kontext von Kunsthandel, Mäzenatentum und Kunstkritik seiner Zeit*, doct. thesis, Salzburg 2002, vol. 2, p. 262.

5 As cited in Sigrid Hinz (ed.), *Caspar David Friedrich in Briefen und Bekenntnissen*, Berlin 1968, pp. 102f.

6 As cited in Hinz 1968, p. 128.

7 Cf. more detailed Martina Haja, "Thema mit Variationen. Schindlers 'Pappelallee bei Plankenberg'", in: Peter Weninger/Peter Müller (eds.), *Die Schule von Plankenberg. Emil Jakob Schindler und der österreichische Stimmungsimpressionismus* (exh.cat. Niederösterreichisches Landesmuseum, Vienna 1991), Graz 1991, pp. 32–37. – the same, "Emil Jakob Schindlers Zyklus 'Die Monate'. Zum 160. Geburtstag und 110. Todestag des Künstlers (1842–1892)", in: *Belvedere. Zeitschrift für bildende Kunst*, no. 2, 2002, pp. 4–17.

8 The diary covers the period from February 4 to the end of May 1879; Österreichische Nationalbibliothek, Sammlung von Handschriften und alten Drucken (Austrian National Library, Department of Manuscripts and Rare Books), cod. ser. n. 38841 Han. It was entirely transcribed by Elisabeth Kamenicek; Kamenicek 2002, vol. 2, pp. 58–124.

9 Carl Moll, *Emil Jakob Schindler (1842–1892). Eine Bildnisstudie*, Vienna 1930, p. 39.

10 Emil Jakob Schindler, "Photographie. Pleinair", typescript, Österreichische Nationalbibliothek, Sammlung von Handschriften und alten Drucken (Austrian National Library, Department of Manuscripts and Rare Books), cod. ser. n. 20745 Han; as cited in Kamenicek 2002, vol. 2, pp. 307f.

11 Emil Jakob Schindler, "Akademische Landschaftsschule", typescript, Österreichische Nationalbibliothek, Sammlung von Handschriften und alten Drucken (Austrian National Library, Department of Manuscripts and Rare Books), cod. ser. n. 20742 Han; as cited in Kamenicek 2002, vol. 2, pp. 283f.

12 Cf. Klaus Albrecht Schröder, "Ferdinand Georg Waldmüller und die Entdeckung der Wirklichkeit", in: the same (ed.), *Ferdinand Georg Waldmüller* (exh. cat. Kunstforum Länderbank, Vienna 1990), Vienna 1990, pp. 9f. and pp. 20–22.

13 Bärbel Holaus, *Studien zu Emil Jacob Schindler*, dipl. thesis, Vienna 1994, vol. 1, p. 107.

14 Heinrich Schwarz, "Vor 1839. Symptome und Strömungen", in: Anselm Wagner (ed.), *Heinrich Schwarz. Techniken des Sehens – vor und nach der Fotografie. Ausgewählte Schriften 1929–1966*, Salzburg 2006, pp. 183–200, esp. pp. 196f. – Hermann Beenken also already found black-and-white photographs of pictures by Waldmüller reminiscent of photographs; Hermann Beenken, *Das 19. Jahrhundert in der deutschen Kunst*, München 1944, pp. 140f.

15 Schwarz 2006, p. 196.

16 Schwarz 2006, pp. 196f.

17 Emil Jakob Schindler, "Photographie. Pleinair", Österreichische Nationalbibliothek, Sammlung von Handschriften und alten Drucken (Austrian National Library, Department of Manuscripts and Rare Books), cod. ser. n. 20745 Han; as cited in Kamenicek 2002, vol. 2, p. 303.

18 As cited in Klaus Herding (ed.), *Realismus als Widerspruch. Die Wirklichkeit in Courbets Malerei*, 2nd. comb. ed., Frankfurt am Main 1984, p. 118.

19 Entry of February 11, 1879, as cited in Kamenicek 2002, vol. 2, p. 64. Schindler means Charles-François Daubigny (1817–1878).

20 February 14, 1879, as cited in Kamenicek 2002, vol.2, p. 66.

21 The picture was shown in 1869 on the First International Exhibition in the Glass Palace in Munich; cf. Kamenicek 2002, vol. 2, p. 113.

22 As cited in Kamenicek 2002, vol. 2, p. 123.

23 March 18, 1879, as cited in Kamenicek 2002, vol. 2, p. 88.

24 See e.g. Ulrich Pohlmann, "'Etudes d'après nature'. Barbizon und die französische Landschaftsphotographie von 1849 bis 1875", in: Michael Clarke/Christoph Heilmann/John Sillevis (eds.), *Corot, Courbet und die Maler von Barbizon. Les amis de la nature* (exh.cat. Haus der Kunst, Munich 1996), Munich 1996, pp. 406–416. – the same, "Von der Künstlerstudie zur Kunstphotographie. Französische Photographie im 19. Jahrhundert", in: Bodo von Dewitz/Roland Scotti (eds.), *Alles Wahrheit! Alles Lüge! Photographie und Wirklichkeit im 19. Jahrhundert* (exh.cat. Wallraf-Richartz-Museum, Cologne 1996/97), Cologne 1996, pp. 414f.

25 February 15, 1879, as cited in Kamenicek 2002, vol. 2, p. 68.

26 March 18, 1879, as cited in Kamenicek 2002, vol. 2, p. 88.

27 Even Heinrich Fuchs mentions in his Schindler catalogue raisonné that the picture No. 300, *Memory of England* (Erinnerung an England) created around 1880, was painted from a photograph; Heinrich Fuchs, *Emil Jakob Schindler*, Vienna 1970, p. 195.

28 Elisabeth Kamenicek, "Emil Jakob Schindler. Zwischen Tradition und Moderne. Unbeachtete Archivalien in der Handschriftensammlung der Österreichischen Nationalbibliothek als wertvolle Ergänzung zum malerischen Œuvre Emil Jakob Schindlers," in: Gerbert Frodl/Verena Traeger (eds.), *Stimmungsimpressionismus* (exh.cat. Belvedere, Vienna 2004), Vienna 2004, pp. 269–279, esp. pp. 274f.

29 In the diary of 1879 he mentions in the entry of March, 10: "We are walking. I am taking a small camera with me." As cited in Kamenicek 2002, vol. 2, p. 82. Later in this or in the following year, pictures were produced from photos from Weißenkirchen, which he visited with Anna in the summer of 1879.

30 In his correspondence to Anna and Carl Moll Schindler reports on his photographic practice; cf. Kamenicek 2002, vol. 2, pp. 275f. – Holaus 1994, vol. 2, p. 71.

31 Roland Barthes, *Camera Lucida*, New York 1981, p. 87.

32 In detail in Timm Starl, *Knipser. Die Bildgeschichte der privaten Fotografie in Deutschland und Österreich von 1880 bis 1980*, Munich 1995.

33 The Munich Secession was founded in Schindler's death year 1892, the Vienna Secession in 1897, the one in Berlin in 1899.

34 Emil Jakob Schindler, "Akademische Landschaftsschule", as cited in Kamenicek 2002, vol. 2, p. 285. – Cf. also Schindler's text "Volksschule", in which he writes: "The square and later the circle constitute the beginnings." As cited in Kamenicek 2002, vol. 2, p. 278.

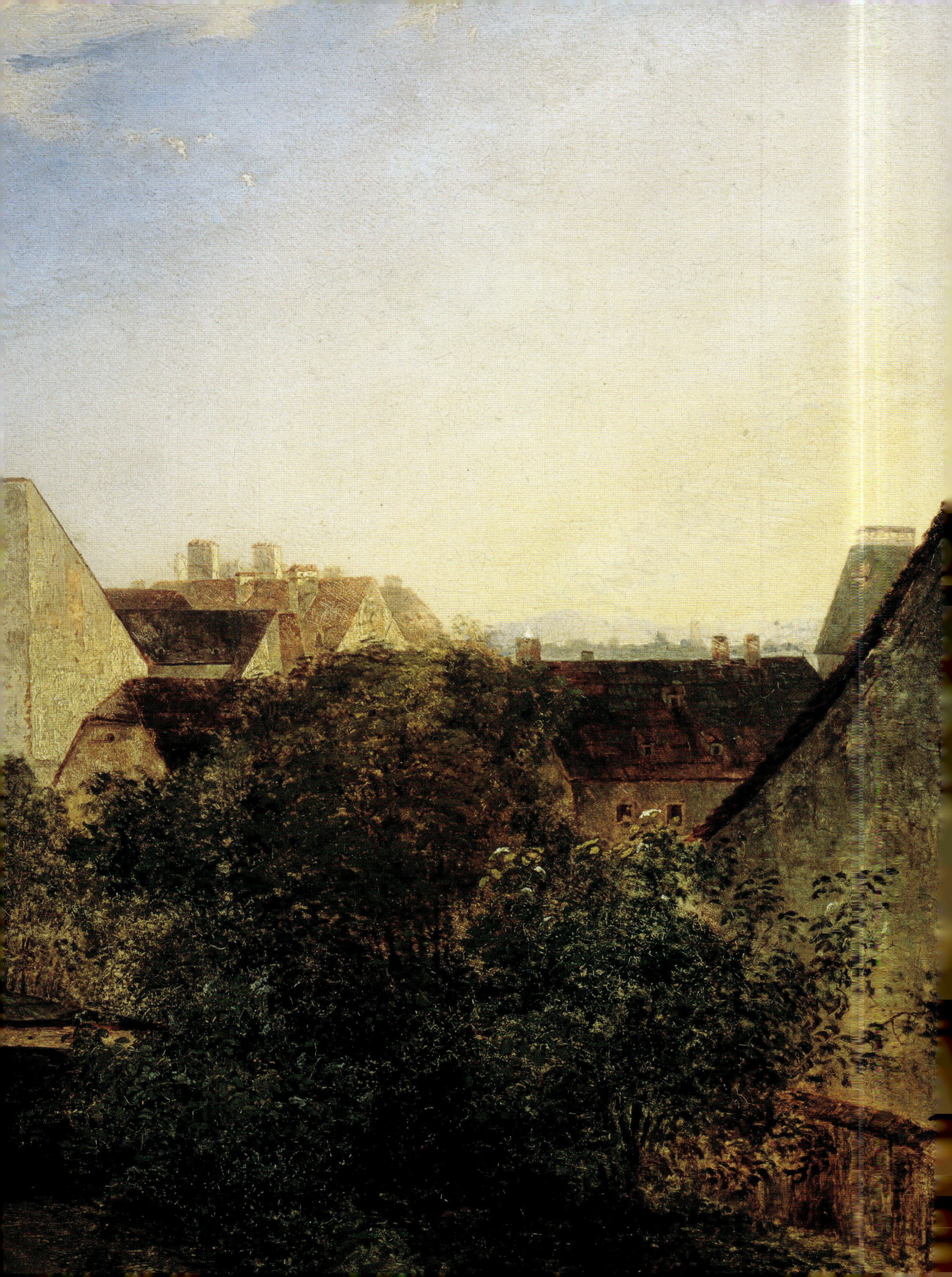

Markus Fellinger

The View of Nature in the Work of Adalbert Stifter and Emil Jakob Schindler

Today, Adalbert Stifter is regarded as *the* nature poet of Austrian 19th century literature. Instead of the Italian wishful landscapes of the early generations, on the trail of the Classicists and Romantics, he discovers the local countryside and cultural landscapes of the Bohemian Forest, the high mountains and the plateaus of the foothills of the Alps as scenes of his narratives. So he allows hikers, surveyors, landscape painters and naturalists to explore the smallest details of the land, and in his historical novels and narrative he also sets the events of the past in the same landscape as the one presented to the reader as a hiking writer.

Thus it is no wonder that Stifter is frequently mentioned as reference in literature on the painting of Austrian Atmospheric Impressionism.[1] The poet of the Bohemian Forest is also rediscovered in Emil Jakob Schindler's forest clearings and moor landscapes, the portrayer of the Upper Austrian foothills of the Alps in the pictures of country roads and park landscapes around Schindler's residence in Plankenberg. In view of the large time difference alone it is not really surprising, however, that this comparability only functions on a rather superficial level and examined critically, does justice neither to Stifter's nor to Schindler's true ambitions. Stifter is part of a completely different epoch. The world of his stories and novels can be found far more in the pictures of his contemporaries, in particular in the Biedermeier realism of a Ferdinand Georg Waldmüller or of a Rudolf von Alt. Accordingly, one can also say that poets of the time, such as Detlev von Liliencron, for example, are much closer to Schindler's "poetic realism" than Stifter.[2] But the fact that some of Stifter's writing also contains certain thoughts that are relevant to Austrian Atmospheric Impressionism, especially in those exciting moments when Stifter's multifaceted artist's personality arrives at more profound considerations beyond the ordered Biedermeier surface, suggests that a more detailed examination would be rewarding.

Biographical Background

Stifter and Schindler probably never met personally. Stifter, born in 1805, was 35 years older than Schindler and spent the last 20 years of his life far from the capital in Linz on the Danube. He died in 1868, taking his own life, which was exactly the year when the young Schindler celebrated his first successes. He grew up in Oberplan in the Bohemian Forest and attended the Kremsmünster Stiftsgymnasium (monastery secondary school) from 1818 to 1826, after which he lived in the Vienna of Metternich's police state.[3] Frustrated and disillusioned after the revolutionary year of 1848, he left the capital and until his death lived in Linz on the Danube, where he accepted a position as a teacher and later a regional school inspector.[4]

The period after the Vienna Congress until the early years of government of

Fig. 1.
Adalbert Stifter
View over Houses in the Suburbs of Vienna (Beatrixgasse)
(Blick über Wiener Vorstadthäuser [Beatrixgasse]), detail, 1839
Belvedere, Vienna

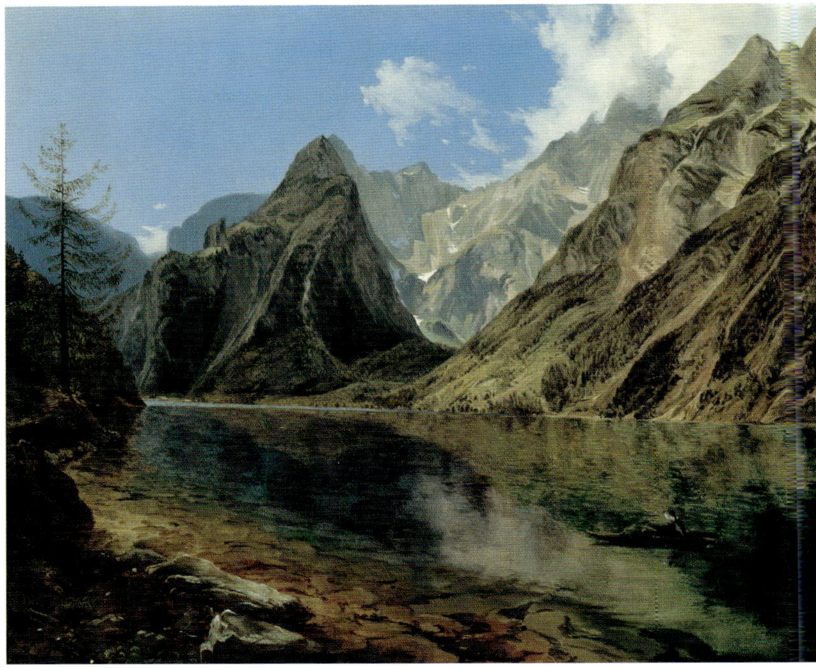

Fig.2.
Adalbert Stifter
Lake Königssee with the Watzmann Mountain
(Der Königsee mit dem Watzmann), 1837
Belvedere, Vienna

Emperor Franz Joseph I was marked by the rigid implementation of the old absolutist social order, which was also to become fundamentally evident in Stifter's mindset. Stifter was basically opposed to any kind of revolution and advocated social progress from the within on the basis of the moral betterment of each individual. For him, above all pedagogics was the means to this end. A comprehensive, scientific and moral education was to enable the citizen to lead a happy and independent life within the scope of the valid norms and conditions. Stifter is entirely in line with the tradition of the Enlightenment. He mentions Goethe as a great role model, and his admiration for Alexander von Humboldt is also expressed in his novels.[5] In particular in *Nachsommer* (Indian Summer) he outlines a conservative utopia in which every individual, from the Emperor to the servant, leads a satisfied and fulfilled life corresponding to his position and possibilities, as a necessary component of a greater whole.

Emil Jakob Schindler, on the other hand, was born as the son of a partner in a trading company in Vienna in 1842.[6] His youth after the revolution of 1848 was marked by the uneasy conditions under the young Emperor Franz Joseph, which were so contrary to Stifter's ideals in such a depressing way. The industrialization of the "Gründerzeit" era of industrial expansion and the increasingly serious conflict of nationalities in the whole Empire, combined with the wars involving heavy losses against France and Sardinia/Piedmont (1859) as well as against Prussia (1866), contrasted Stifter's ideas of a quiet, orderly and above all peaceful state with a completely different social development. Against the backdrop of these developments, his contemporaries could no longer follow his idealism, and even before his death, Schindler's literature was regarded as anachronistic, his description of art was considered excessively pedantic and long-winded. Friedrich Hebbel even bestowed the famous title the "buttercup and beetle poet" on him.[7]

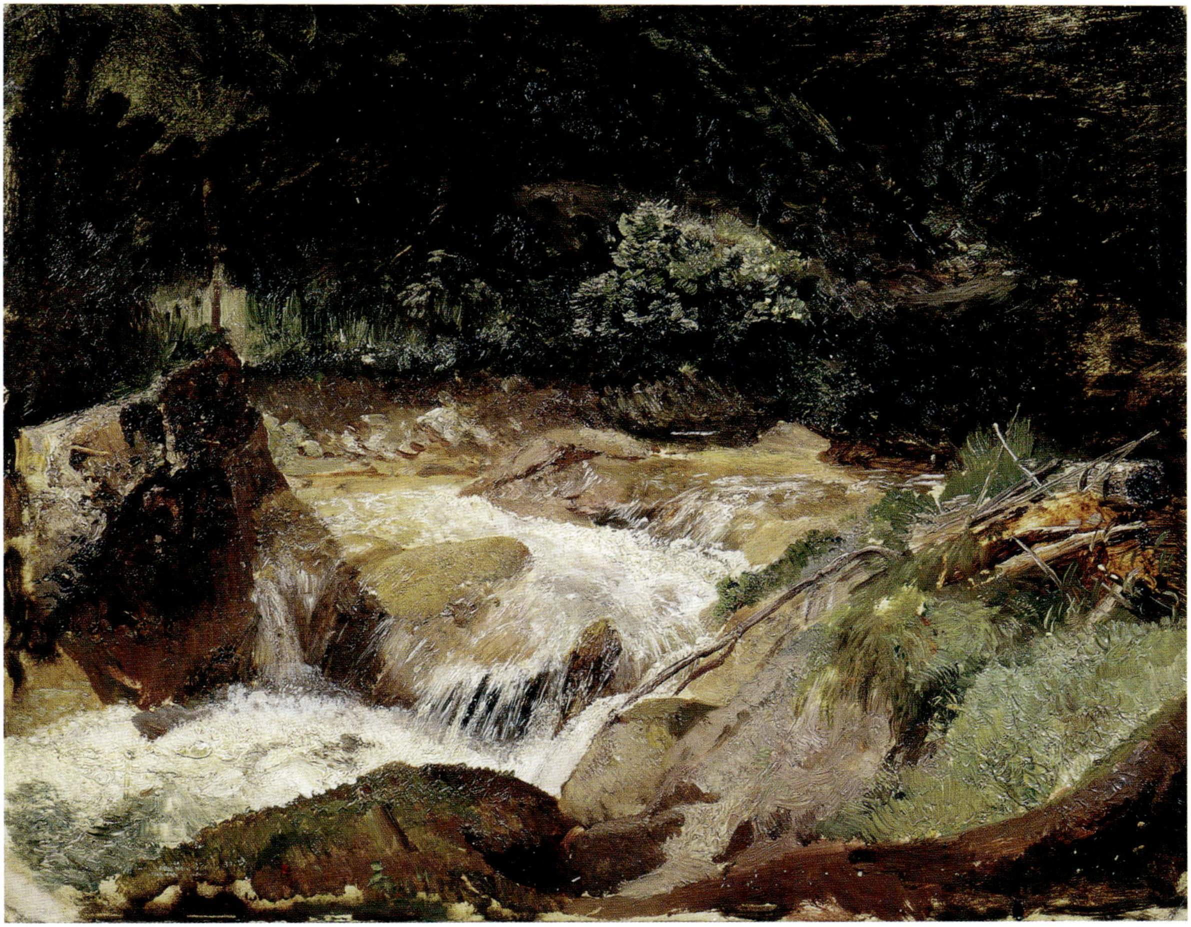

Fig.3.
Emil Jakob Schindler
Mountain Stream in the Ramsau
(Gebirgsbach in der Ramsau), c. 1868
Belvedere, Vienna

The great stars of the new era were artists such as Richard Wagner and Hans Makart, while the placid art of the Biedermeier period had long lost its attraction for Emil Jakob Schindler's generation.
Against this background, a direct reference of Schindler's painting to Adalbert Stifter's stories and thinking does not seem to be plausible. Yet Schindler's own activity as a landscape painter is still a linking element in this context; in his early years he was more active as a landscape painter than as a writer.[8] Self-educated, he had no solid education and so had to seek advice from befriended painters. As late as in the 1850s, he had to finally declare that he had failed in his dream of achieving true mastery as a painter and henceforth limited himself to his successful career as a writer.
Stifter's painting is fairly inconsistent. He primarily painted mountain landscapes in the Biedermeier style, as well as cityscapes such as the *View over Houses in the Suburbs of Vienna (Beatrixgasse)*[9] (fig. 1), which in their simple and unspectacular observation are reminiscent of the first photographic snapshots.
It is above all striking that Stifter's painting hardly conforms with his own literary style. Even though the natural-science view of his narratives is often found again in the meticulous details in the painting's foreground, the lack of technical

knowledge prevented him from coherently employing this style in complex paintings of the sort that Waldmüller, for example, was a master. Schindler's simpler and plainer compositions that do without meticulous detail are generally regarded as his most successful, for example *Lake Königssee with the Watzmann Mountain*[10] (fig. 2) or *View over Houses in the Suburbs of Vienna (Beatrixgasse)*. While Stifter the author is often matter-of-fact and austere, as a painter he often tends to pathos. In paintings, he wants to impress with motifs such as thunderstorms and nights of full moons, and thus contradicts his own, meanwhile famous foreword to his story collection *Bunte Steine* (Colorful Stones), in which – referring to the critics of his descriptive style – he explicitly speaks against the (literary) representation of extraordinary natural phenomena and advocates the common and the small as the truly significant: "I consider the wafting of the air, the trickling of the water the growing of crops, the rippling of the sea the greening of the earth the shining of the sky, the sparkling of the star to be awesome: I do not think that the magnificently incoming thunderstorm, the lightning that cracks the houses, the storm driving up the surf, the mountain spitting fire, the earthquake burying countries are greater than the above manifestations; yes, I consider them more as insignificant, because they are only the effects of much higher laws. They appear at individual locations and they are the results of one-sided causes."[11]

For these reasons, in the following the main emphasis will be on Stifter's literary work rather than on Stifter as a painter. To this end, three representative works will be considered: the early narrative *Der Hochwald* (The High Forest), the main work from his middle years *Der Nachsommer* (Indian Summer) and the late narrative *Nachkommenschaften* (Descendants)[12]. In these works, Schindler examines nature and to some extent landscape painting particularly intensively. In addition, they reveal a personal development that makes it possible to deduce common features with and differences from Schindler.

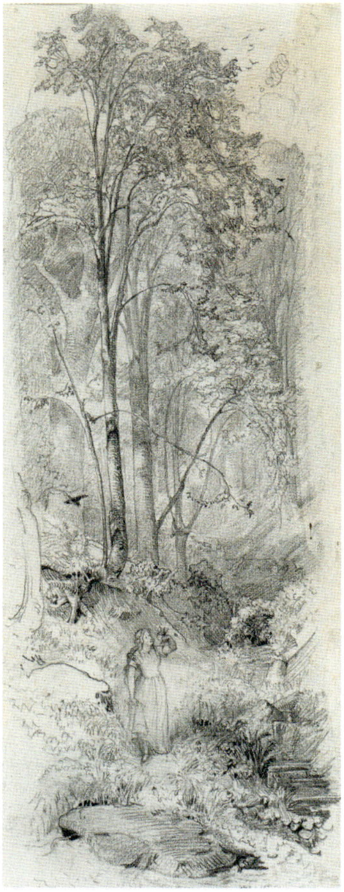

Fig.4.
Emil Jakob Schindler
"*Waldfräulein*" *Grows Up*
(Waldfräulein wächst heran), before 1868
Private collection

Der Hochwald (The High Forest)

In his early narrative *Der Hochwald* (1841) Stifter tells of a journey through the Bohemian Forest by an old knight with his two young daughters and his son. He wants to bring them to safety from the dangers of the Thirty Years' War in a hiding place by a forest lake. The daughters, Johanna and Klarissa, at first experience the forest as something threatening, but then gradually lose their timidity and become immersed in nature: "Anyone who looks at the girls' faces – how they are floating double, purely and tenderly against the dark ground of the forest foliage, how they glance bloomingly and gaily out of the flowing white veil of the headgear – would have never thought that they only recently feared and shrank so much from these woods. Johanna remained almost always at the top, as much as previously, in accordance with her nature, she was utterly terrified, so now she was also utterly delighted."[13]

The deeply romantic, fairytale-like nature of this story is obvious, but is relegated to its historical dimension as early as at the beginning. The narrator is a wanderer from Stifter's time who – after a thorough description of the Bohemian Forest – at the sight of the ruin of Wittinghausen castle retells the events that ended 200 years earlier with the castle's destruction. But the story does not focus on the historic events. Stifter's intention becomes obvious in the details of the description of life in the lonely, but wildly romantic nature of the Bohemian Forest.

The teacher figure of the hunter Gregor serves as counter-image to the two maidens. He is a former companion of the lord of Wittinghausen castle. This experienced man of nature drives out the young girls' superstition and the prejudices against the natural world. He takes away the girls' irrational fear of the unknown wilderness by providing them simple natural scientific explanations for phenomena that popular belief links with supernatural ideas, and he exposes old stories as products of a too lively imagination of an unknown wilderness. Yet seemingly Schindler attaches great importance to the fact that this wilderness does not lose its wondrous beauty as a result: "[...] but do see since I gradually became acquainted with the forest and understood how full of miracles it was even without people weaving their fables into it [...]"[14]

Emil Jakob Schindler's early work is also marked by wild forest landscapes (fig. 3). His earliest known works are small studies of the forests of the Bavarian and Austrian Alpine valleys, to which his teacher Albert Zimmermann regularly traveled with his students. Schindler still shows the wild mountain streams, clearings and forest mills in excessive romantic pathos. But they are already reminiscent of the later realism. From 1868 Schindler worked on illustrations of the fairytale *Das Waldfräulein* (The Woodland Girl) by Joseph Christian von Zedlitz. Ca. 21 pencil drawings and the painting "*Waldfraulein's*" *Birth*[15] (fig. p. 19) were produced. In the first place, the refined sheets show wild romantic forest views of the Spessart Forest, in which the fairytale is set. The protagonists of the narrative are treated as mere extras, they appear tiny and are in most cases so completely integrated into the surrounding woodland that at first glance they are often unnoticeable. Especially through a dynamic play of light and shadow full of contrast, Schindler successfully captures the enchanted fairytale atmosphere of Zedlitz's story. The tale is about a girl whose mother became pregnant out of wedlock, escaped to the forest and died when the girl was born. Yet the girl is rescued and brought up by a fairy, until she herself falls prey to the temptations of love. The "*Waldfräulein*" is the romantic figure of a child who lives innocently in complete harmony with nature, similar to the two girls in Stifter's *Hochwald*, after they lost their fear of nature.

Only a little later Schindler's art experienced a complete change of direction. With the *Steamer Station* (fig. p. 75) around 1871/72 he painted his main early work that put him on the tracks of the Barbizon School and the *Paysage intime*.[16]

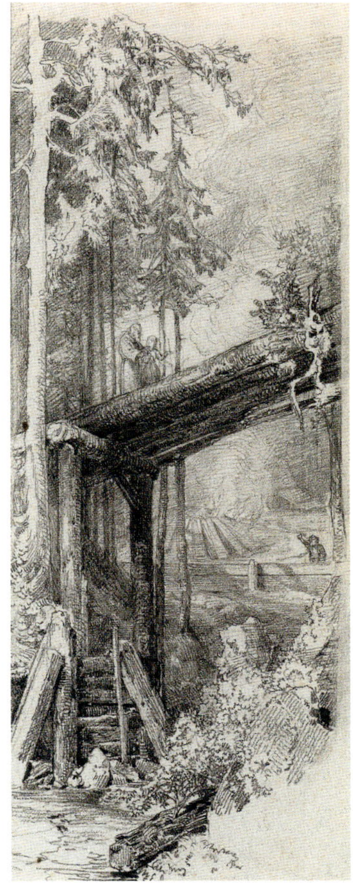

Fig.5.
Emil Jakob Schindler
"*Waldfräulein*" *is Threatened by the Charcoal-Burner Cyprus and Freed by the Hermit*
(Waldfräulein wird vom Köhler Cyprus bedroht und vom Einsiedel befreit),
before 1868
Private collection

Der Nachsommer (Indian Summer) – the Garden

Der *Nachsommer* (1857) is one of Stifter's main works. It is a *Bildungsroman* and at the same time a utopian parable, in which Stifter contrasts the disappointing conditions of his time with the design of a fulfilled life through voluntary order, discipline, moral values and not least through science and education. Stifter remarks to his publisher: "Presumably [I] have accomplished the work because of the badness which in general with some exceptions predominates in the conditions of the states in the world, both as regards the ethical life of these and the art of writing [...] In this work, I wanted to draw a deeper and richer life, as it generally occurs, and this to perfection."[17]

In the first and second chapters the development of the young Heinrich Drendorf toward independence and his gradual cutting ties with his parents' home in the city initially correspond with an increasingly deep immersion in nature.[18] The personal developmental path runs from the bourgeois existence in Vienna via increasingly extensive trips to the surrounding villages up to the

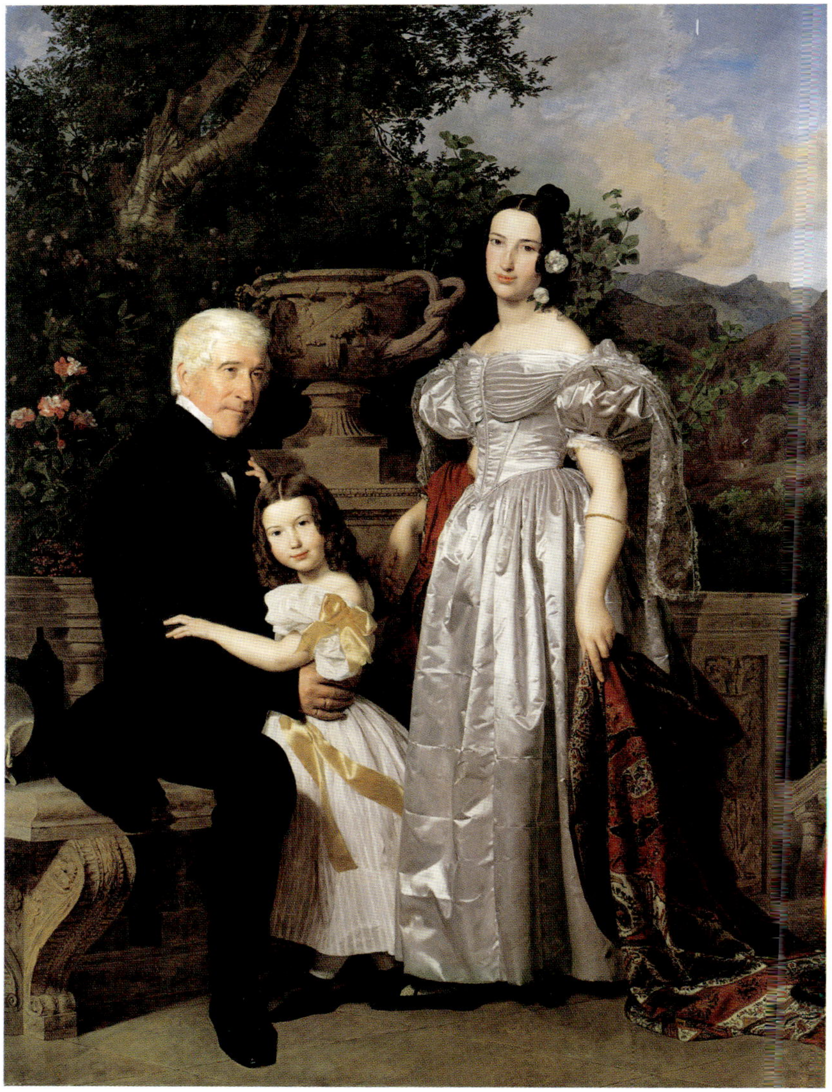

Fig.6.
Ferdinand Georg Waldmüller
Prince Esterházy's Councillor Mathias Kerzmann with his Second Wife, née Countess Majlath, and his Daughter Maria
(Der fürstliche Esterházysche Rat Mathias Kerzmann mit seiner zweiten Gattin, geb. Gräfin Majlath, und seiner Tochter Maria), 1835
Belvedere, Vienna

discovery of the wilderness of the high mountains. The ordered world of urban civilization with its restrictive life is increasingly exchanged with the freedom of the unspoiled natural world. Yet Heinrich is not idle; he concerns himself with natural science, does empirical nature research and learns about the processes in nature and agriculture. But above all he is interested in geological formations in the mountains. He collects rocks and samples of earth. This lonely effort comes to an end, however, when the young researcher seeks refuge on a large farm in a thunderstorm and finds a new mentor in the house's new owner, Baron Risach. The idyllic conditions in the *Rosenhaus* (Rose House), in which every detail is arranged cleverly and thoughtfully, become the alternative draft to a chaotic reality that lacks order, spirit and knowledge. In the Rose House's garden, the plants are not only more beautiful than elsewhere, but also completely healthy. No vermin or sicknesses disturb growth and the beautiful sight of flowers and

trees.[19] This condition is not achieved through the use of poison and fertilizer, but simply through the skilful use of natural-science knowledge referring to gardening and organic farming, which Stifter explains in every detail. Where despite every precaution there are wilted leaves, they are immediately removed by hand so they do not disturb the perfect order.[20] The knowing response to the natural needs of every plant and every living being in their complicated interplay turns the host into a model for people in positions of social responsibility. So Risach's garden also serves as the basis of an ideal state in microcosm. But unlike with Plato, the ideal ruler is now no longer a philosopher – Risach explicitly rejects philosophy[21] – but he is an authority on natural history and an art lover.
Stifter's ideas can most closely be compared with pictures by Waldmüller, for example with the picture of the Kerzmann family (fig. 6), who are shown on their terrace in their idyllic landscape garden. The left of the picture even displays some roses. One looks in vain for such a claim in Schindler's garden paintings. For Schindler, the garden is also a symbol of the ideal world, but he is more realistic in this respect and also accepts the incomplete in nature, indeed, even this aspect has an individual charm for him. In Schindler's *Flower Garden in Weißenkirchen* (p. 87) the lush vegetation overgrows the entire setting, including the architectural elements. Even though flowerbeds and a path are recognizable, with regard to aesthetic aspects the garden as a whole appears rather chaotic and neglected.
While Schindler's garden pictures represent almost an opposite to Stifter's *Rosenhaus* garden, Schindler is closer to Stifter in his theoretical writings. In the manuscripts on his planned art historical treatise, Schindler also left a chapter on horticulture, in which he describes the various historical types of design. Contrary to the current style of the English landscape garden and its imitation of unspoiled nature, he polemicizes in his usual sharp way: "We used to have a garden art, today we have a nursery and we forget that the garden can never be a piece of nature and will never be one."[22] Here Schindler clearly admits the architectural function of the garden, which is openly artificial and is to reveal itself as a piece of art, as he shows it in his painting *In the Garden at Schloss Niederweiden* (p. 79).

Nachkommenschaften (Descendants) – the Moor

In *Nachkommenschaften* (1865) Stifter describes a young landscape painter who, like Stifter himself, wealthy and self-taught, has committed himself to his art out of sheer enthusiasm.[23] Far away from his home town, Vienna, in which he is socially well integrated, Friedrich Roderer paints the moorland in the small village of Lüpfing. Tirelessly, he completes studies of the marshy area, intending to bring it together in a large landscape painting. Yet the moor landscape in Lüpfing is endangered: "But there is not much to paint since an unreasonably rich man has bought Firnberg castle there and now has had so many rocks and earth carried onto the moor and so many trenches drawn away from it that the moor has become smaller and the fever has reduced. He then harvested a bit of grass and very poor oats on the moor."[24]
The original moorland is thus cultivated for economic interests. What was previously a breeding-ground for Malaria, is now planted with oats. Here, a subtle criticism of capitalism, which sacrifices unspoiled nature for the pursuit for profit, comes to light: "[…] I say it was not worth mentioning what one could paint in the moor – but I have to paint it since the rich man will finally destroy it all and then there will be nothing to paint at all."[25]

However, Stifter dispenses with being indignant at this fact – the landscape painter afterwards rather befriends the castle owner. The drainage is accepted as necessary progress. Apparently, at this point Stifter had sufficiently recognized the signs of the times and knew that industrialization was unstoppable. Everywhere, unspoiled nature was falling victim to the modern frenzy to regulate, which was steadily expanding through the invention of various machines.
Here, Stifter and Schindler are as close as never before. Similar to the young Friedrich Roderer in Stifter's story, Schindler also looks for unspoiled spots of nature in the local moorland and meadow landscape, in order to record them before they are destroyed (fig. 7). Many of the scenes from the Danube meadows that Schindler painted around the year 1870 were destroyed very soon afterwards in the course of the regulation of the Danube (fig. 8, 9).
It is also remarkable how Stifter's Friedrich Roderer approaches the painting of the moor: "[...] because I wanted to begin with painting moor in the morning light, moor in the early noon light, moor in the noon light, moor in the afternoon light and paint at the corresponding sheet every day during the suitable hours, as long as the sky would allow it. I already had planned to paint the moor in the rain, from my window. I have not yet thought about the moor in the mist."[26]
Such a working method is also often found with Schindler. Before he started on a large oil painting, Schindler often produced a series of oil studies on the subject showing the motif in the most varied atmospheres, weather conditions and times of day. As with Schindler in most cases, in Stifter's *Nachkommenschaften* these studies culminated in the creation of a single large painting of the moor in Lüpfung, which, however, was ultimately all destroyed by the artist since it could not "[...] depict the dreariness, the simplicity and the sublimity of the moor."[27] Not only does Stifter here introduce a working method that is comparable to Schindler, but the idea of the atmosphere picture, which is so central for Schindler's understanding of art, also already comes to light: "Here, it is important to sense the solemn moments. Every religion has its festive days and the priests of the nature cults also have to function in some sort of vestment. One has to see the feast day in every work of art, as one also recognizes it in nature. The festive hours are not all too frequent, but nature has them, and they are to be sensed through illusions, through tranquility, through the harmony of color shades in the same way as the one whose senses are less tender and finer can recognize them in the respective weather and even in the completely dead gray of a day full of endless rain."[28]
In the *Nachkommenschaften*, only some ten years after Stifter had introduced a model design of the scientist's rational view of the world in *Nachsommer*, he described the profound, emotional and partly also tragic view of nature of the landscape painter of the *Paysage intime*.

The Objective and Subjective View of Nature

It is perspective that is the essential difference between the world view in Schindler's paintings and in Stifter's works. It is true that some of Schindler's paintings – not all of them by far – reveal Stifter's detailed description of nature. Yet Schindler is always mainly concerned with the harmonious whole of the pictorial impression. He binds atmospherically the heterogeneous elements together and underlays them with a consistent fundamental tone. His compositions thus become pictures of the fleeting moment. His works are always recordings of the moment.

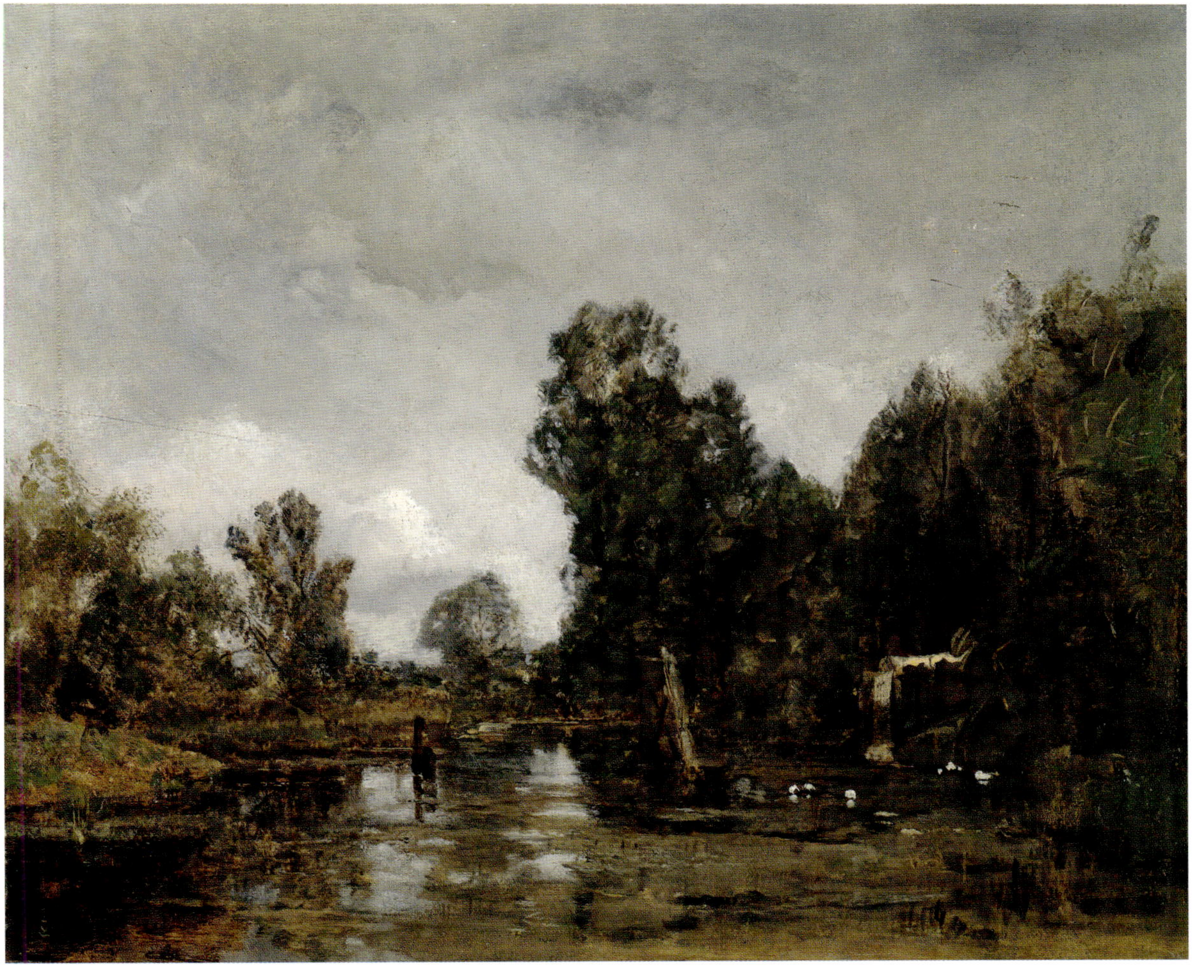

Fig.7.
Emil Jakob Schindler
Motif from the Vienna Prater (Krieau)
(Motiv aus dem Wiener Prater [Krieau]), 1876
Private collection

The whole scene could have a completely different effect just a moment later. Nevertheless his pictures are always a balanced whole. Like hardly any other painter, Schindler is concerned with the weather, with the change in the light, with humidity and the mist, and not in the least with the effect of the wind, which influences the portrayal of the plants and trees through the movement of the leaves. Schindler is well aware of the fact that the crown of a tree looks different in a picture of the moment when there is no wind than it does when the wind has set it in motion.

Stifter, too, does not stop at the observation of details. He, too, subsumes them into a larger picture, but unlike Schindler he does not achieve this in the form of a atmospheric "snapshot". Especially in *Nachsommer*, he rather strives for the construction of a "world landscape". He does not restrict himself to a small extract of reality, but he builds a macrocosm based on the sum of the individual descriptions. While in his art-history writings, taking the example of mountain paintings, Schindler describes precisely this claim as an impossible task for the painter – that is, to convincingly represent the larger whole in the view to the distance and at the same time the detail in a close-up view[29] – Stifter attempts to

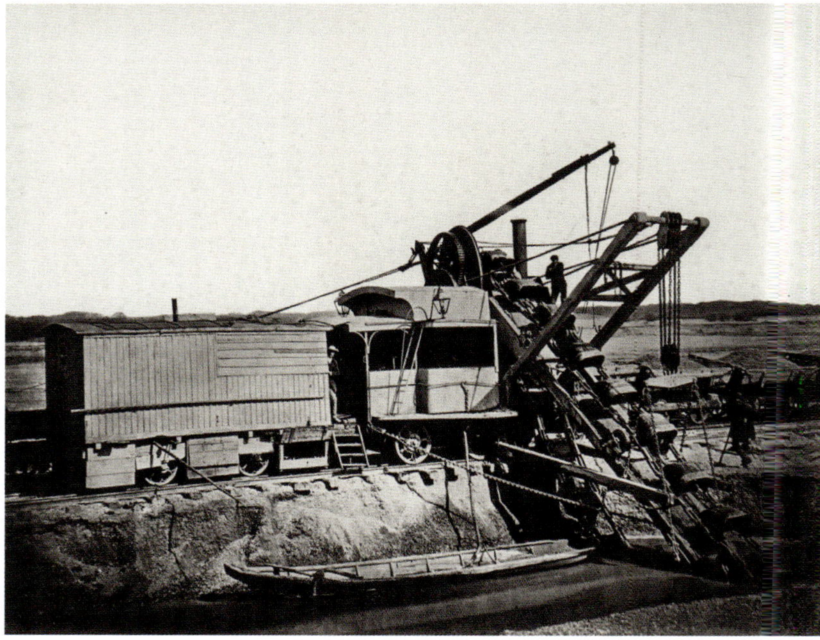

Fig.8.
Oskar Kramer
Excavateur (Front View),
(Excavateur [vordere Ansicht]), 1873/76
Albertina, Vienna

achieve this in his novels. He, too, was often criticized because in his works the general picture was allegedly lost behind the long-winded descriptions of detail.[30] Especially in *Nachsommer*, Stifter lays out the world of the Upper Austrian foothills of the Alps encyclopedically for his reader, cataloguing it like a natural scientist. He precisely enumerates their individual components and explains how these interact with each other. Stifter's view of the world is mechanical and in most cases also objective, nevertheless leaving room for the unexpected and the wonderful. In Stifter one often finds expressions of a sentimental view of nature, in which the astonished individual is confronted with it, although the objectivity of things is never called into question. The objective-scientific view of the world is only briefly interrupted here by a poetic-aesthetic one.

With his atmospheric pictures, Schindler, however, captures almost exclusively the aesthetic and subjective moment. The above quote from this writings shows how much his painting differs from Stifter's encyclopedic view of nature.

Schindler does not show any interest in the objects portrayed as such, but only in their effect in the aesthetic context of the artwork. The realism of his style goes only as far as his showing an optical impression of the objects, but only in poetically charged form. His landscapes primarily convey a feeling, a atmosphere or a poetic sentiment which the artist puts into them and which is to be sensed by the viewer when looking at the picture.[31] This becomes particularly evident in the fleeting oil sketches, in which the artist examines the atmosphere of the respective landscape in its prevailing tone and thereby fathoms its potential with regard to the effect on the viewer (p. 92, 102).

The numerous reviews that Stifter published on the exhibitions in the Linz Kunstverein (art association) show that he was aware of the technical difficulties of landscape painting.[32] Yet in his literature he remains far from applying such an approach – he does not "paint" landscapes in an atmospheric context, but

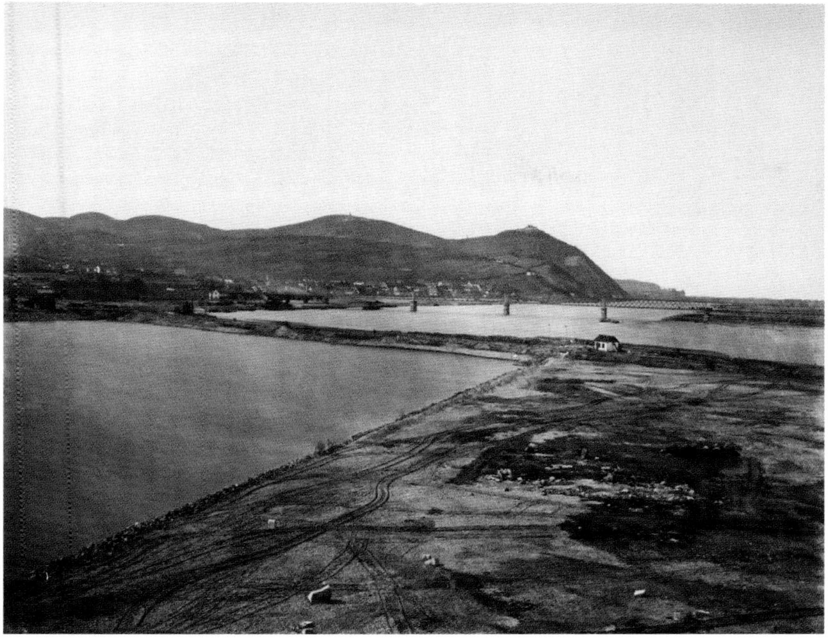

Fig.9.
Oskar Kramer
Upper Overflow Basin and the Roller-Dam
(Oberes Durchstich-Bassin mit dem Roller-Damme), April 10, 1875
Albertina, Vienna

describes details and assembles these into a picture. In *Nachsommer* Stifter describes a method of painting that is related to this approach: in the natural-science illustration or in the draft design for buildings and interior designs, everything is aimed at the clear record of the depicted object's structure and its composition: "Until now I had drawn objects in reference to my field of study with the characteristics as the most important aspect. These had to be expressed in the drawing with emphasis on the features distinguishing a given object from related ones."[33]

Neither does Stifter's protagonist conceal that his attempts in drawing and painting start in this field, and here he is also much more successful than in the far more difficult art of landscape painting. Apparently, Stifter deliberately resorted to this style in his novels and tales in order to show the "true reality" as clearly and as purely as possible. This is also confirmed by an almost programmatic statement by the young painter Friedrich Roderer in *Nachkommenschaften*: "True, it is said that it would be a major mistake for one to depict the real too realistically: one would become dry, craft-oriented and would destroy the entire poetic fragrance of work. Free zest, free judgment, free flight of the artist would be necessary, then a free, light and poetic work would emerge. Otherwise, everything would be in vain and finished. – This is what people who cannot depict reality say. Yet I am saying: why did God make the real so realistically at all and most realistically in his artwork, and yet achieved in it the highest impetus, which you cannot achieve even with all your panache? The world and its parts contain the utmost poetic wealth and the most heart-breaking violence. Do make reality as realistic as it is, and do not change the zest, which is in it anyway, and you will bring about more wonderful works than you believe and than you do if you merely paint after reality and say: now it has zest."[34]

Here, the difference from Schindler is above all evident in the fact that Stifter is very little concerned with reproducing a poetic feeling from out of himself or a particularly individual mood through his (landscape) descriptions. For Stifter the poetry as such is already present in nature itself in its most complete form, not in the person of the artist. Stifter's description is therefore mostly as subject-oriented and prosaic as it can ever be. He only directs the view and the reader's attention to nature and does not try to intensify its beauty poetically. It is the naturalist's curious view, not that of the poet. Schindler, however, despite all the realism of his landscapes, still always sees himself as a poetic observer, who does not look at nature objectively but in his very subjective mood, deliberately charged with emotion.[35] He faces nature like a person with whom he is communicating, he dismantles and re-forms it, as it deems appropriate to him for his artistic end product.[36] For him, nature has a magic that he wants to explicitly express by artistic means. For Schindler, a purely objective description such as with Stifter, which only reproduces reality without having it translated into a new form by the artist's eyes, soul and hands, would not have the power to convey nature's poetry hidden beneath the surface. "The absolute landscapist will never be in a position to copy nature, but he certainly has to discern it. He needs an unfathomable knowledge and in this context, the real sciences support him only very little. His plant cannot be found in any botanical work, his stone is not part of any mineralogy. In all things, he only has to deal with the extract that his eye may see in their existence. This eye must be emotionally enhanced through the soul, so that it becomes a second soul."[37]

Here, the concept of empathy aesthetics, which was conceived at about the same time by Friedrich Theodor Vischer and especially by his son Robert is already anticipated. This concept was of utmost importance for the development of Modernism.[38] Stifter is very noticeably still obliged to the classical tradition of Alexander Baumgarten and Georg Wilhelm Friedrich Hegel, according to which beauty is only inherent in the objects' qualities, so that it can be basically objectively and universally experienced. Empathy aesthetics, to the contrary, considers the aesthetic experience taking account of the subjective condition of the individual viewer, who himself empathizes with his object. Stifter's and the Biedermeier painters' realism and the sensitive approach to nature have remained with Schindler. Yet empathy with nature was a new development of his time.

In summary, the following conclusion can be drawn with regard to the differences in the approach to nature: Stifter is above all an objective admirer of nature; Schindler in contrast is a subjective interpreter. Both positions have their justification and certainly also their respective significance for Modernism: Schindler's expression of the artist's personality in an artistically re-formed nature as predecessor of expressionistic developments, Stifter's austere objectivity in dealing with nature in the New Objectivity of the 1920s and 1930s.

1 Carl Moll, "Wie der Schüler seinen Meister sieht", in: *Emil Jakob Schindler 1842–1892. Gedächtnisausstellung* (exh.cat. Galerie des 19. Jahrhunderts, Vienna 1942), Vienna 1942, p. 8. – Ulla Weich, "Sehnsuchts-, Flucht- und Schicksalsort. Über das Verhältnis zu Natur und Landschaft im Österreich der 2. Hälfte des 19. Jahrhunderts anhand literarischer Beispiele", in: *Natürlichere Natur. Österreichische Malerei des Stimmungsrealismus* (exh.cat. Kunsthaus Mürzzuschlag, Mürzzuschlag 1994), Mürzzuschlag 1994, pp. 36f. – Klaus Demus, "E. J. Schindlers Zyklus 'Die Monate' und der Stimmungsimpressionismus", in: *Mitteilungen der Österreichischen Galerie*, 3. yr., No. 34–36, 1959, p. 38.
Above all Stifter's claim to produce a "realistic reality" (Adalbert Stifter, *Nachkommenschaften*, in: Johannes John/Sibylle von Steinsdorff [eds.], *Adalbert Stifter. Werke und Briefe. Historisch-kritische Gesamtausgabe*, Stuttgart 2002 [in the following: WuB], vol. 3,2, p. 65) tended to be applied to the painting of the Schindler-circle: Gerbert Frodl, "Die Landschaftsmalerei", in: *Das Zeitalter Kaiser Franz Josephs: 1. Teil. Von der Revolution zur Gründerzeit* (exh.cat. Niederösterreichisches Landesmuseum, Schloss Grafenegg 1984), Vienna 1984, p. 468. – Cf. also the exhibition title *Natürlichere Natur* (A More Realistic Nature) in Mürzzuschlag 1994.

2 Hermann Bahr distinguishes Liliencron particularly as a "atmospheric artist" ("Das jüngste Deutschland", in: *Studien zur Kritik der Moderne*, Weimar 2005, pp. 140–141).

3 Moriz Enzinger, *Adalbert Stifters Studienjahre (1818–1830)*, Innsbruck 1950.

4 On Stifter's biography cf. Kurt Gerhard Fischer, *Adalbert Stifter. Psychologische Beiträge zur Biographie*, Linz 1961. – Wolfgang Matz, *Adalbert Stifter oder Diese fürchterliche Wendung der Dinge*, Munich/Vienna 1995.

5 Adalbert Stifter, *Indian Summer*, trans. by Wendell Frye, 4th ed., Bern 2009, p. 57. – On Stifter's relationship to Humboldt cf. also Franziska Schößler, "Der Weltreisende Alexander von Humboldt in den österreichischen Bergen. Das naturwissenschaftliche Projekt in Adalbert Stifters Nachsommer", in: Sabina Becker/Katharina Grätz (eds.), *Ordnung – Raum – Ritual. Adalbert Stifters artifizieller Realismus*, Heidelberg 2007, pp. 261–286.

6 Peter Weninger/Peter Müller, *Die Schule von Plankenberg*, Graz 1991, p. 15.

7 *Leipziger Illustrierte Zeitung*, September 4, 1858. – Friedrich Hebbel, "Der Nachsommer von Adalbert Stifter", in: Richard Maria Werner (ed.), *Friedrich Hebbel. Sämtliche Werke. Historisch-kritische Ausgabe*, sect. I, vol. 12. – On Hebbel's criticism cf. also Lothar Schneider, "Das Komma im Frack. Adalbert Stifter, von Hebbels Kritik aus betrachtet", in: Hartmut Laufhütte/Karl Möseneder (ed.), *Adalbert Stifter – Dichter und Maler, Denkmalpfleger und Schulmann. Neue Zugänge zu seinem Werk*, Tübingen 1996, pp. 105–118.
On the subject of the early Stifter-reception cf. Moriz Enzinger, *Adalbert Stifter im Urteil seiner Zeit*, Vienna 1968. – Alfred Doppler, "Die Nachrufe auf Stifters Tod", in: Johann Lachinger (ed.), *Adalbert Stifter. Studien zu seiner Rezeption und Wirkung I: 1868–1930*, Linz 1995, pp. 11–20.

8 On Stifter's painting cf. Fritz Novotny, *Adalbert Stifter als Maler*, 4th ed., Vienna 1979. – Franz Baumer, *Adalbert Stifter der Zeichner und Maler*, Passau 1979. – Brigitte Hauptner, *Adalbert Stifter und die zeitgenössische Landschaftsmalerei*, dipl. thesis, Vienna 1996. – Karl Möseneder, "Stimmung und Erdleben. Adalbert Stifters Ikonologie der Landschaftsmalerei", in: Laufhütte/Möseneder 1996, pp. 18–57.

9 Adalbert Stifter, *Blick über Wiener Vorstadthäuser (Beatrixgasse)*, 1839, Belvedere, Vienna, inv. no. 1284.

10 Adalbert Stifter, *Der Königsee mit dem Watzmann*, 1837, Belvedere, Vienna, inv.no. 517.

11 Adalbert Stifter, *Bunte Steine*, in: WuB, vol. 2,2, pp. 14f. [As to the translation cf. note 12, translation of the passage: Dörte Eliass.]

12 [Very few of Stifter's works have been translated into English. Of those mentioned in this essay only *Nachsommer* (Indian Summer) is available: trans. by Wendell Frye, 4th ed., Bern 2009]

13 Adalbert Stifter, *Der Hochwald*, in: WuB, vol. 1,4, p. 236. [Translation of the passage: Dörte Eliass.]

14 Stifter, *Der Hochwald*, in: WuB, vol. 1,4, p. 267. [Translation of the passage: Dörte Eliass.]

15 Emil Jakob Schindler, *Waldfräuleins Geburt*, 1868, Akademie der bildenden Künste Wien (Academy of Fine Arts Vienna).

16 At the latest, Schindler had the occasion to become acquainted with the painters of Barbizon on the I. International Art Exhibition in the Glass Palace in Munich 1869, at which he exhibited two works himself (No. 506: *Wood Scene* [Waldpartie], No. 620: *Alp* [Alpe]). A large number of the Barbizon painters were represented there. Five paintings were exhibited by Díaz de la Peña, four each by Corot and Troyon, three by Harpignies, two by Daubigny and one by Rousseau: *Katalog zur I. Internationalen Kunstausstellung im Königlichen Glaspalaste zu München*, Munich 1869.
As early as in December 1868, pictures by Rousseau, Daubigny, Troyon, Jacque and others were

exhibited in the Künstlerhaus (House of Artists) in Vienna. Cf. Martina Haja, "Der österreichische Stimmungsimpressionismus", in: Götz Czymmek (ed.), *Landschaft im Licht. Impressionistische Malerei in Europa und Nordamerika 1860–1910* (exh.cat. Wallraf-Richartz Museum, Cologne 1990, Kunsthaus Zürich, Zurich 1990), Cologne/Zurich 1990, p. 158.

17 Adalbert Stifter, *Sämmtliche Werke*, Prague 1929, vol. 19, pp. 93f. [Translation of the passage: Dörte Eliass.] – Christian Begemann, "'Realismus' oder 'Idealismus"? Über einige Schwierigkeiten bei der Rekonstruktion von Stifters Kunstbegriff", in: Laufhütte/Möseneder 1996, pp. 6f.

18 Adalbert Stifter, *Indian Summer*, trans. by Wendell Frye, 4th ed., Bern 2009, pp. 9–30.

19 Stifter, *Indian Summer*, trans. by Wendell Frye, 4th ed., Bern 2009, vol. 1, ch. 5.

20 Stifter, *Indian Summer*, trans. by Wendell Frye, 4th ed., Bern 2009, vol. 1, p. 140ff.

21 Stifter, *Indian Summer*, trans. by Wendell Frye, 4th ed., Bern 2009, vol. 2, p. 199ff.

22 As cited in Elisabeth Edith Kamenicek, *Emil Jakob Schindler (1842–1892). Sein schriftliches Werk im Kontext von Kunsthandel, Mäzenatentum und Kunstkritik seiner Zeit*, doct. thesis, Salzburg 2002, vol. 2, pp. 247f.

23 Adalbert Stifter, *Nachkommenschaften*, in: WuB, vol. 3,2, pp. 25–94.

24 Stifter, *Nachkommenschaften*, in: WuB, vol. 3,2, p. 32. [Translation of the passage by Dörte Eliass.]

25 Stifter, *Nachkommenschaften*, in: WuB, vol. 3,2, p. 32. [Translation of the passage by Dörte Eliass.]

26 Stifter, *Nachkommenschaften*, in: WuB, vol. 3,2, p. 38. [Translation of the passage by Dörte Eliass.]

27 Stifter, *Nachkommenschaften*, in: WuB, 3,2, p. 92. [Translation of the passage by Dörte Eliass.]

28 As cited in Kamenicek 2002, vol. 2, p. 262.

29 Kamenicek 2002, vol. 2, p. 298.

30 Erzinger 1968, p. 203.

31 According to this view, Schindler can neither be appropriately characterized as a realist nor as a naturalist. Following the line of thought which he develops in his theoretical writing, he neither truly focuses on reality nor nature in his work, but really on the art of painting as such. Another quote demonstrates that Schindler, too, only came to this realization after a long search: "In order to achieve this, we lack what the worst color paint mixer of Poussin or Claude [Lorrain] intuitively knew, the rule, the principle, the general basis and the compositional theory of painting. There is no artwork without it. One may be as reluctant to admit it as you like. I lost 20 years of my life in this battle; many lost their whole life with it." (As cited in Kamenicek 2002, vol. 2, pp. 224f.)

32 Adalbert Stifter, *Schriften zur bildenden Kunst*, in: WuB, vol. 8,4.

33 Adalbert Stifter, *Indian Summer*, trans. by Wendell Frye, 4th ed., Bern 2009, p.195.

34 Stifter, *Nachkommenschaften*, in: WuB, vol. 3,2, p. 65. [Translation of the passage by Dörte Eliass.]

35 Schindler explicitly asks his students to educate their own personality and soul in their artistic work. Cf. Elisabeth Kamenicek's contribution in this volume on p. 53, notes 17, 18.

36 Carl Moll's description is significant: he describes how Schindler replaces individual pictorial objects by others during painting and overpaints them. Thus the artwork is autonomized in the painting process before the immediate depiction of nature. Cf. on this the quote in Andrea Winklbauer's contribution in this volume on page 26.

37 As cited in Kamenicek 2002, vol. 2, p. 262.

38 On the concept of 'empathy aesthetics' cf. Thomas Friedrich/Jörg H. Gleiter (eds.), *Einfühlung und phänomenologische Reduktion*, Berlin 2007.

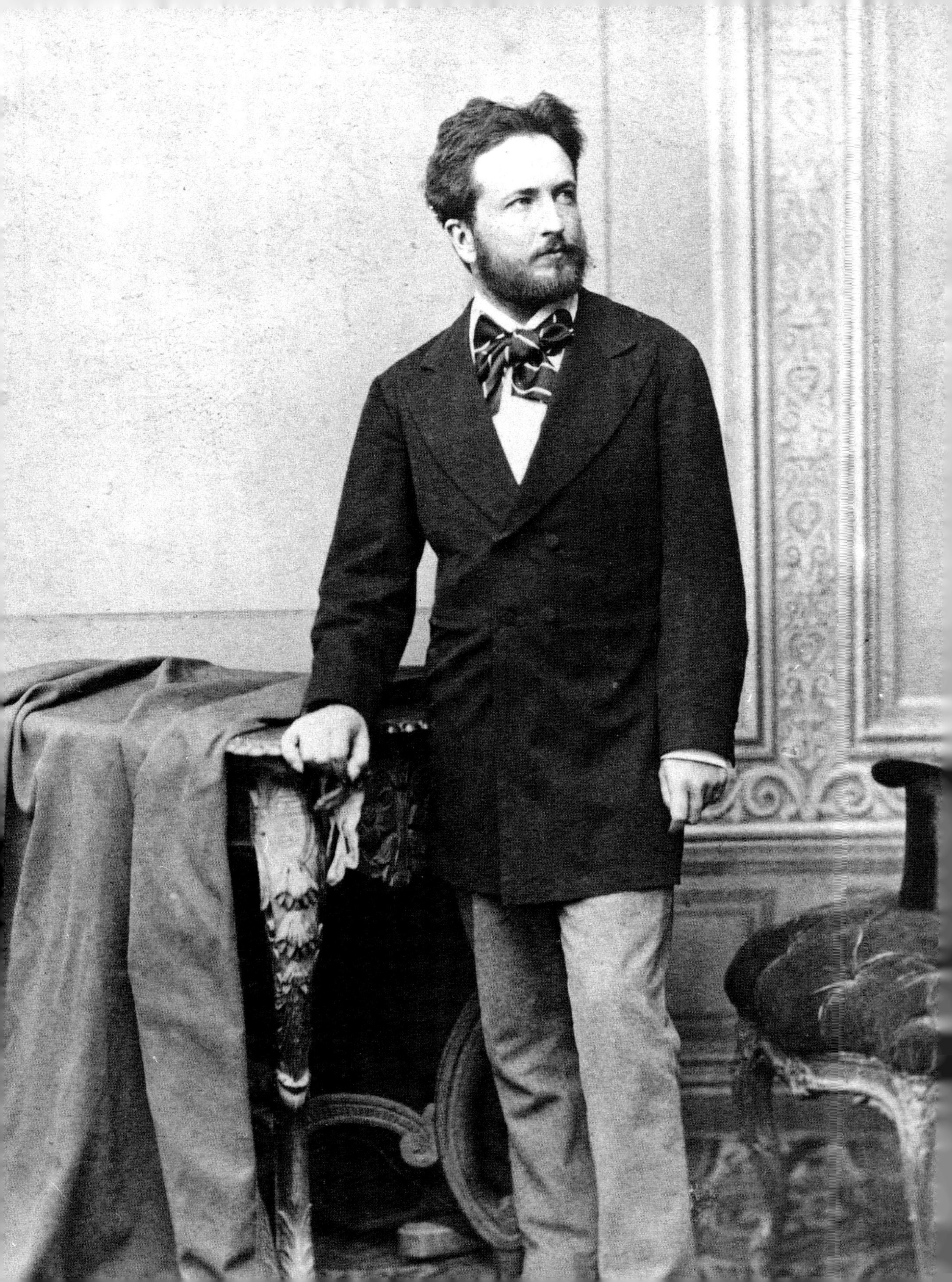

Elisabeth Kamenicek

Nature.Composition
Theoretical Fragments on Landscape Painting

"To my mind, what I want and try to achieve is the culmination of the most important modern branch of the fine arts, landscape painting."[1] On April 13, 1879 Emil Jakob Schindler writes this confidentially in his diary, in which he mostly briefly also documents his artistic process (fig.2–4).[2] The artist systematically revealed his views on issues of landscape painting in the unfinished rough draft of a planned and never published book. This work was most probably written from 1885 to 1892 and has come down to us as a fragment in the form of a typescript (fig.5–6). And as artistic mentor of the "Plankenberg School of Painting", the artist who as early as in the 1870s taught students such as Marie (1846–1879) and Luise von Parmentier (later Begas-Parmentier, 1850–1920) and at the beginning of the 1880s Olga Wisinger-Florian (1844–1926), Marie Egner (1850–1940) and Carl Moll (1861–1945) as a result had good reason to theoretically examine the education and thus also the problems of painting.
In his "fragment" Schindler preferably refers to "old masters" such as Jacob van Ruisdael (1628/29–1682), Allart van Everdingen (1621–1675) and to his student Meindert Hobbema (1638–1709), Rembrandt Harmensz van Rijn (1606–1669), Nicolas Poussin (1593/94–1665) and Claude Lorrain (1600–1682). With regard to his own century, he mentions above all the names of the brothers Andreas (1815–1910) and Oswald Achenbach (1827–1905), sometimes also several painters of the Munich School of Painting, and some pages are dedicated to the French Barbizon School. However, it is remarkable that references to other European art movements are lacking, for example to John Constable (1776–1837) and William Turner (1775–1851) or to the French Impressionists, who were active at the same time.

Landscape in the Aesthetic Discourse

The number of treatises and theoretical essays on landscape painting between the 18th and 20th century is immense.[3] In this context, for example, Christian Ludwig Hagedorn's (1712–1780) *Betrachtungen über die Mahlerey*, which were published in 1762 in two volumes and contributed decisive aspects to the development of German taste through the communication of the primarily French art literature, should be mentioned.[4] Salomon Gessner (1730–1788) had been unusually successful in Germany, but also in France with his work *Idylle*, which had already been published anonymously in Zurich six years earlier: a collection of prose pieces of bucolic nature. "It captured the atmosphere of the loss of nature with its descriptions of a life without conflict of sensitive shepherds living free and without any needs, 'which are caused only by the unhappy detachment from nature' (*Foreword* 1756)."[5]

Fig.1.
Karl Herberth
Emil Jakob Schindler, c. 1875
ÖNB (Austrian National Library), Picture Archive, Vienna

In 1771 and 1774 Johann Georg Sulzer (1720–1779), who was active in Berlin, presented two volumes of his encyclopedia of aesthetics under the title *Allgemeine Theorie der Schönen Künste*, also comprising a whole contribution on the landscape that in essential parts draws on Lairesse[6] and Hagedorn and highlights the great esteem accorded to landscape painting.
Johann Wolfgang von Goethe's (1749–1832) short essay on "imitation, manner and style"[7] in 1789 undoubtedly influenced the considerations of the Goethe-admirer Schindler. In his essay Goethe takes up the problem of the various kinds of imitation and their relationship to the invention of the image. He differentiates between the subjective need for expression and the insight into the essence of things. "Manner", the form of production between imitation and style, occupies most of the article.[8] Goethe's essay on Jacob van Ruisdael probably also exerted some influence on Emil Jakob Schindler's observations on this most influential and often copied Dutch landscape artist of the 17th century.
The education as a landscape painter in the 19th century was, however, above all marked by the writings of Pierre-Henri de Valenciennes (1750–1819), a student of Claude-Joseph Vernet (1714–1789). Around 1800 this artist edited the possibly most significant work on landscape painting.[9] "Valenciennes must have felt that the landscape, the forms of nature were to be the true object of the coming century [...] he felt that it was not the pursuit of mathematical rules that was promising for the future but the observation of the changeable and irregular."[10]
Lithography played an important role in the spreading of the new attitudes and teaching methods in the field of landscape painting. As early as 1820 maps with lithographs were published that were destined for students of the academy who wanted to educate themselves further in the subject of landscape painting – for example the *Leçon de paysage* by Alexandre Calame (1810–1864), the landscape painter, graphic designer and draughtsman of series such as *Esquisse d'après nature*.[11]

From Open Air into the Studio

Schindler's theoretical conception of a landscape painter's good education, i.e. "the free development"[12] of a student, starts for him as early as in "primary school". According to him, in the "academic landscape school" the student would already master perspective, drawing and painting from models and "leaf ornaments" before he or she would "work from nature".[13] "One simply had to have plain ornaments from all realms translated from nature, from the ancient Indian through the Egyptian, Greek, Roman, Gothic, Roman, Moorish up to the Renaissance and to the plait [i.e. the age of Baroque], albeit from existing originals, but still freely translated from nature in the sense of all these past genres of style. Thus the student will learn one thing, namely that there is no art form that does not result from a form of nature. So he will easily sense the underlying nature study from any really existing art."[14]
For Schindler, the student could now already "proficiently draw, paint, model, he can reproduce everything he sees in front of him in form and color. He has sincerely gone to the limit of what is worth knowing [...]".[15] Yet although he could now imitate nature, this would have nothing in common with the "painter's soul". His pictures convey the impression of a "nature study founded

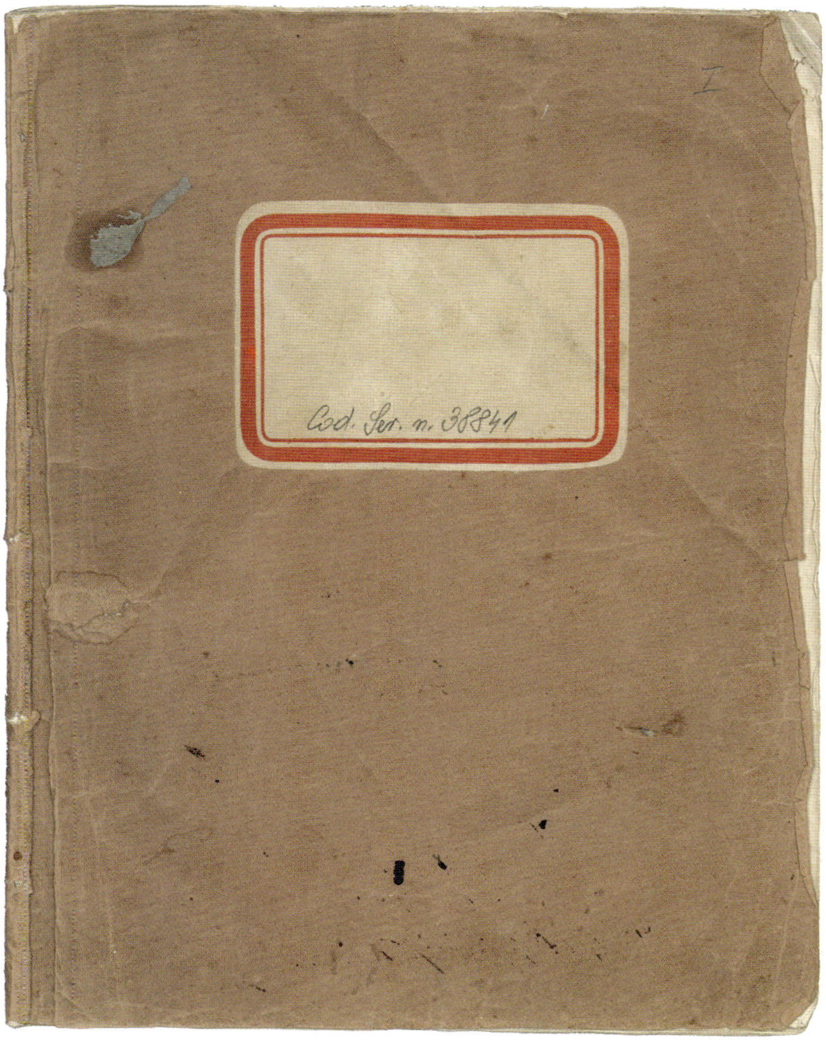

Fig.2.
Emil Jakob Schindler
Diary with Work List, 1879
Cover front
ÖNB (Austrian National Library),
Department of Manuscripts and Rare Books,
Vienna

under favorable auspices", from this moment the further process was "nothing more than a recovery of what [...] really already existed in the child, before it got the first pencil in its hand".[16] The student's task was now above all to look for himself"[17]. He would see in advance "as a border the artwork, his own soul that he has to draw on for support in creating"[18].

Dream Images in the Temple of Art

Schindler describes the artwork as "something independent, [as] a creation and dependent on nature only insofar as it is impossible for the human mind to go beyond the forms and appearances of it"[19]. Even though the artist would be entirely aware of the dependence on nature ("only the elements can design"[20]), he had yet to go to the furthest edge of space, to the ultimate limits of the sciences and the arts, yes, even far beyond these.

Schindler describes the artistic process as follows: "Visual [art] is the detachment from the appearance, in other words the idea, the concept of the material existence."[21] While science would dissect and analyze nature and use its forces, art would "form" and "create" and would thus even be on a "higher level."[22] Yet art as well as the natural sciences would remain "forged on nature"[23]. This would also apply to music and the art of poetry, even though painting was the most direct of the arts. "The art of poetry condenses and forms the existence, music the sound, the visual arts the appearance."[24] But all the arts had in common that "the only priests permitted to enter their temples would be those who had all the ordinations [...] The ordained are now all those who have dared to make the big step from nature beyond it towards the work of art [...] who were able to crystallize the artistic action from the works of art."[25] Schindler pointedly summarizes these lines of thoughts: "If the student [...] has clearly understood that he has to thoroughly examine nature for it to shine through in the work of art, if he has understood that an image is no reflection but a newly created, [...] a most precious dream image, he may enter the temple of art."[26]

Plein-air and Photography

It might therefore be at first surprising that Schindler also used photography as a completely new medium of the 19th century. This can also be deduced from his diary entries: "A few strokes of charcoal from a photographic study. Suitable for a very fine picture with mist [...] Towards the evening started the little picture from the photography [...] I took the French photographic image still on the table and put it into the right atmosphere. I have to start it all over again [...] Tina was here. I painted at the French photographic picture, in the one that I drew yesterday. It may turn out well. Intuited in the mood. In any case, [it] must become a fine evening. The photograph's atmosphere is of a nameless charm. Whatever I painted today then, may only be regarded as a panel ground, and hardly that [...] I have worked on the French photographic picture by gaslight."[27]

All the more has Schindler to radically distinguish between photography and the artistic process: "What the painters demand of the photographic image is either relief in the collection of materials or disintegration into movements that elude the normal eye because they take place so quickly, or else simply that sort of study painting in which the hand, eye or mind are completely still. This sort of painting is very popular today. This artistically obscene attitude, however, results in an entire series of often really excellent pictures that without entering into contact with our soul only address our eye and are forever dismissed by it with a brief glance."[28] As Schindler further writes, these pictures are marked by an absolute correctness of forms and shadows and rank high above everything that art has achieved so far. Yet they are to be ranked by far below the products of even the worst artistic periods as far as the ability to impress and the artistic language is concerned. "And what is it, after all? This art appears down from the canvas as listless as even the most penetrating observer passes by in nature, only even more indifferent, since the canvas still misses a lot of things that are always inherent in nature."[29] Because, according to Schindler, art does not aim at "forming a mirror image of nature", but at the "most accomplished ability of expression in the poetic parallel to nature."[30] However, Schindler already anticipates that art will have to change after the invention of photography.

In the section "Pleinair", Schindler also discusses the achievements of landscape painting in the 19th century. Similar to the Barbizon School, which regards

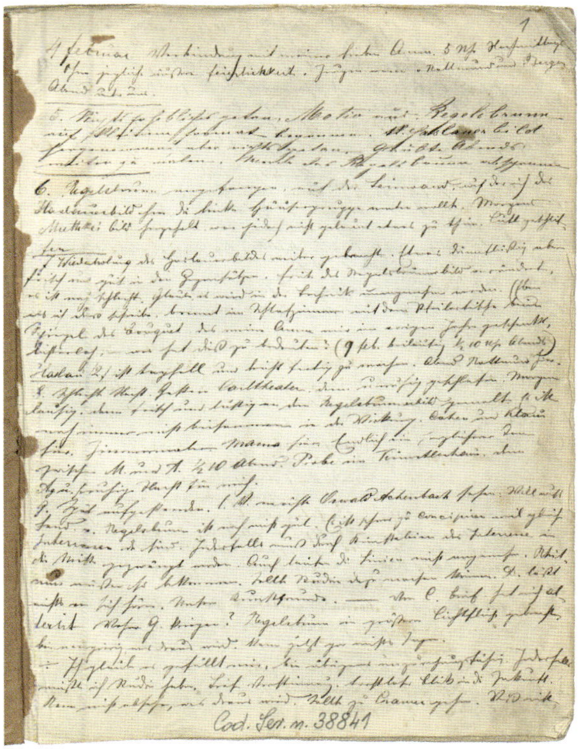

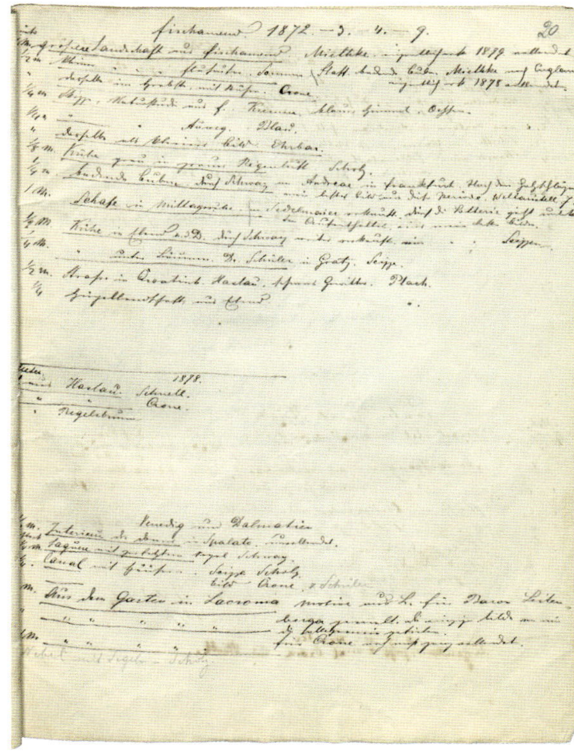

painting en plein-air as progress as opposed to the academically mannered way of painting, Schindler also sees it as a liberation, despite conceding that the "daylight art" was only blessed in connection with the so-called "luminism" of a Rembrandt.[31]

Fig.3.
EMIL JAKOB SCHINDLER
Diary with Work List, p. 1r
ÖNB (Austrian National Library), Department of Manuscripts and Rare Books, Vienna

Fig.4.
EMIL JAKOB SCHINDLER
Diary with Work List, p. 20r
ÖNB (Austrian National Library), Department of Manuscripts and Rare Books, Vienna

The Painter's Script[32]

For Schindler, the brushstroke is not only the painter's script, but it also represents at the same time a recitation of his poetry. The colorist's ductus was a "sung word", "a song". Schindler differentiates between the "one who knows" and the "one who feels" and talks in this context about the "power of naturalism visualizing with every stroke and tone the absent nature," and he underlines the "freedom that may follow its own heart and carries nature already in transformed form in itself."[33] In this sense Schindler regards Peter Paul Rubens (1577–1640) as the best "technician", far beyond any of the modernists. "His brushstroke is that of someone who knows, of the omniscient, and I think of him whenever I speak of the awareness of the brushstroke [...] He pours the [art necessities] into the art form as if they come naturally."[34]

Yet the artistically successful brushstroke would always also need the auxiliary sciences. Among them Schindler includes stylism, anthropology, art history and in parallel world and cultural history, zoology, botany, mineralogy and geology, geometry, perspective, anatomy of the real world and of the appearances, the ultimately perfect drawing of the human being and of the animal as necessary basis for everything. "Since now all these things have to be passed before the first picture is created, I now call it all together technique."[35]

While central perspective, the major invention of the Renaissance, successively loses in significance in 19th century painting, Schindler regards the study of perspective as highly important: "However, only very few know that the most profound knowledge of this auxiliary science is the first and most important condition for everything later on. Yet even the teachers do not want to know it, since this science would be of little use to them unless they were able to teach it. Without it there is no sound stroke and no possible shade of color, without it there is only blind luck and blind coincidence in visual art."[36]

As early as in the first year of his education, Schindler wants the future young artist to "already have an ingrained awareness [...] of perspective so that a fine net of lines visible to the inward eye will permeate and cover all objects when looking at them, thus, that he will sense even the smallest deviation from nature's rightness"[37].

Air – Light – Color

Schindler decidedly rejects the Impressionists' technique of breaking down the colors: "The clearer the individual colors are kept distinct, the closer is their appearance to the vulgar concept of exposure through sunlight."[38] In his opinion: "The more tenderly condensed air interweaves the colors, the more comfortable is the appearance to the educated eye. If all shades of the rainbow jumble up so that it is impossible to differentiate one from the other, as is the case in the rain landscape, the appearance that we call gray replaces the colors even though it contains all the colors of the rainbow."[39]

According to Schindler, the "air" is the "tuning fork", the tone-setting factor in the picture, it is the carrier of the light, the atmospheric value that regulates and controls the value of all tones in the picture.[40] It is the space in front of which everything the painter wants to tell takes place. With the finest, almost invisible change of the air, "every atom of color immediately changes in the whole natural process. So [for] me it is impossible to study air and landscape independently of each other"[41]. For him, the term "air" really includes the entire "concept of tone"[42]. The appearance of air in nature was hardly perceived, however, apart from those cases, he says, when, for example, summer clouds move across a "hard [...] blue ground"[43].

Landscape as Décor

According to Schindler, landscape painting is not without paradox: "An image of the landscape has to suffice and fulfill the requirements in two directions: firstly, and there it enters a difficult competition with the figure and the still life – the interior space as such – it has to be decorative; then it has to be a description of a process in nature, of a certain atmosphere in open nature that can be sensed and recognized by everyone. Unfortunately these two things contradict themselves particularly for the landscape."[44] The more magnificent the experience of nature, the smaller in most cases is the decorative value, "so that this value is sometimes altogether missing in the most beautiful nature studies"[45].

Under the "decorative" Schindler understands the harmonious integration of a panel painting into the middle-class apartment of the 19th century with "walls decorated in dark colors and wood-paneled rooms. There are artists who are always suitable to being hung both in exhibitions and in apartments. I believe that these [...] paid heed to the selection of motifs, the distribution of light and

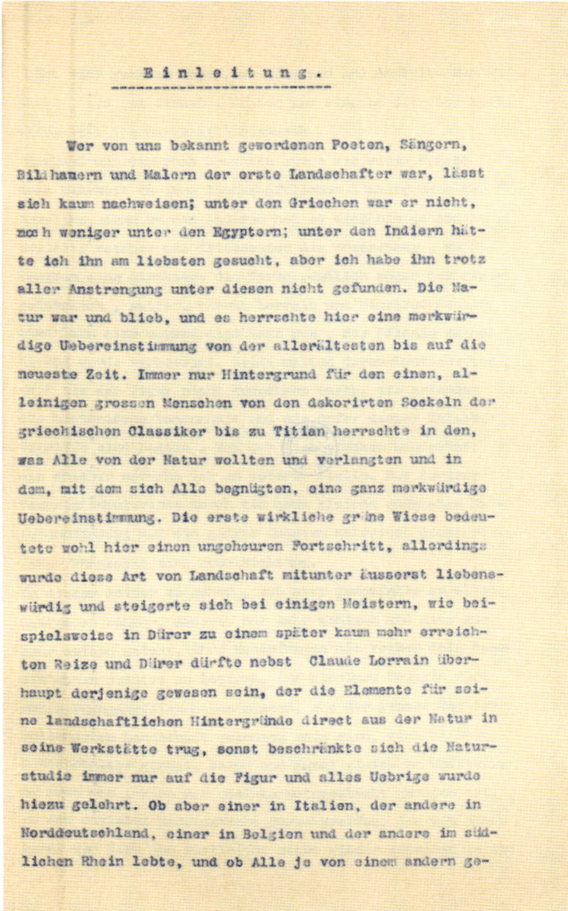
Einleitung.

Wer von uns bekannt gewordenen Poeten, Sängern,
Bildhauern und Malern der erste Landschafter war, lässt
sich kaum nachweisen; unter den Griechen war er nicht,
noch weniger unter den Egyptern; unter den Indiern hät-
te ich ihn am liebsten gesucht, aber ich habe ihn trotz
aller Anstrengung unter diesen nicht gefunden. Die Na-
tur war und blieb, und es herrschte hier eine merkwür-
dige Uebereinstimmung von der allerältesten bis auf die
neueste Zeit. Immer nur Hintergrund für den einen, al-
leinigen grossen Menschen von den dekorirten Sockeln der
griechischen Classiker bis zu Titian herrschte in den,
was Alle von der Natur wollten und verlangten und in
dem, mit dem sich Alle begnügten, eine ganz merkwürdige
Uebereinstimmung. Die erste wirkliche grüne Wiese bedeu-
tete wohl hier einen ungeheuren Fortschritt, allerdings
wurde diese Art von Landschaft mitunter äusserst liebens-
würdig und steigerte sich bei einigen Meistern, wie bei-
spielsweise in Dürer zu einem später kaum mehr erreich-
ten Reize und Dürer dürfte nebst Claude Lorrain über-
haupt derjenige gewesen sein, der die Elemente für sei-
ne landschaftlichen Hintergründe direct aus der Natur in
seine Werkstätte trug, sonst beschränkte sich die Natur-
studie immer nur auf die Figur und alles Uebrige wurde
hiezu gelehrt. Ob aber einer in Italien, der andere in
Norddeutschland, einer in Belgien und der andere im süd-
lichen Rhein lebte, und ob Alle je von einem andern ge-

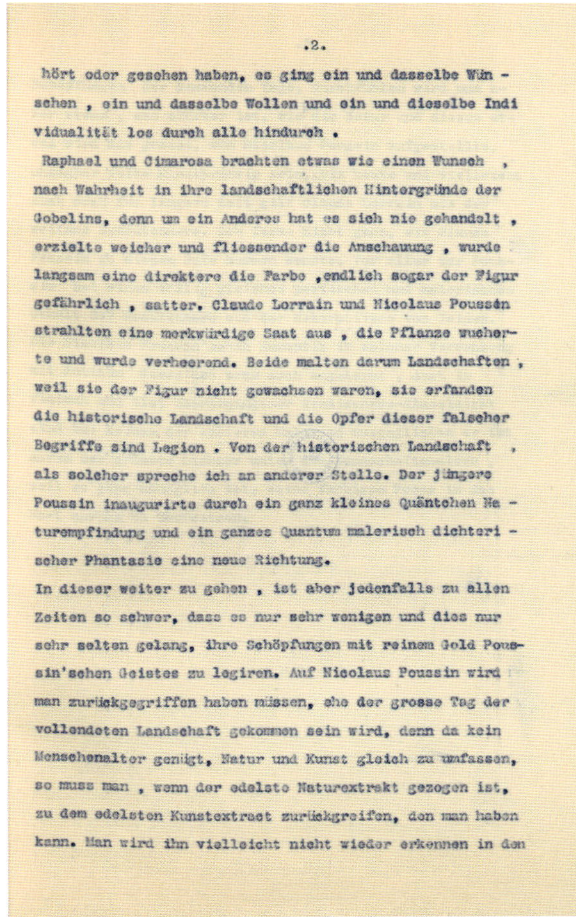
.2.
hört oder gesehen haben, es ging ein und dasselbe Wün -
schen , ein und dasselbe Wollen und ein und dieselbe Indi
vidualität los durch alle hindurch .
Raphael und Cimarosa brachten etwas wie einen Wunsch ,
nach Wahrheit in ihre landschaftlichen Hintergründe der
Gobelins, denn um ein Anderes hat es sich nie gehandelt ,
erzielte weicher und fliessender die Anschauung , wurde
langsam eine direktere die Farbe ,endlich sogar der Figur
gefährlich , satter. Claude Lorrain und Nicolaus Poussin
strahlten eine merkwürdige Saat aus , die Pflanze wucher-
te und wurde verheerend. Beide malten darum Landschaften ,
weil sie der Figur nicht gewachsen waren, sie erfanden
die historische Landschaft und die Opfer dieser falscher
Begriffe sind Legion . Von der historischen Landschaft ,
als solcher spreche ich an anderer Stelle. Der jüngere
Poussin inaugurirte durch ein ganz kleines Quäntchen Na -
turempfindung und ein ganzes Quantum malerisch dichteri -
scher Phantasie eine neue Richtung.
In dieser weiter zu gehen , ist aber jedenfalls zu allen
Zeiten so schwer, dass es nur sehr wenigen und dies nur
sehr selten gelang, ihre Schöpfungen mit reinem Gold Pous-
sin'schen Geistes zu legiren. Auf Nicolaus Poussin wird
man zurückgegriffen haben müssen, ehe der grosse Tag der
vollendeten Landschaft gekommen sein wird, denn da kein
Menschenalter genügt, Natur und Kunst gleich zu umfassen,
so muss man , wenn der edelste Naturextrakt gezogen ist,
zu dem edelsten Kunstextract zurückgreifen, den man haben
kann. Man wird ihn vielleicht nicht wieder erkennen in den

Fig.5.
Emil Jakob Schindler
Theoretical Writings, Typescript on the Artists, p. 1
ÖNB (Austrian National Library),
Department of Manuscripts and Rare Books,
Vienna

Fig.6.
Emil Jakob Schindler
Theoretical Writings, Typescript on the Artists, p. 2
ÖNB (Austrian National Library),
Department of Manuscripts and Rare Books,
Vienna

ultimately the way of painting insofar as they have already tested their pictures in their apartment at all possible and impossible places. Clarity of conception, brightly shining colors and favorable ornaments in form and color and a completely deliberate, simple alla prima painting technique; thus excellent qualities like these give the artist this infallibility in all contingencies."[46] In such an ambiance, the Dutch landscape had a particularly "decorative,"[47] yes, even intoxicating effect! Schindler states that the effect of naturalism would not be decorative. The "bad era of Biedermeier painting" and thus in particular also the "alpine landscape" seems to be particularly unharmonious to him.[48]

Rottmann, Schleich and Lessing

Which models from the early 19th century are now particularly important for Schindler? His subjective selection of German painters, above all from the Munich and Düsseldorf painting school, allows an insight into his development. In the first place, Schindler mentions Carl Rottmann (1797–1850); Romantics such as Caspar David Friedrich (1774–1840) and other painters from the first half of the 19th century, who are regarded as far more influential today, do not play any role in the passages on the development of landscape painting.
Schindler characterizes Rottmann as a titan – similar to Beethoven. For

Schindler, Rottmann is one of the most significant landscape painters of his century! "He has the best line, better than everybody else, and the unique look to see only what he wanted to see. He was the most cruel, but most spirited despot towards nature, he always strove to reach his aim across a field of corpses, without pity and love." Schindler criticized Rottmann's works because they "had no trace of real knowledge about our nature, no trace of romanticism, no love and no humaneness,"[49] yet for him Rottmann is the "most matchless narrator of all that happens in the air".[50]
Likewise, Schindler admires Eduard Schleich the Elder (1812–1874), a "truly modern man. It is said that there were nature studies by his hand which are intended as the utmost of childlike sensations and mere nature worship."[51] But: "He created a scale for himself which included [everything] from the brightest light of modern pleinairists to the deepest black of the darkened pictures of past periods. From the utmost depths to the brightest light he worked up and down the scale in golden and silvery-gray shades. He confidently mastered this scale and was a great man within these narrow confines."[52] But according to Schindler, form played no role for Schleich.[53] Yet this does not diminish Schindler's great admiration for Schleich, and he pointedly regrets that Schleich did not achieve recognition in Munich. "If he had been understood with regard to these high-standing aspects of color, which give evidence of a very unusual spiritual ability, Munich today would have the first landscape school in Europe while de facto the landscape in Munich still suffers from the Schleich-disease today, or, as you say there, it is 'angeschlichen' [i.e. in a creeping state]."[54]
In addition, Schindler admires a third painter of the Romantic school: Karl Friedrich Lessing (1808–1860). "There was a time when I considered Lessing to be the greatest word imaginable. When I stood in front of one of Lessing's landscapes for the first time, I said to myself that his trees were talking. And I was delighted to hear a tree talk. I also heard trees talking later, but they told a great story, a far-reaching one, one about their becoming, about their youthful sorrows, about their fight for existence and their height."[55] But the rapture conveyed does not prevent Schindler from describing Lessing as a bloodless Romantic. So according to his criticism, even though Lessing did not lack seriousness, solemnity and artistic feeling, he was too soft, too "dimly-Romantic" and ultimately lacked classical schooling.[56]

The Pinnacle of Modern Painting

Among his contemporaries, Schindler thinks highly of the two brothers Andreas and Oswald Achenbach from Düsseldorf, who are hardly known to us today, "who had already achieved world fame during their lifetimes"[57].
Schindler talks about them as the most significant landscape painters of his time. "Andreas has reached the pinnacle of modern painting […] he has surpassed his predecessors by far. All, even those who are devoutly admired today, even Hobbema and Ruisdael, have fallen behind him by far, as Claude Lorrain and Poussin fell behind Oswald."[58] "If Andreas Achenbach had not shown the world in a new light, one would still unswervingly believe in Ruisdael today"[59] – that painter who was such a great model for Schindler.
Schindler believes that Oswald Achenbach was poetic throughout his entire work, even when he painted lightning and thunderstorms. Thus he would be comparable to Mozart, "while Andreas, even if he extracted the most charming

from nature, would not attach much importance to the beautiful sound. His orchestra does not always have the time to test all the instruments with regard to the delicacy of their tones, so that he always remains austere and serious and often becomes unharmonious himself. This would be the much-desired difference between the two of them."[60]

In his diary, Schindler also refers back to Andreas Achenbach – in the context of his considerations on the central significance of landscape painting for modern art which I quoted at the beginning –, Achenbach here becomes a metaphor for euphoria and downhill, an image Schindler eventually wishes to identify himself with: "Sculpture has reached its peak in Fidias, painting in Rembrandt, and if both art forms go downwards, one for 2000 years, the other for 200, the landscape, the singing sister of music, comes to life with it again in our century, and will reach its peak in my school – not in myself because I lack the necessary talent and am too badly brought up. It will do so even without me because the existence of a human being does not hinder such a large movement. It would have reached its highpoint in Rousseau if all the Eisenmengers of his period had not half starved him to death. It would have had its climax in Andreas Achenbach if he had not been a factory owner. I thought that I could have reached it myself – but it was a brief illusion, I have given up on it [...]."[61] This multi-level, finely distinguished statement most pointedly describes the wide field of tension that gave rise to Schindler's artistic work. For him, landscape painting was not only a special genre but also the genuine object of modern fine art. And as far as that goes, Schindler's fragment on landscape painting, which should also serve the education of future artists, is an important key to understand Schindler's artistic oeuvre, particularly through its very deliberately designed fragmentariness, through its subjectivity – a theoretical work renouncing any explicit reference to all previous theories of landscape painting.

"Nature gave us looking / but art teaches us seeing" – Schindler quotes this aphorism in one of the chapters of his book fragment.[62] In this sense, the artist is as it were creator of nature. It is his act of creation that allows us "to see". And thus, not the mere depiction of and from nature is at stake, as favored by the contemporary Impressionists, but a principle of composition according to which the "impressions" of nature are clarified, stylized and synthesized also by going back to the traditions of perspective painting. Schindler demands line, mass and color from this composition following the rhythm of the painter. And the artistic process does not take place through the overwhelming, immediate impression of nature, but in the artist's memory: through mnemonics as a suitable description of the experience of nature.

And thus the picture becomes a "dream", a form of waking dream, in which other images from various levels of reality, from the observed, from knowledge and insight, from imagination and desire inscribe themselves into the image inspired by nature. Schindler is looking for a new language of art, based on this artistic drive – so to speak a dream language. Mallarmé calls the suggestive means to produce a dream "chanting" ("Fr. chant"), the depicted a "condition of the soul" ("état d'âme").[63] Schindler's major effort is to let the forces of the soul cling together in the atmosphere, which goes hand in hand with the idea of a harmony between the human being and nature. A so-to-say "premodern" as well as "modern" project – a large build-up of tension, a great ambivalence runs all the way through Schindler's work. This might precisely constitute the fascination for a modern audience, who thus learn how to take a new look at the genesis of so-called Modernism.

1 Emil Jakob Schindler, as cited in Elisabeth Edith Kamenicek, *Emil Jakob Schindler (1842–1892). Sein schriftliches Werk im Kontext von Kunsthandel, Mäzenatentum und Kunstkritik seiner Zeit*, doct. thesis, Salzburg 2002, vol. 2, p. 99.

2 Emil Jakob Schindler's diary can be found in the manuscript collection of the Österreichische Nationalbibliothek (Austrian National Library). His theoretical writings in the form of a 160-page typescript are also kept there – the respective manuscript is still considered lost. The art historical writings include those themes that the artist has been concerned with all his life, such as the basic problems of painting, the education as an artist, his relationship to the Academy and to important artistic models from the past, but also to contemporary artists in France, Germany and the Austro-Hungarian Empire, his artistic self-understanding vis-á-vis the Künstlerhaus (House of Artists in Vienna), the public and society and many more. Schindler's theoretical writings and his diary were published and edited for the first time in my dissertation.

3 Cf. Oskar Bätschmann, *Entfernung der Natur. Landschaftsmalerei 1750–1920*, Cologne 1989.

4 Hagedorn was in the diplomatic service and afterwards director of the art academies of Dresden and Leipzig. Schindler's teacher and professor at the k. k. Akademie der bildenden Künste (Academy of Fine Arts) in Vienna, Albert Zimmermann (1809–1888) studied in Dresden. Cf. Bätschmann 1989, p. 262.

5 Bätschmann 1989, document 7, Salomon Gessner (1730–1788), "Selbstunterricht des Landschaftsmalers", p. 265.

6 Cf. Bätschmann 1989, document 1, Gérard de Lairesse (1641–1711), "Landschaft als ergötzlichster Gegenstand der Malkunst", pp. 242–244.

7 [Original title of the English translation: *Simple Imitation of Nature, Manner and Style*, trans. by John Gage, Berkeley and Los Angeles, 1980.]

8 Cf. Bätschmann 1989, pp. 291–293.

9 Bätschmann 1989, p. 298.

10 Bätschmann 1989, p. 298.

11 Cf. John Sillevis, "Pastoral und pittoresk. Alte Meister und neue Theorien", in: the same/Michael Clarke/Christoph Heilmann (eds.), *Corot, Courbet und die Maler von Barbizon. Les amis de la nature* (exh. cat. Haus der Kunst, Munich 1996), Munich 1996, pp. 18–22.

12 As cited in Kamenicek 2002, vol. 2, p. 283.

13 As cited in Kamenicek 2002, vol. 2, p. 283.

14 As cited in Kamenicek 2002, vol. 2, p. 281.

15 As cited in Kamenicek 2002, vol. 2, p. 286.

16 As cited in Kamenicek 2002, vol. 2, p. 286.

17 As cited in Kamenicek 2002, vol. 2, p. 286.

18 As cited in Kamenicek 2002, vol. 2, p. 286.

19 As cited in Kamenicek 2002, vol. 2, p. 286.

20 As cited in Kamenicek 2002, vol. 2, p. 287.

21 As cited in Kamenicek 2002, vol. 2, p. 287.

22 As cited in Kamenicek 2002, vol. 2, p. 287.

23 As cited in Kamenicek 2002, vol. 2, p. 287.

24 As cited in Kamenicek 2002, vol. 2, p. 287.

25 As cited in Kamenicek 2002, vol. 2, p. 287.

26 As cited in Kamenicek 2002, vol. 2, p. 288.

27 As cited in Kamenicek 2002, vol. 2, pp. 64–68.

28 As cited in Kamenicek 2002, vol. 2, p. 303.

29 As cited in Kamenicek 2002, vol. 2, p. 303.

30 As cited in Kamenicek 2002, vol. 2, p. 304.

31 As cited in Kamenicek 2002, vol. 2, p. 305.

32 Kamenicek 2002, vol. 2, p. 289.

33 As cited in Kamenicek 2002, vol. 2, p. 289.

34 As cited in Kamenicek 2002, vol. 2, p. 289.

35 As cited in Kamenicek 2002, vol. 2, p. 291.
36 As cited in Kamenicek 2002, vol. 2, p. 295.
37 As cited in Kamenicek 2002, vol. 2, p. 295.
38 As cited in Kamenicek 2002, vol. 2, p. 244.
39 As cited in Kamenicek 2002, vol. 2, p. 244.
40 Kamenicek 2002, vol.2, p. 239.
41 As cited in Kamenicek 2002, vol. 2, p. 239.
42 As cited in Kamenicek 2002, vol. 2, p. 236.
43 As cited in Kamenicek 2002, vol. 2, p. 237.
44 As cited in Kamenicek 2002, vol. 2, p. 222.
45 As cited in Kamenicek 2002, vol. 2, p. 223.
46 As cited in Kamenicek 2002, vol. 2, p. 223.
47 As cited in Kamenicek 2002, vol. 2, p. 222.
48 As cited in Kamenicek 2002, vol. 2, p. 224.
49 As cited in Kamenicek 2002, vol. 2, p. 314.
50 As cited in Kamenicek 2002, vol. 2, p. 315.
51 As cited in Kamenicek 2002, vol. 2, p. 317.
52 As cited in Kamenicek 2002, vol. 2, p. 317.
53 Kamenicek 2002, vol. 2, p. 317.
54 As cited in Kamenicek 2002, vol. 2, p. 318.
55 As cited in Kamenicek 2002, vol. 2, p. 319.
56 Kamenicek 2002, vol. 2, p. 318.
57 Martina Sitt, "Das A und O der Landschaft – Zwei Malerkarrieren im Spiegel von Selbstzeugnissen und zeitgenössischen Kritiken", in: the same (ed.), *Das A und O der Landschaft. Andreas und Oswald Achenbach* (exh. cat. Kunstmuseum Düsseldorf, Düsseldorf 1997/98), Cologne 1997, pp. 24–27.
58 As cited in Kamenicek 2002, vol. 2, p. 331.
59 As cited in Kamenicek 2002, vol. 2, p. 313.
60 As cited in Kamenicek 2002, vol. 2, p. 334.
61 As cited in Kamenicek 2002, vol. 2, p. 99f.
62 As cited in Kamenicek 2002, vol. 2, p. 232.
63 As cited in Kerstin Thomas, "Un Paysage est un État de l'Âme. Landschaft als Stimmung bei Paul Gauguin", in: Werner Busch/Oliver Jehle (eds.), *Vermessen. Landschaft und Ungegenständlichkeit*, Zurich/Berlin 2007, p. 177.

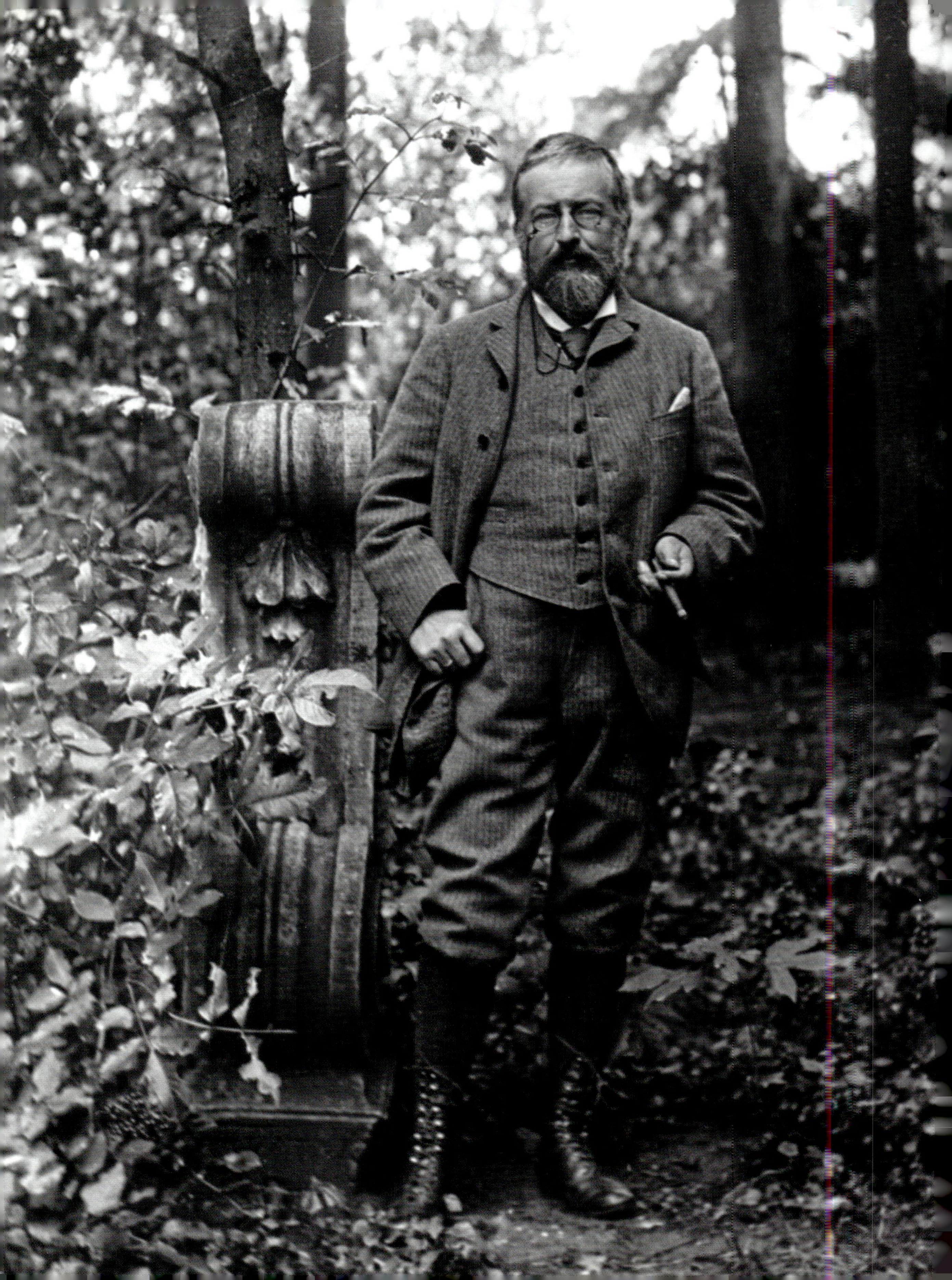

Stephanie Auer

"Sensing instead of painting"
Plankenberg Castle as School of Seeing

"The landscapists are starting to move into loneliness; one does not encounter them so often in far-off countries any longer but sees them escaping from the cities' mist. They do not want to strive to see sights as travelers, but one finds them in small circles in close quarters, where they teach one another to see into the depths of nature. Such groups, who move out of the city in order to get close to nature in the village again, are the characteristic of the landscape of our entire century."[1]

Fig.1.
Emil Jakob Schindler in the park of Plankenberg Castle, c. 1885/90
ÖNB (Austrian National Library), Picture Archive, Vienna

Plankenberg Castle as an "Artists' Colony"

In Plankenberg Castle between Tulln and Neulengbach, from 1885 to 1892 Emil Jakob Schindler found the ideal place for his life and work (fig. 1). For him the empty castle in the middle of an old park, "almost the withered garden of his dreams,"[2] represented the "fulfillment of his most secret [...] wishes"[3] (fig. 2, 3). The surrounding landscape was for Schindler an inexhaustible source for the study of nature, in which he taught his students looking and seeing, the sensing of nature.[4] Rented in the winter of 1884 for 300 guilders a year, the castle became Schindler's family residence and the artistic and social centre of his life during the summer months (fig. 4).

Entirely in line with Schindler's conviction to attach himself closely to his students as a teacher,[5] they constituted an essential part of social life at Plankenberg Castle. Here Carl Moll (1861–1945) occupied a special position. Accepted by Schindler as his student in the autumn of 1881, he was soon promoted to become his personal assistant and spent the following years until Schindler's early death primarily in the artist's family circle.[6] Besides Carl Moll, with Marie (1846–1879)

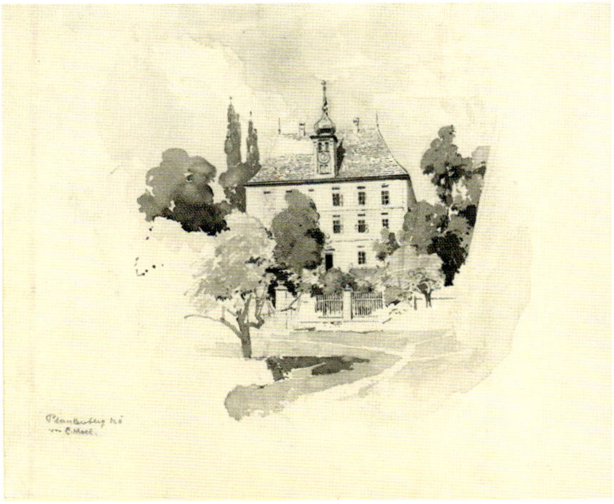

Fig.2.
Carl Moll
Plankenberg Castle (Schloss Plankenberg), c. 1885
Wien Museum

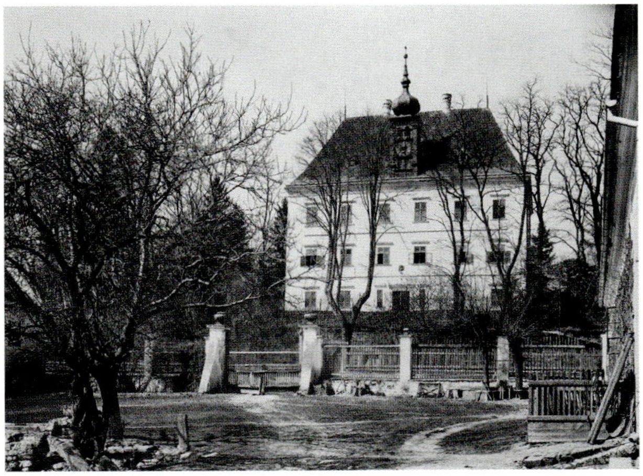

Fig.3.
Plankenberg Castle, c. 1900
ÖNB (Austrian National Library), Picture Archive, Vienna

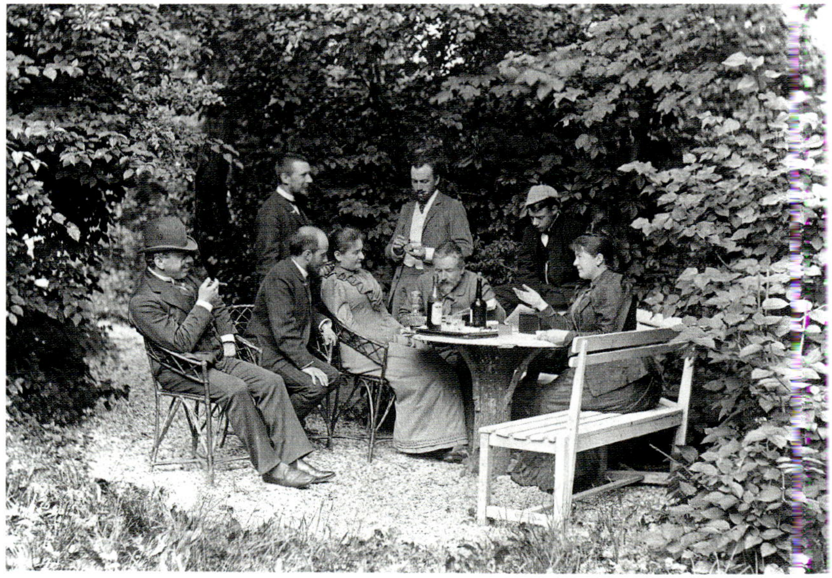

Fig.4.
Emil Jakob Schindler, (center, sitting) with his wife Anna Bergen, Carl Moll (behind Schindler, standing) and others in the park of Plankenberg Castle, c. 1890
ÖNB (Austrian National Library), Vienna, Picture Archive, Vienna

and Luise von Parmentier (1850–1920), Olga Wisinger-Florian (1844–1926) and Marie Egner (1850–1940) several women painters were also among Schindler's students. Since women were not admitted at the Academy of Fine Arts Vienna at that time, this form of private tuition was the only chance they had of receiving an in-depth education. While Marie Egner took lessons from Schindler from 1882 and spent the years in Plankenberg at first as an active student, Olga Wisinger-Florian contacted Schindler only occasionally, because after around four years of education he ended the teacher-student relationship in the spring of 1885.[7] Marie Egner, however, only began increasingly to detach herself from her mentor in 1887/88, by accepting a position as art teacher in England.
In order to ensure his family's subsistence regardless of his success, Schindler had decided as early as in October 1879 to become a private tutor.[8] While at the beginning of his teaching activity he still undertook regular field excursions with his students and spent some time in Goisern in the Salzkammergut, in the last seven years of his life – apart from a few journeys – Plankenberg had become the starting point for joint nature studies. The landscape in and around the small palace must have entirely corresponded to Schindler's ideas, since it contained numerous subjects which he had repeatedly taken up in the course of his entire creative work: the park (p. 90, 105) and the in-house vegetable garden (fig. 5), the mill (p. 92), the river course (p. 96) or the pond. These recurring motifs had already allowed Schindler to observe "the changeable in the consistent"[9] during the years when he had no fixed place of residence and had thus no opportunity to thoroughly examine a motif over the changing seasons and times of day. Schindler's interest in the changing atmospheric appearance of nature is most obvious in the numerous open-air sketches he made during his years in Plankenberg on the poplar-lined avenue close to the castle, which resulted in three large-format paintings (see fig. p. 17).

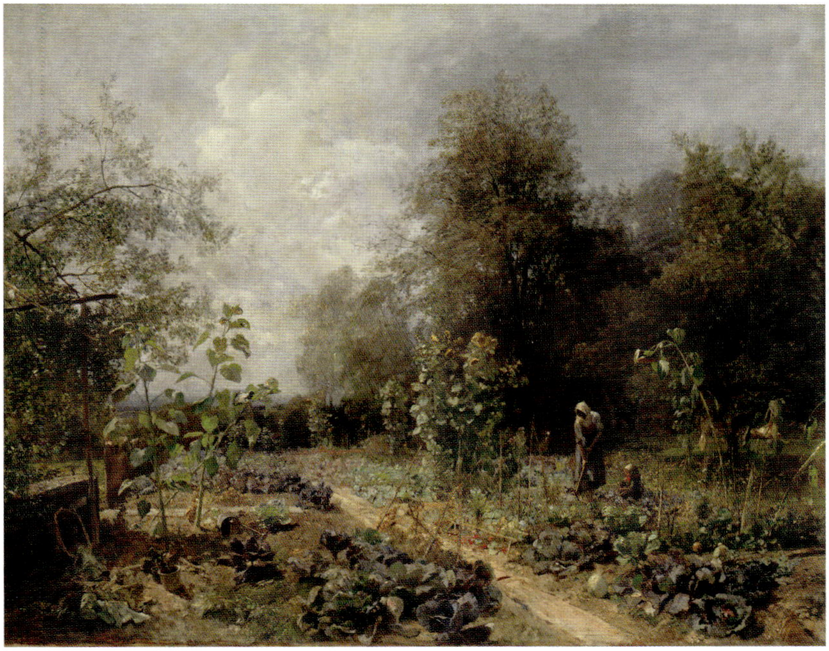

Fig.5.
EMIL JAKOB SCHINDLER
Vegetable Garden in Plankenberg in September
(Gemüsegarten in Plankenberg im September),
1885
Bayerische Staatsgemäldesammlungen
(Bavarian State Painting Collections), Munich

The "Academic Landscape School"

Emil Jakob Schindler's remarks on the subject of the academic school of landscape painting underline the significance he attributed to the study of nature as part of his teaching activity. Thus he already wanted to make the first field excursion a key event for his students,[10] which seems to have been successful in the case of Wisinger-Florian, who described her first day face to face with nature as the "most beautiful day in her life" so far. [11] Schindler regarded the mastering of painting and drawing as a basic precondition for the study of nature, since the student should not have to deal with technical issues in this respect. To his mind, the student's task was to understand and to grasp nature.[12] In the biographical recordings on this "master", Moll says that his teaching activity and talent were mainly limited to precisely this seeing and learning to see. "He taught his students how to sense, instead of to paint."[13]

Despite the great significance of the open-air sketch, painting from nature was for Schindler only a necessity for the pictorial invention and not the aim as such, which still consisted for him in the production of large-format compositions and their completion in the studio. The study of nature as a means to an end would show very little of the individuality, the "painter's soul," as this would only be revealed in the course of the artwork's completion.[14] According to him, this very aspect, however, turned the artwork into something independent, a creation which was only dependent on nature inasmuch as the human mind was unable to go beyond the natural forms and appearances, in short, to capture something beyond the world in its depiction.[15] Only if the student succeeded in making the big step beyond nature to the artwork would the painter in him or her become an artist.[16] Schindler saw it as a danger for the future artist to dwell too long on nature studies, since this risked his not being able to detach himself from it.[17] Despite Schindler's conviction that the teacher should bond closely with his students, he

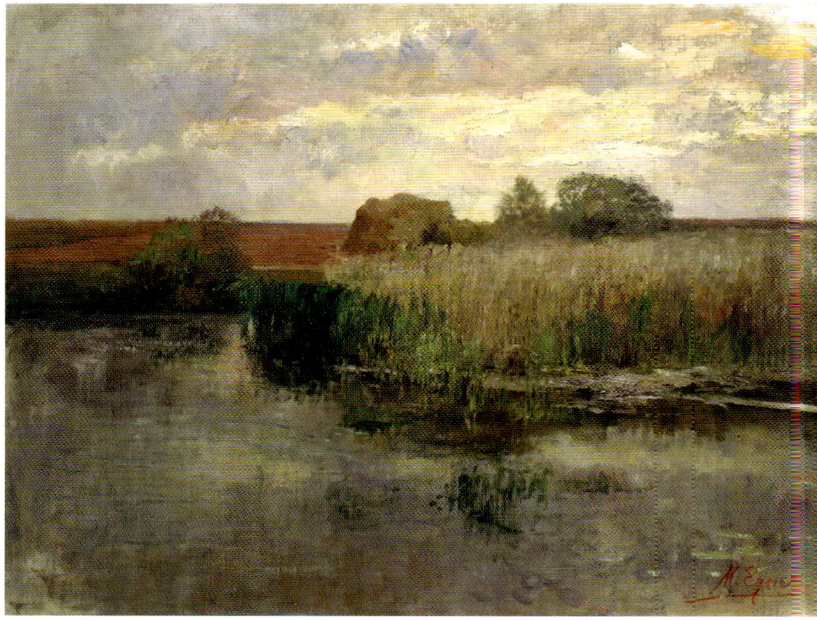

Fig.6.
Marie Egner
Evening Atmosphere in Stillfried on the River March
(Abendstimmung in Stillfried an der March), c. 1883
Private collection

was dubious of the concept of the landscape school as a master class. To his mind, the students would run the risk of adopting their teacher's individual expression and style if they spent too much time with him.[18]

The "Plankenberg School"

Schindler was to be proved right. Those painters who finished his "landscape school" and learnt to see and sense nature through his eyes, approached their admired teacher so much during their years of study that they were already subsumed under the term the "Plankenberg School"[19] (fig. 6, 7, 8). Even though all of them succeeded in detaching themselves from Emil Jakob Schindler's model and developing an individual form of expression, they share individual habits of seeing and interpretation that go back to Schindler's power of persuasion and ability to convey his ideas during the common experience of nature.

1 Cornelius Gurlitt, *Die deutsche Kunst des 19. Jahrhunderts*, Berlin 1900, p. 590.
2 Carl Moll, *Emil Jakob Schindler (1842–1892). Eine Bildnisstudie*, Vienna 1930, p. 40.
3 Moll 1930, p. 40.
4 Cf. Moll 1930, p. 9.
5 Cf. Elisabeth Edith Kamenicek, *Emil Jakob Schindler (1842–1892). Sein schriftliches Werk im Kontext von Kunsthandel, Mäzenatentum und Kunstkritik seiner Zeit*, doct. thesis, Salzburg 2002, vol. 2, p. 283. – Emil Jakob Schindler, "Akademische Landschaftsschule," Österreichische Nationalbibliothek, Sammlung von Handschriften und alten Drucken (Austrian National Library, Department of Manuscripts and Rare Books), cod. ser. n. 20742 Han.
6 Cf. Bärbel Holaus, *Studien zu Emil Jakob Schindler*, dipl. thesis, Vienna 1994, appendix, letters no. 14–18.
7 Wisinger-Florian noted in her diary on April 7, 1885: "With Schindler, he in Plankenberg, he will now abandon me as student [...]", and on April 11, 1885: "[...] Last visit as student, I now stand on my own feet, want to work on my own. This moment too has come!" as cited in Bärbel

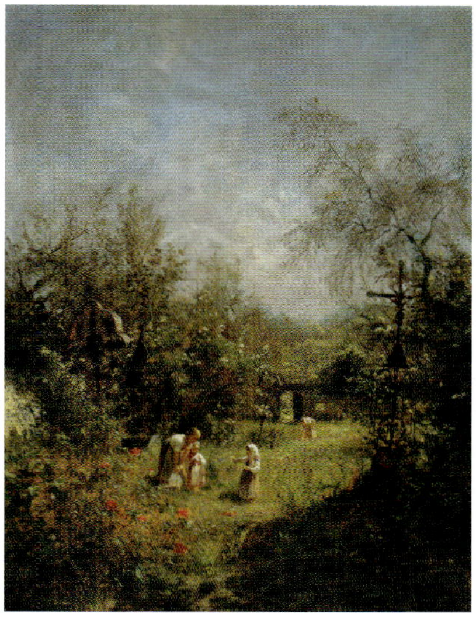

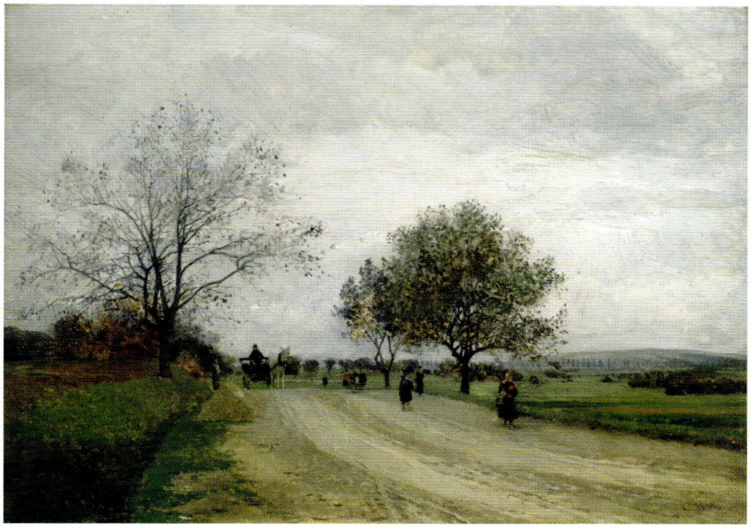

Holaus, "Olga Wisinger-Florian – Weibliches Talent mit … 'riesiger männlicher Energie'", in: Gerbert Frodl/Verena Traeger (eds.), *Stimmungsimpressionismus* (exh. cat. Österreichische Galerie Belvedere, Vienna 2004), Vienna 2004, pp. 289–304.

8 Cf. Emil Jakob Schindler, diary entry, October 15, 1879, as cited in Holaus 1994, appendix, letters no. 14–18, p. 39.

9 Martina Haja, "Thema mit Variationen – Schindlers ‚Pappelallee bei Plankenberg'", in: Peter Weninger/Peter Müller (eds.), *Die Schule von Plankenberg. Emil Jakob Schindler und der österreichische Stimmungsimpressionismus* (exh. cat. Niederösterreichisches Landesmuseum, Vienna 1991), Graz 1991, p. 32.

10 "The teacher organizes the first excursion as a great and serious celebration. It is one of the things that you experience only once, such as the first love, the most beautiful memory for life […]" as cited in Kamenicek 2002, p. 283.

11 Holaus 1994, p. 32.

12 Kamenicek 2002, vol. 2, p. 283.

13 Moll 1930, p. 9.

14 Kamenicek 2002, vol. 2, p. 284.

15 Kamenicek 2002, vol. 2, p. 287.

16 Kamenicek 2002, vol. 2, p. 287.

17 Kamenicek 2002, vol. 2, p. 287.

18 Kamenicek 2002, vol. 2, p. 283.

19 Weninger/Müller 1991.

Fig.7.
Olga Wisinger-Florian
Decayed Cemetery (Verfallener Friedhof), 1884
Belvedere, Vienna

Fig.8.
Carl Moll
Country Road near Plankenberg
(Landstraße bei Plankenberg), 1890
Eisenberger collection, Vienna

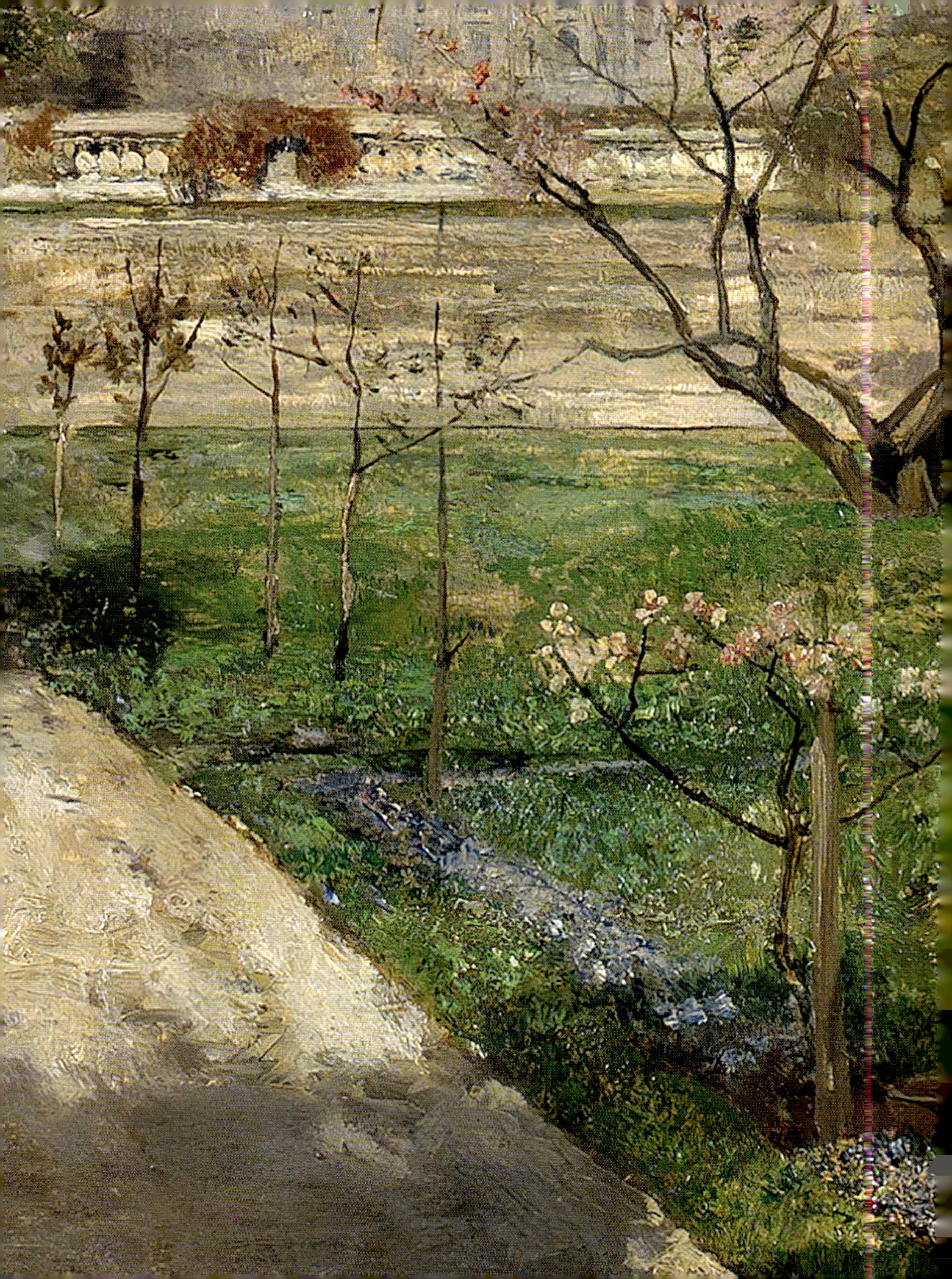

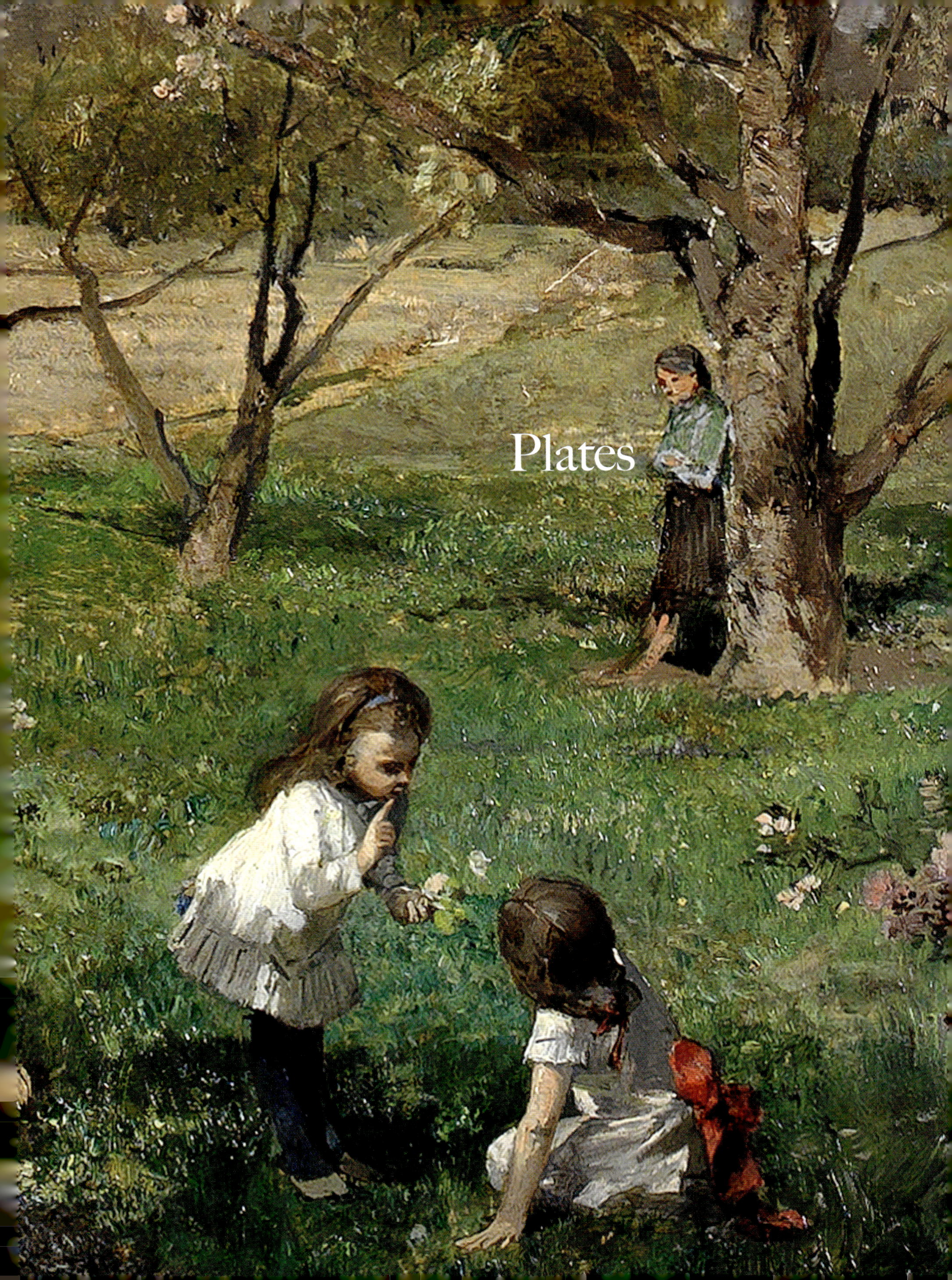

Plates

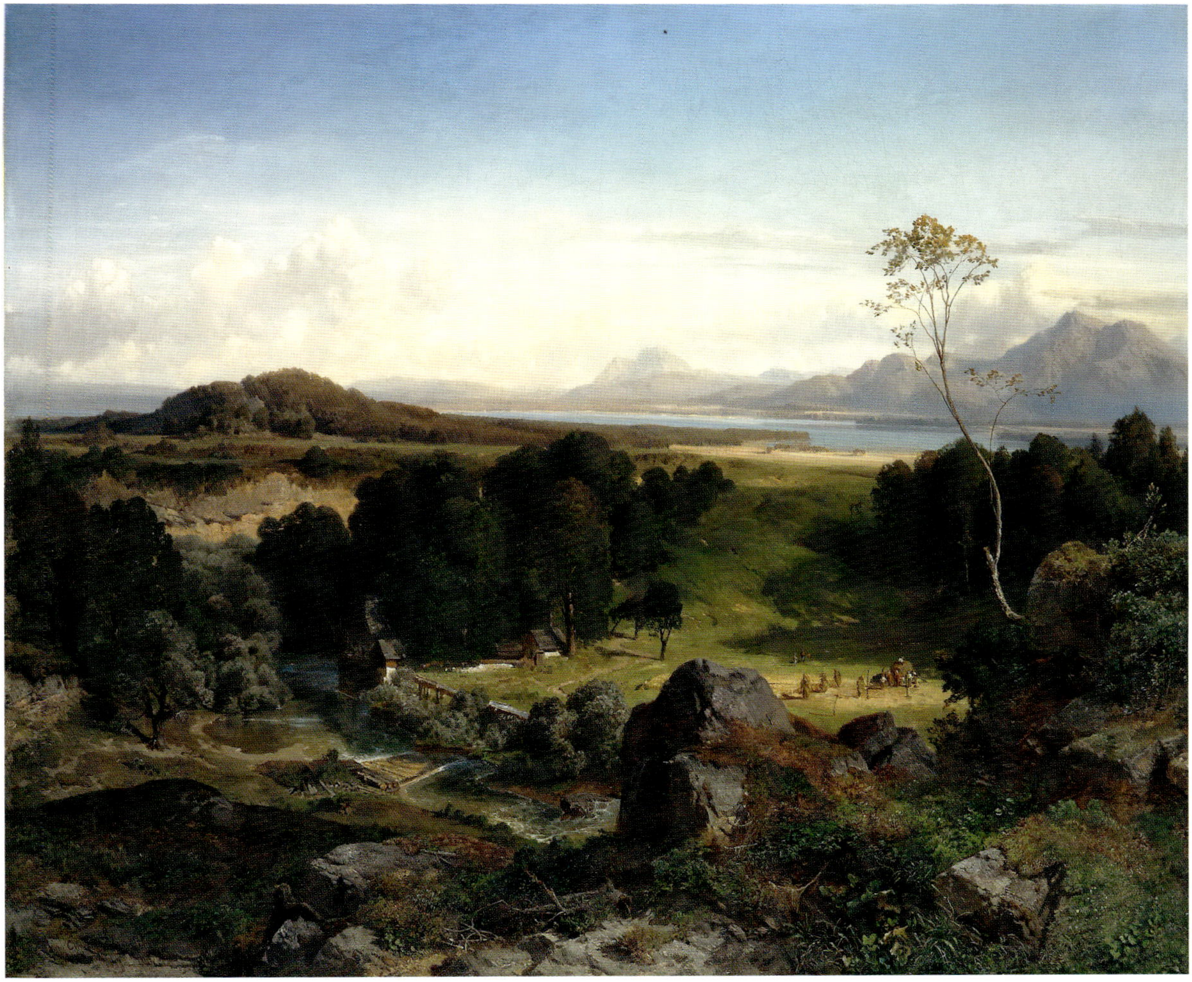

Emil Jakob Schindler, *Old Mill at the Lake Chiemsee* (Alte Mühle am Chiemsee), 1869, oil on canvas, 98 x 120 cm, private collection, Singapur, Courtesy Galerie Martin Suppan

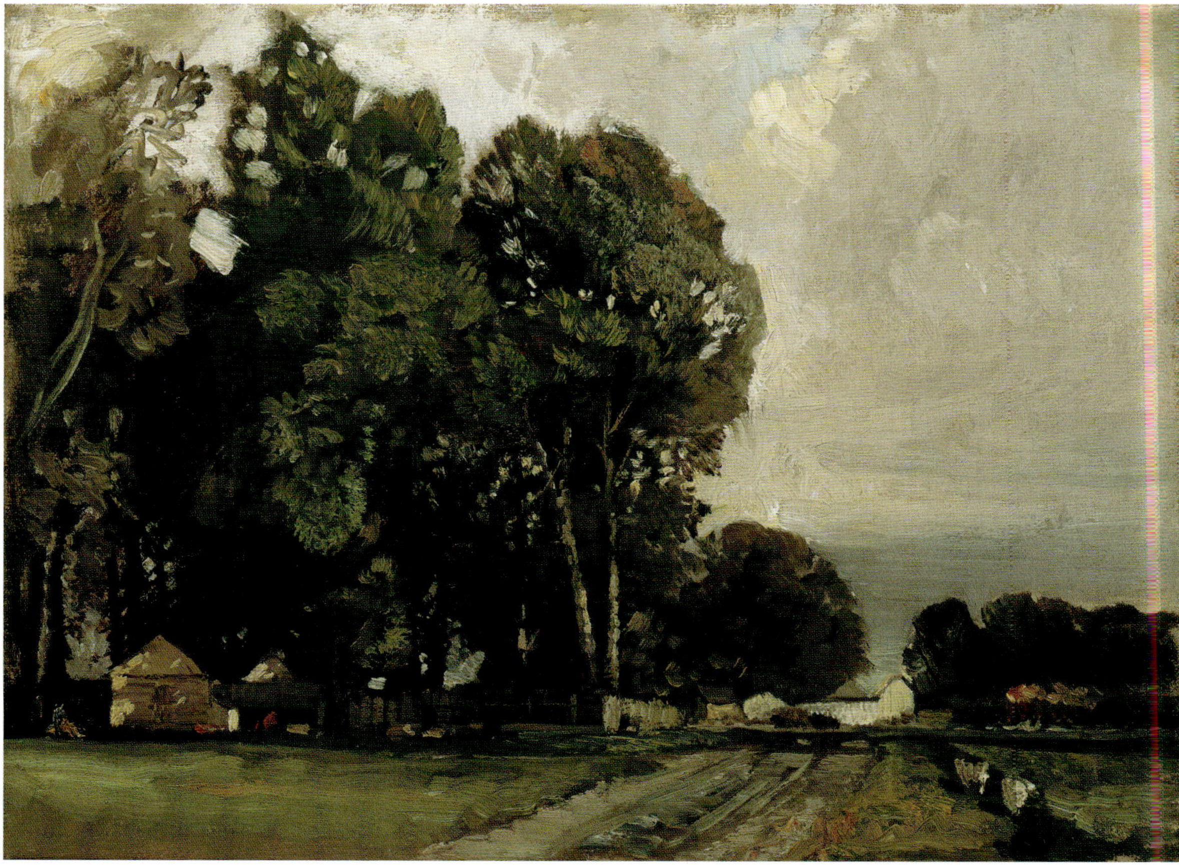

EMIL JAKOB SCHINDLER, *Motif from the Prater – Krieau* (Motiv aus dem Prater – Krieau), c. 1873/74, oil on cardboard on canvas, 27 x 37 cm, Belvedere, Vienna

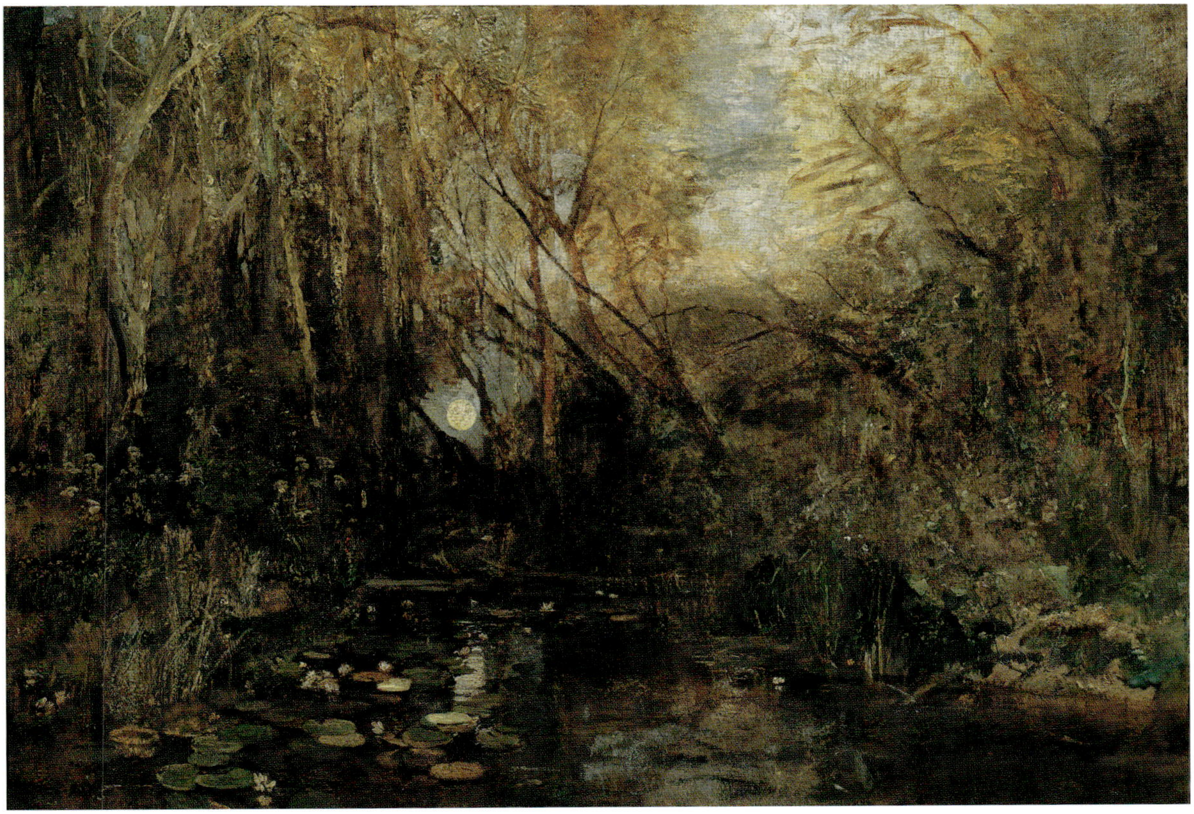

Emil Jakob Schindler, *Moonrise in the Prater Meadows* (Mondaufgang in der Praterau), c. 1877/78, oil on canvas, 105.5 x 154.5 cm, Belvedere, Vienna

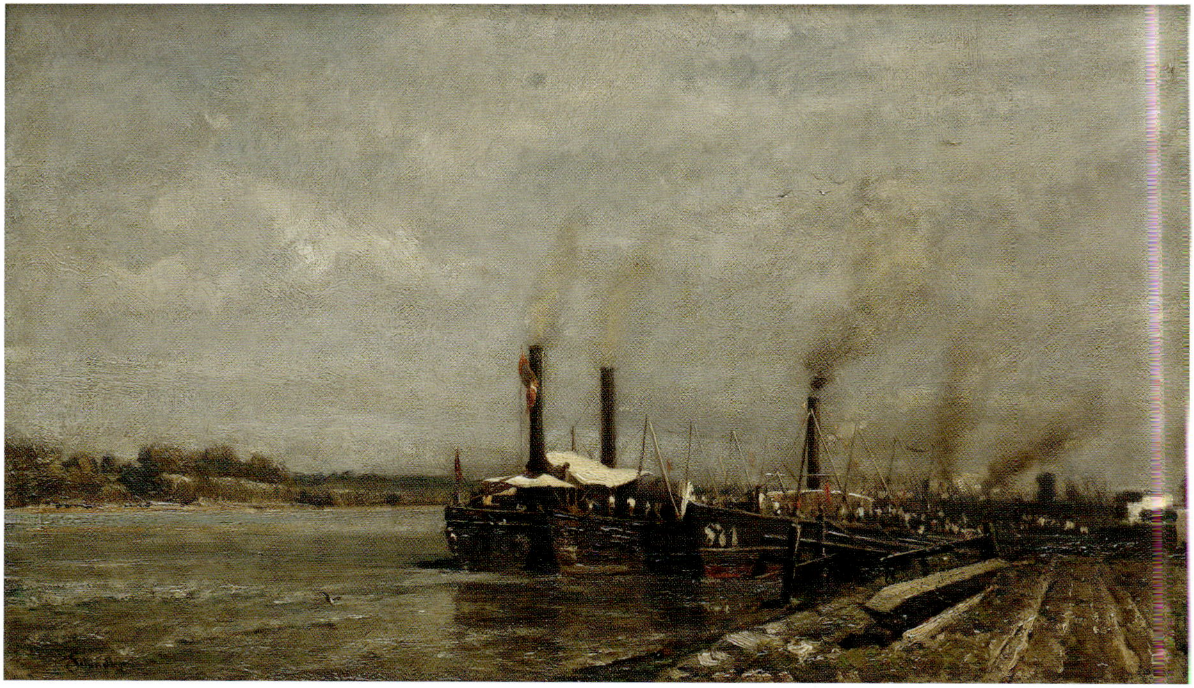

Emil Jakob Schindler, *Danube Steamers at the Landing Stage* (Donau-Dampfschiffe am Anlegeplatz), c. 1871, oil on wood, 21 x 34 cm, Landesmuseum Niederösterreich, St. Pölten

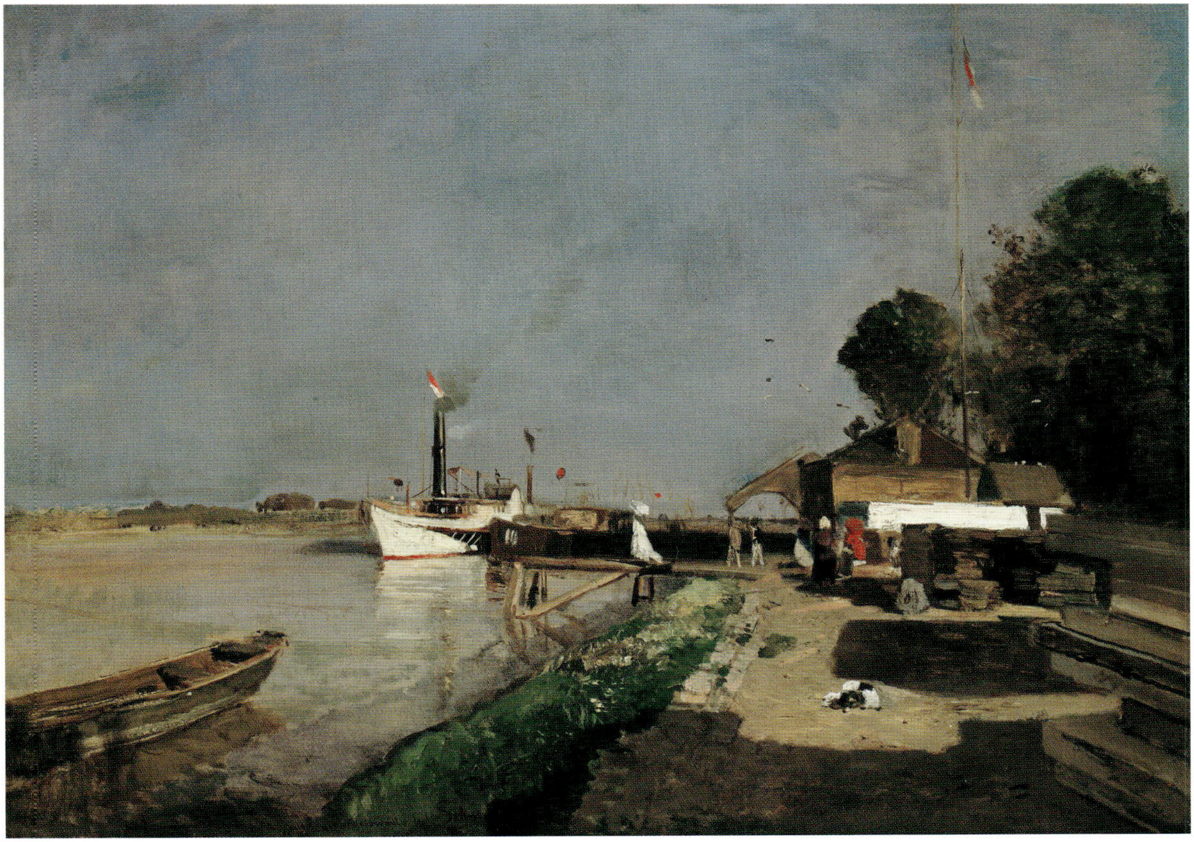

Emil Jakob Schindler, *The Steamer Station on the Danube opposite Kaisermühlen* (Die Dampfschiffstation an der Donau gegenüber Kaisermühlen), c. 1871/72, oil on canvas, 55 x 78.5 cm, Belvedere, Vienna

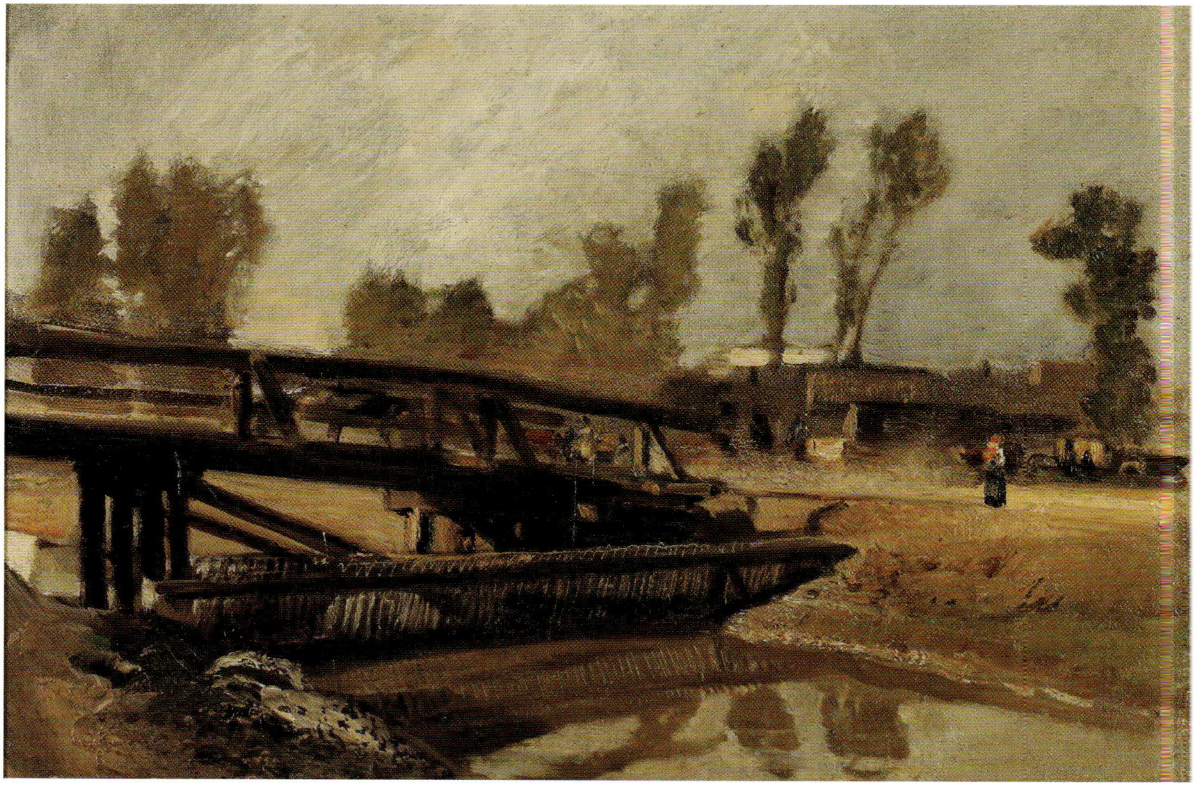

Emil Jakob Schindler, *Kaisermühlen on the Danube* (Kaisermühlen an der Donau), c. 1870/72, oil on canvas on cardboard, 27 x 41.5 cm, Landesmuseum Niederösterreich, St. Pölten

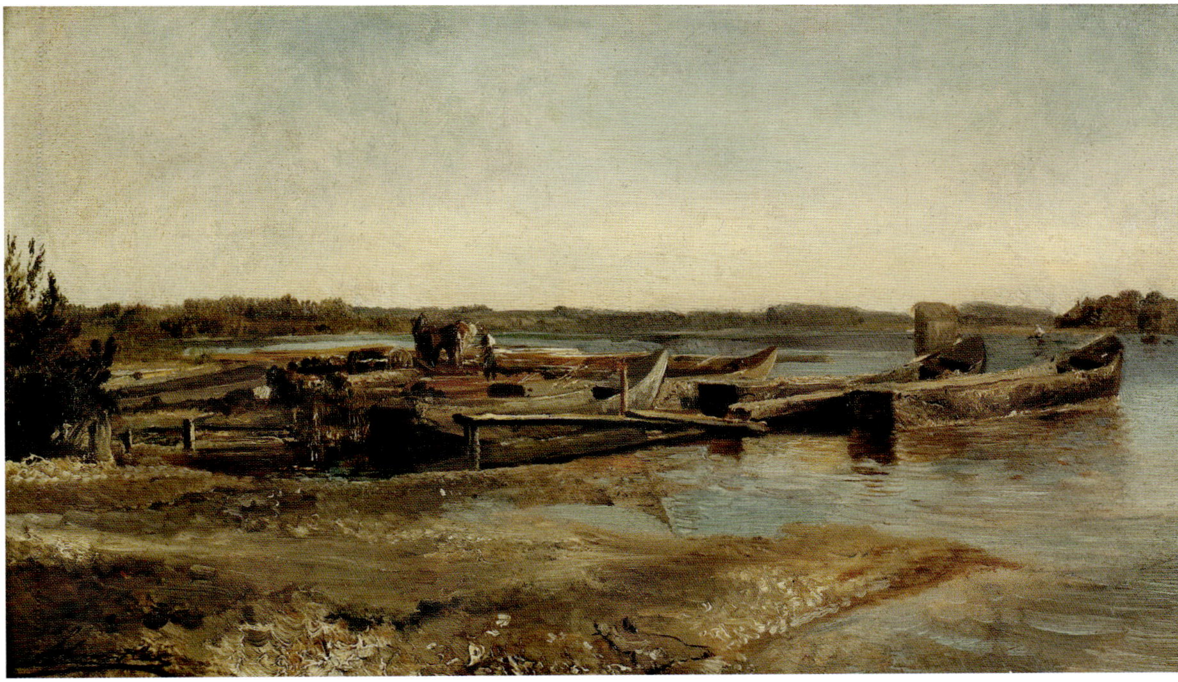

EMIL JAKOB SCHINDLER, *Boats on the Danube* (Boote an der Donau), c. 1870/1872, oil on paper on wood, 17.3 x 30.5 cm, Landesmuseum Niederösterreich, St. Pölten

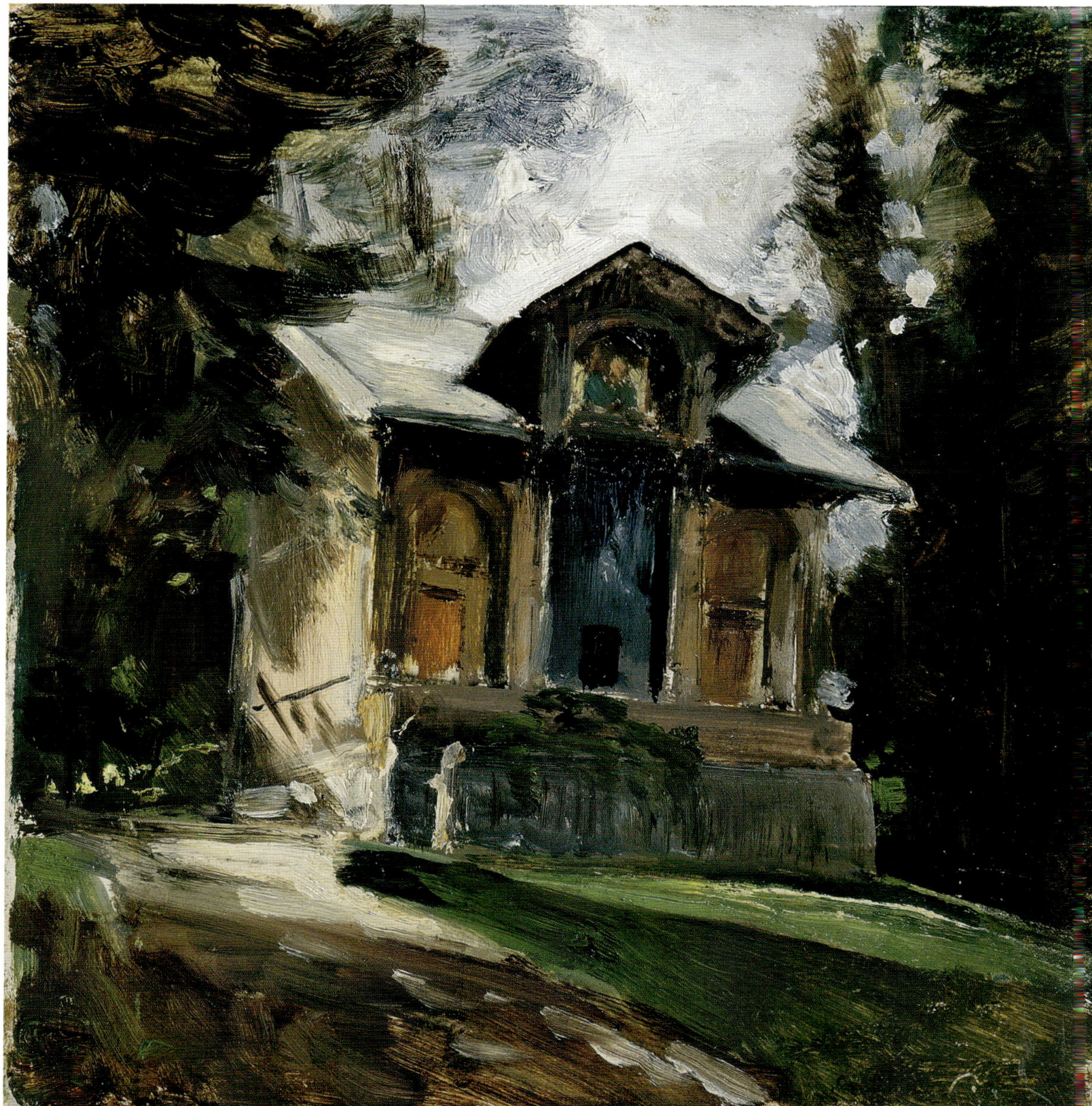

Emil Jakob Schindler, *Studio of the Painter Heinrich von Angeli in Reichenau*
(Das Atelier des Malers Heinrich von Angeli in der Reichenau), 1884, oil on wood, 22 x 22 cm, Belvedere, Vienna

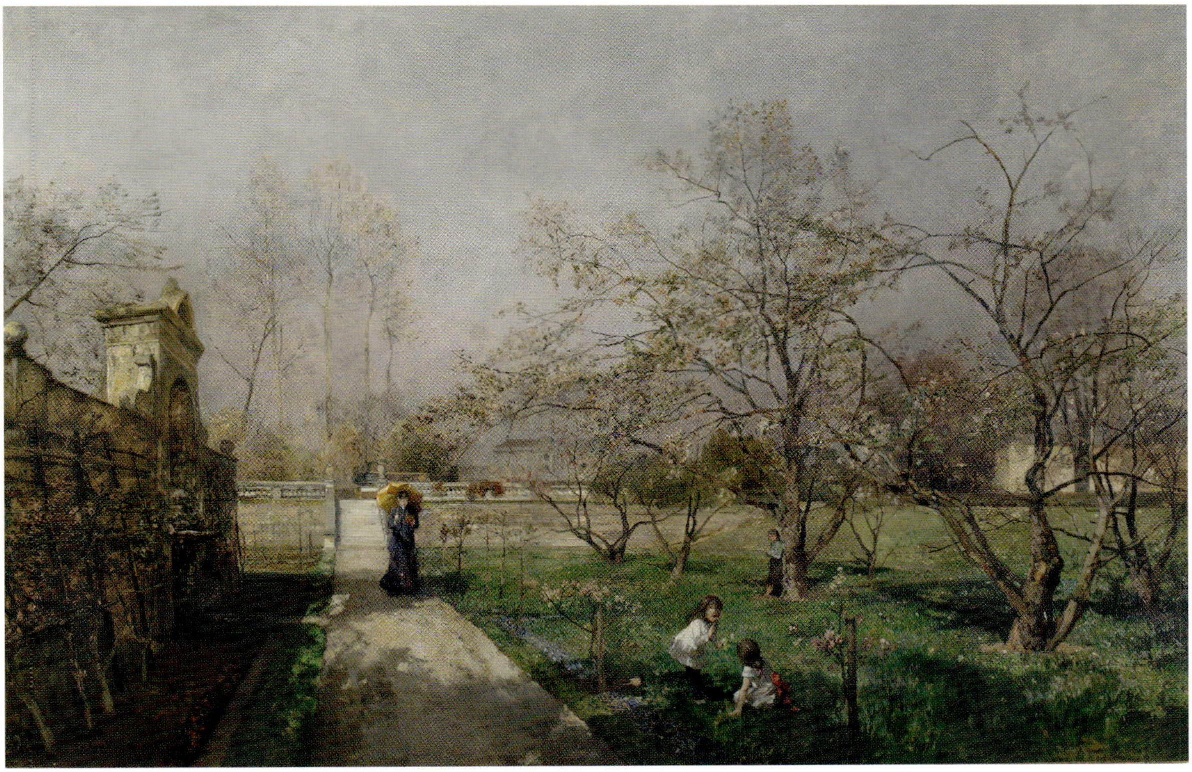

EMIL JAKOB SCHINDLER, *In the Garden at Schloss Niederweiden* (Im Garten von Schloss Niederweiden), 1885, oil on wood, 48 x 75 cm, private collection

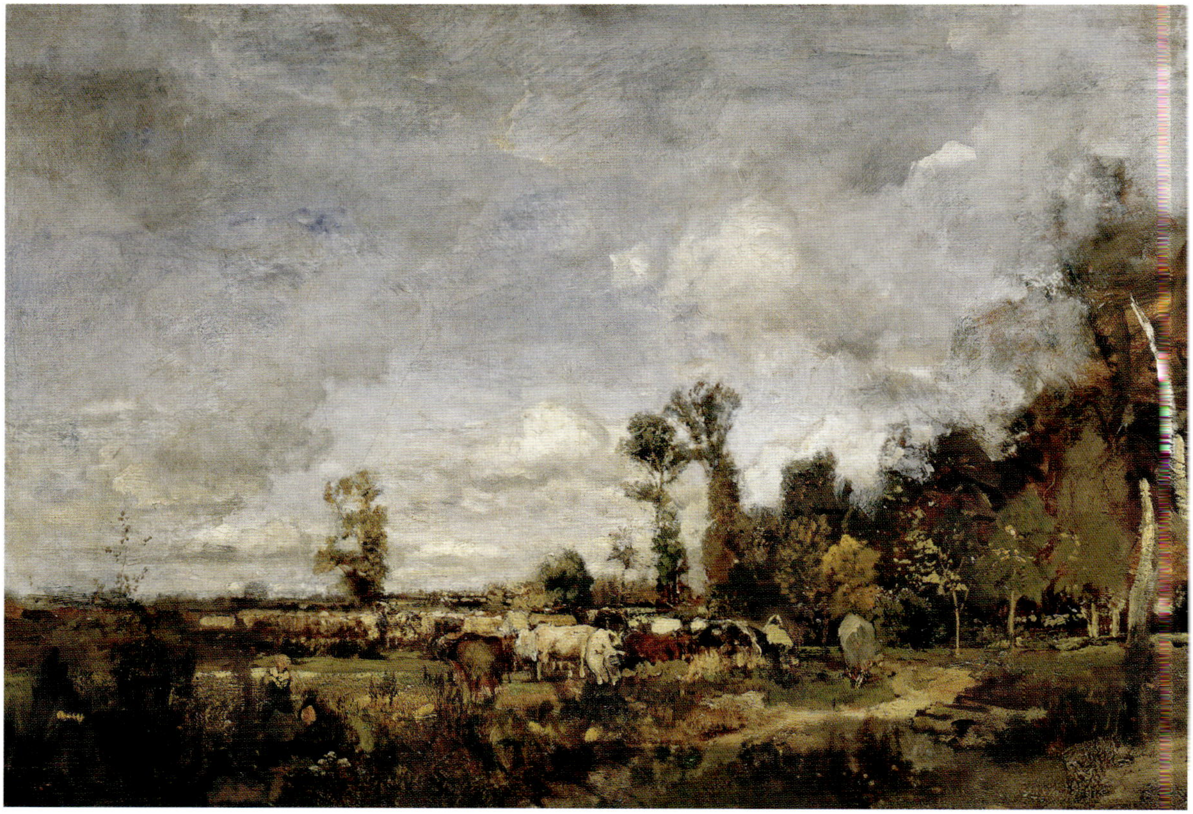

Emil Jakob Schindler, *Grazing Cattle in Holland* (Weidendes Vieh in Holland), c. 1875, oil on canvas, 55.5 x 82 cm, Belvedere, Vienna

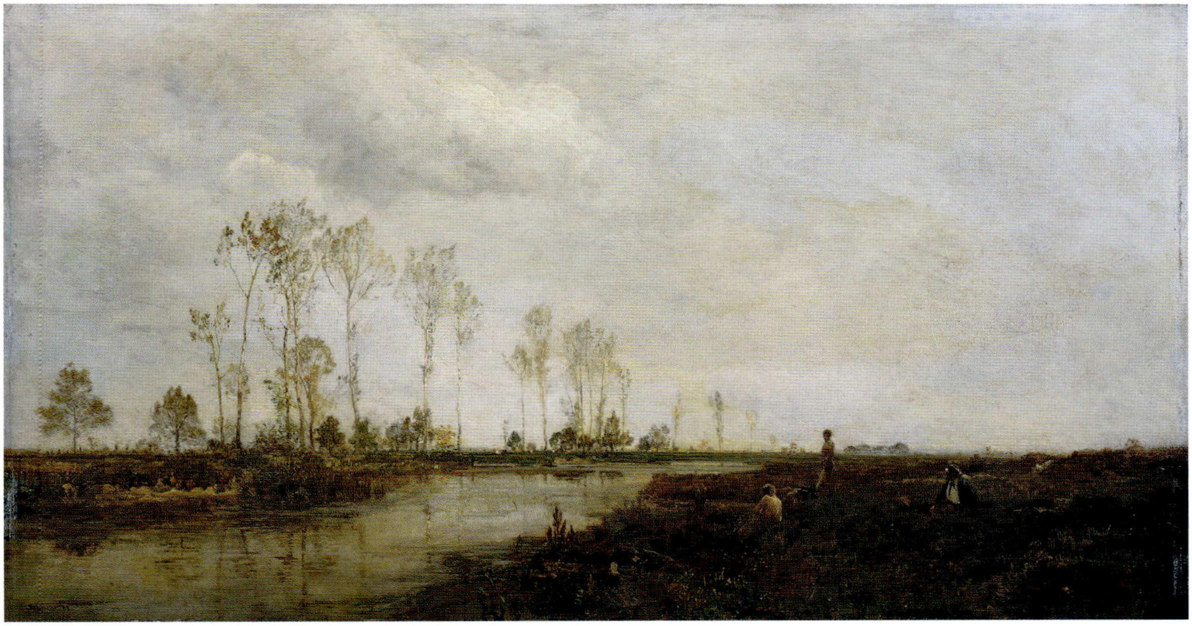

Emil Jakob Schindler, *On the Thaya near Lundenburg I* (An der Thaya bei Lundenburg I), 1877, oil on wood, 39.5 x 74 cm, Belvedere, Vienna

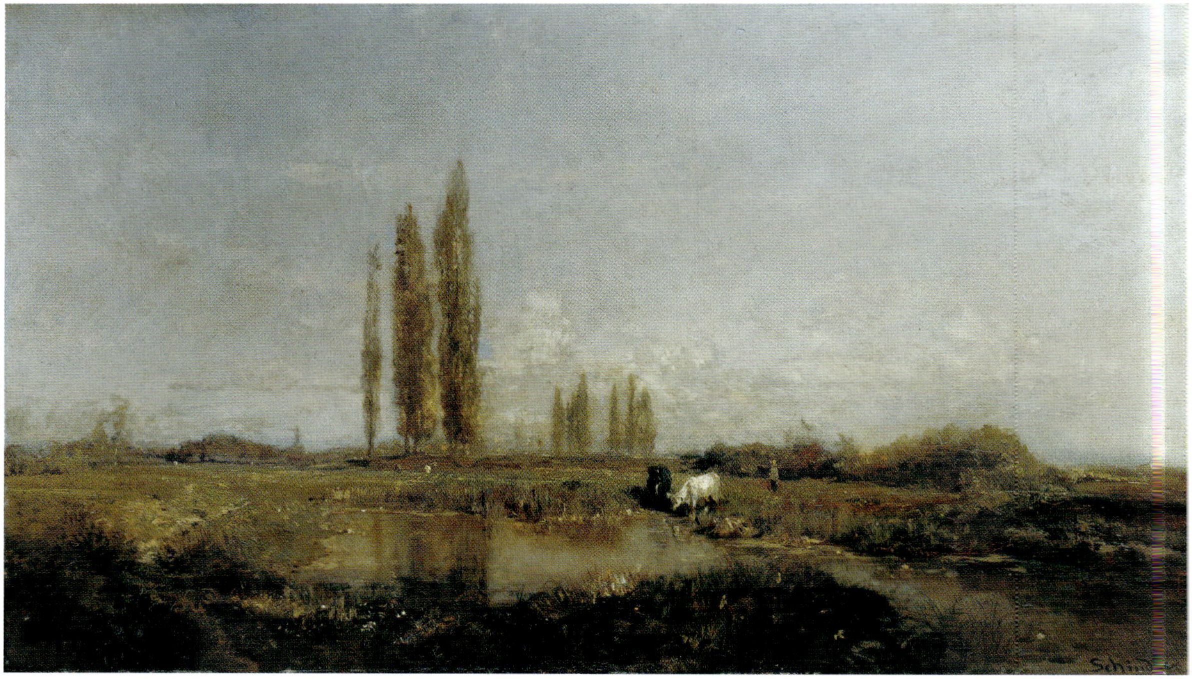

Emil Jakob Schindler, *On the Thaya near Lundenburg* (An der Thaya bei Lundenburg), 1883/84, oil on wood, 36.5 x 63 cm, Belvedere, Vienna

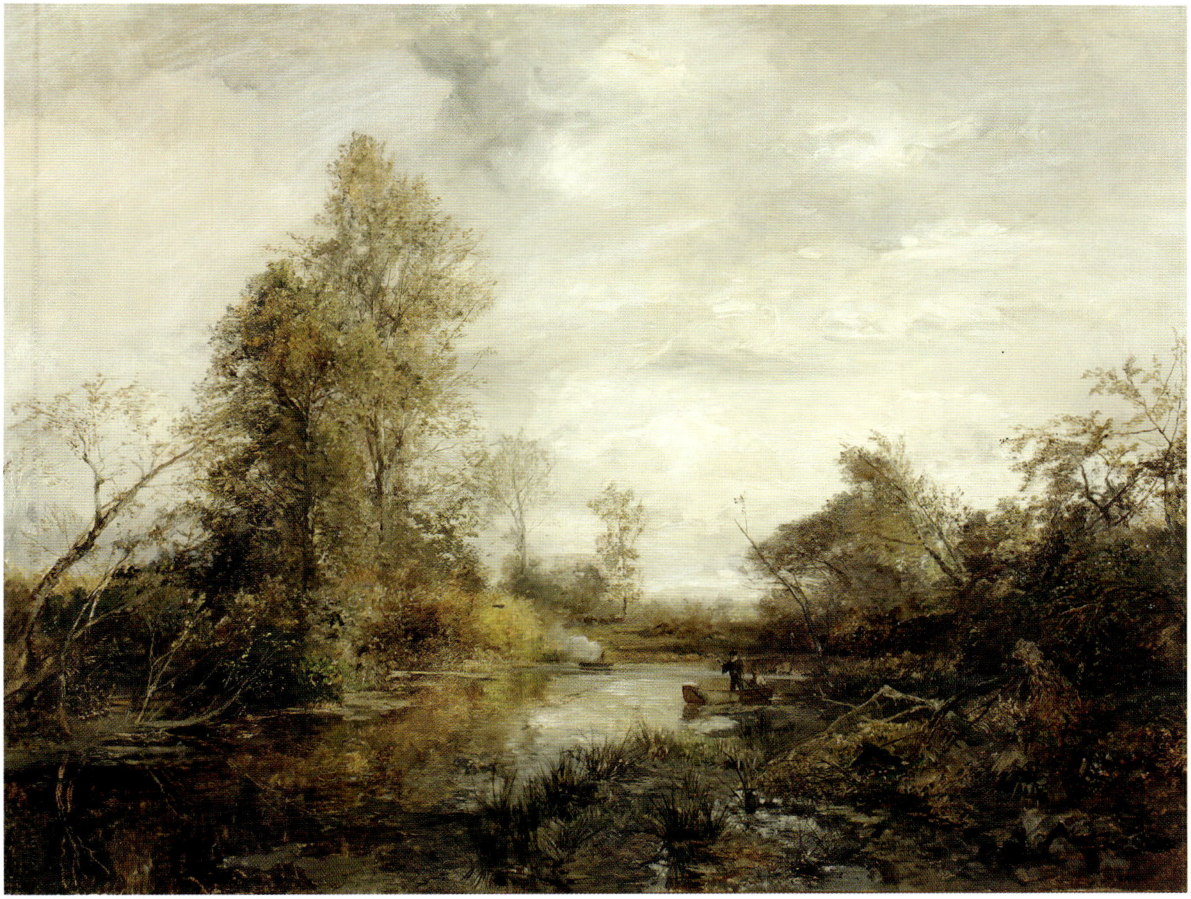

Emil Jakob Schindler, *Duck Hunting in the Prater* (Entenjagd im Prater), c. 1881, oil on canvas, 74 x 100 cm, Belvedere, Vienna

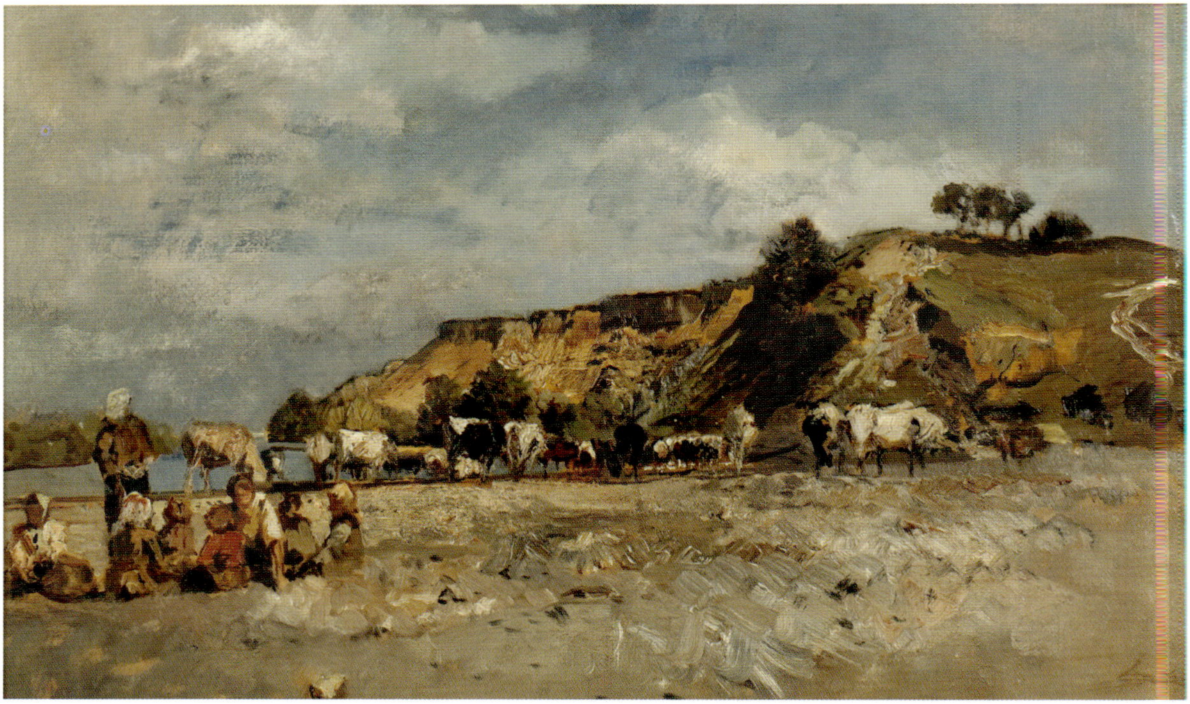

Emil Jakob Schindler, *Cows on the Danube near Haslau* (Kühe an der Donau bei Haslau), 1878/80, oil on canvas, 34 x 58 cm, Landesmuseum Niederösterreich, St. Pölten

Emil Jakob Schindler, *Old Farm in Weißenkirchen* (Alter Hof in Weißenkirchen), c. 1880, oil on canvas, 97.5 x 74 cm, Landesmuseum Niederösterreich, St. Pölten

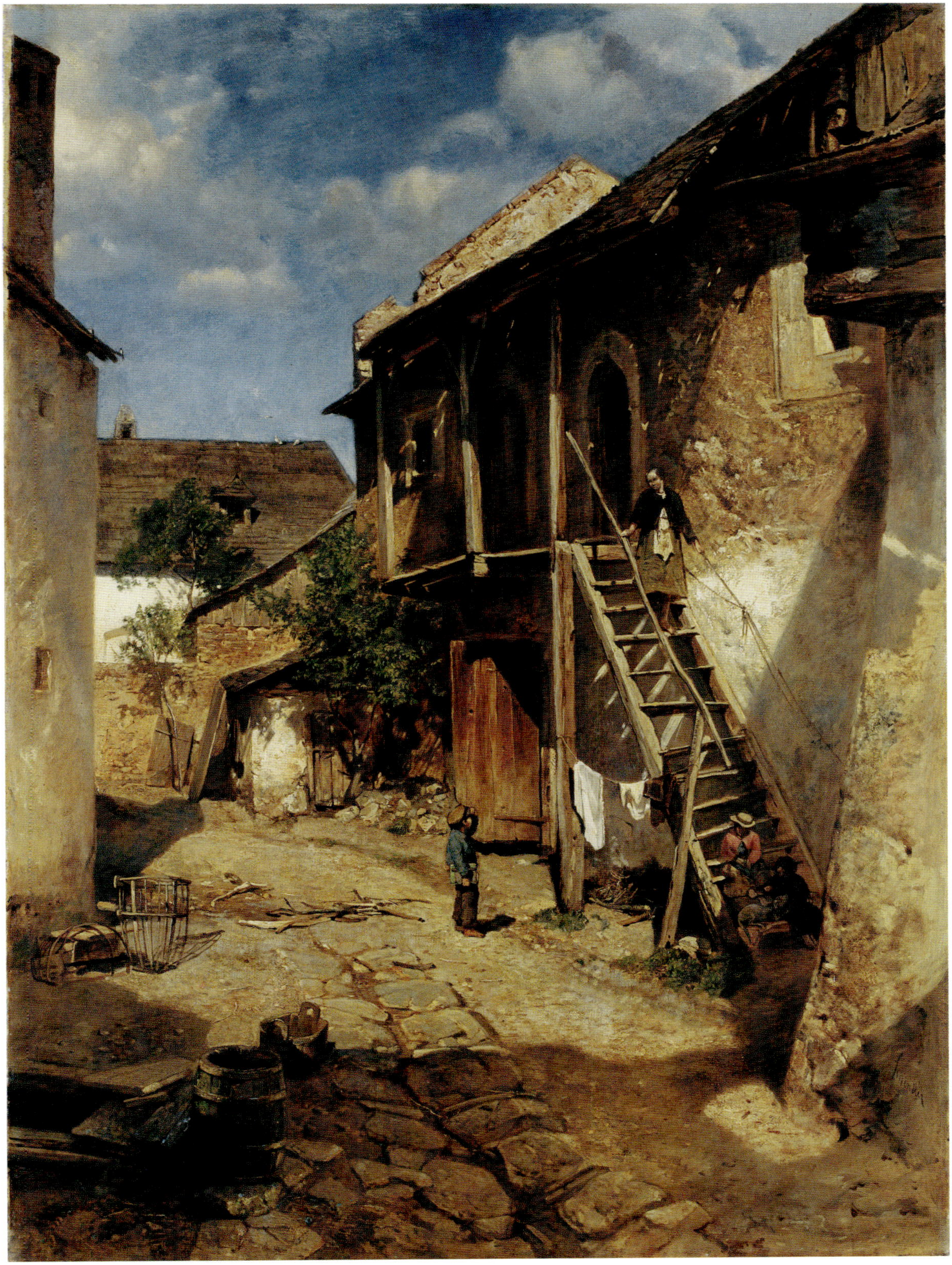

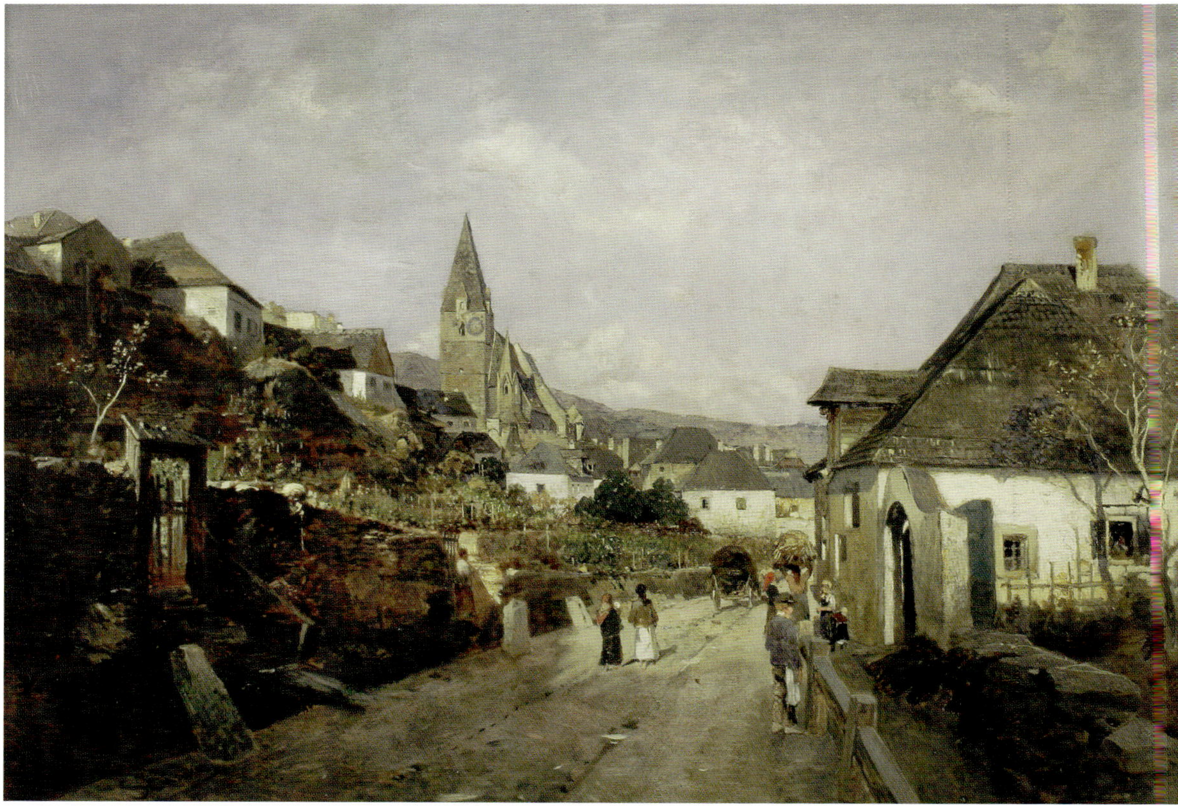

Emil Jakob Schindler, *Scene from Weißenkirchen* (Partie aus Weißenkirchen), 1878/79, oil on wood, 34 x 50 cm, Oberösterreichische Landesmuseen, Linz

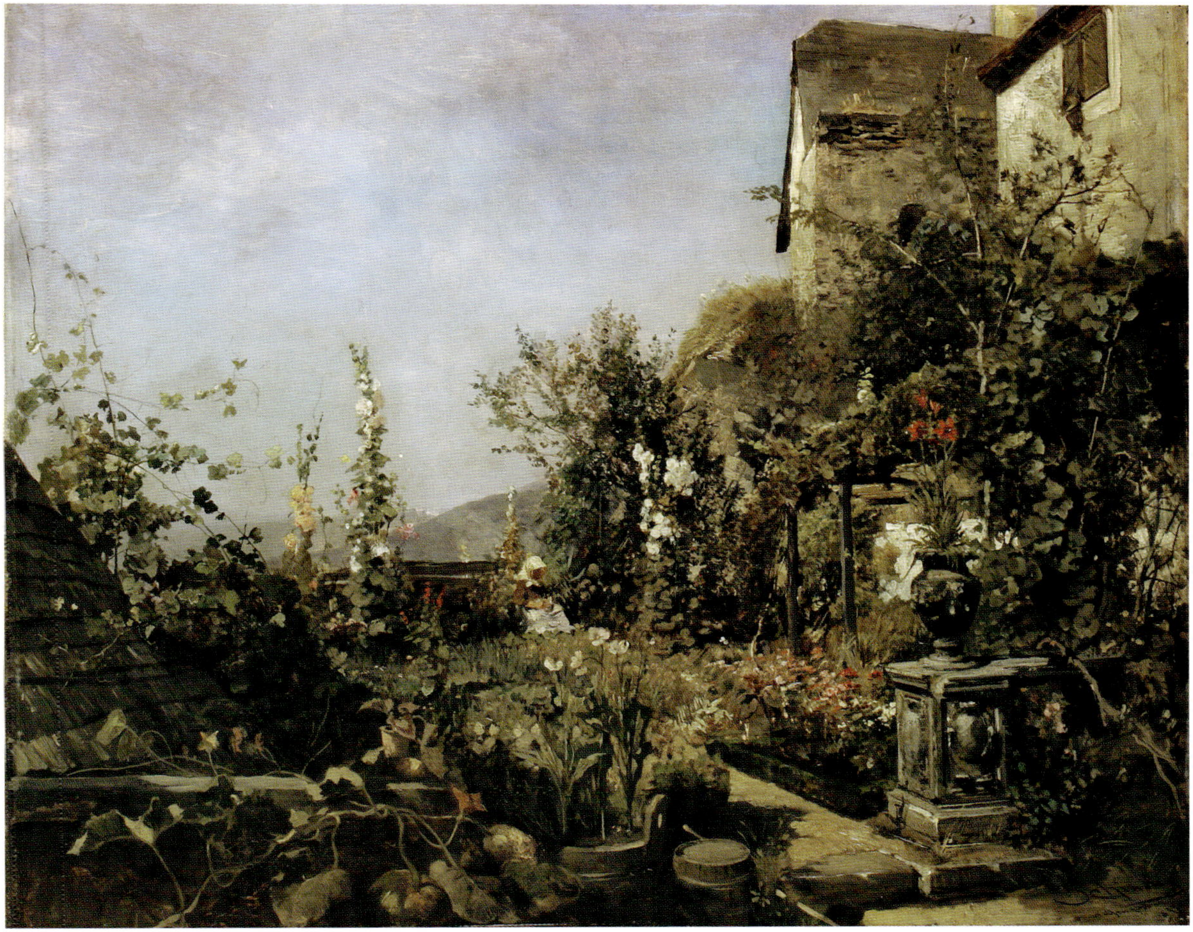

Emil Jakob Schindler, *Flower Garden in Weißenkirchen* (Blumengarten in Weißenkirchen), 1879, oil on mahogany, 41.5 x 53 cm, Oberösterreichische Landesmuseen, Linz

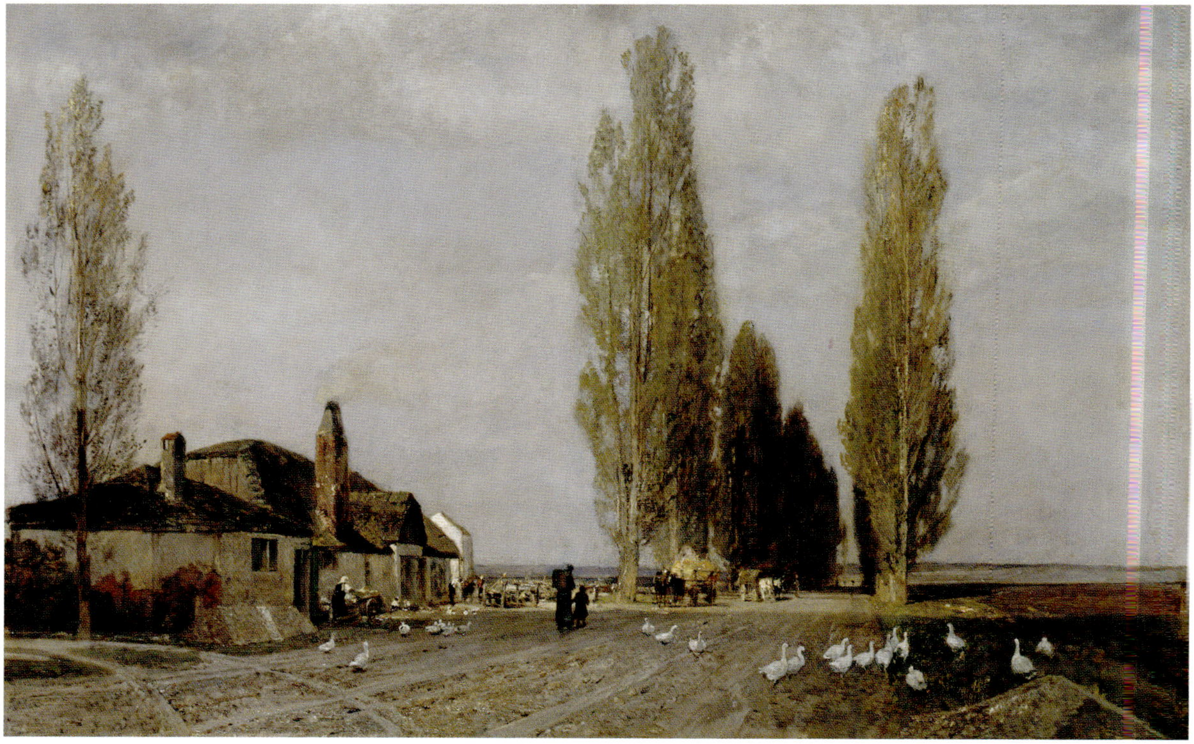

Emil Jakob Schindler, *On the "Imperial Road" to Streithofen* (An der Reichsstraße bei Streithofen), 1890, oil on wood, 43 x 67 cm, Eisenberger collection, Vienna

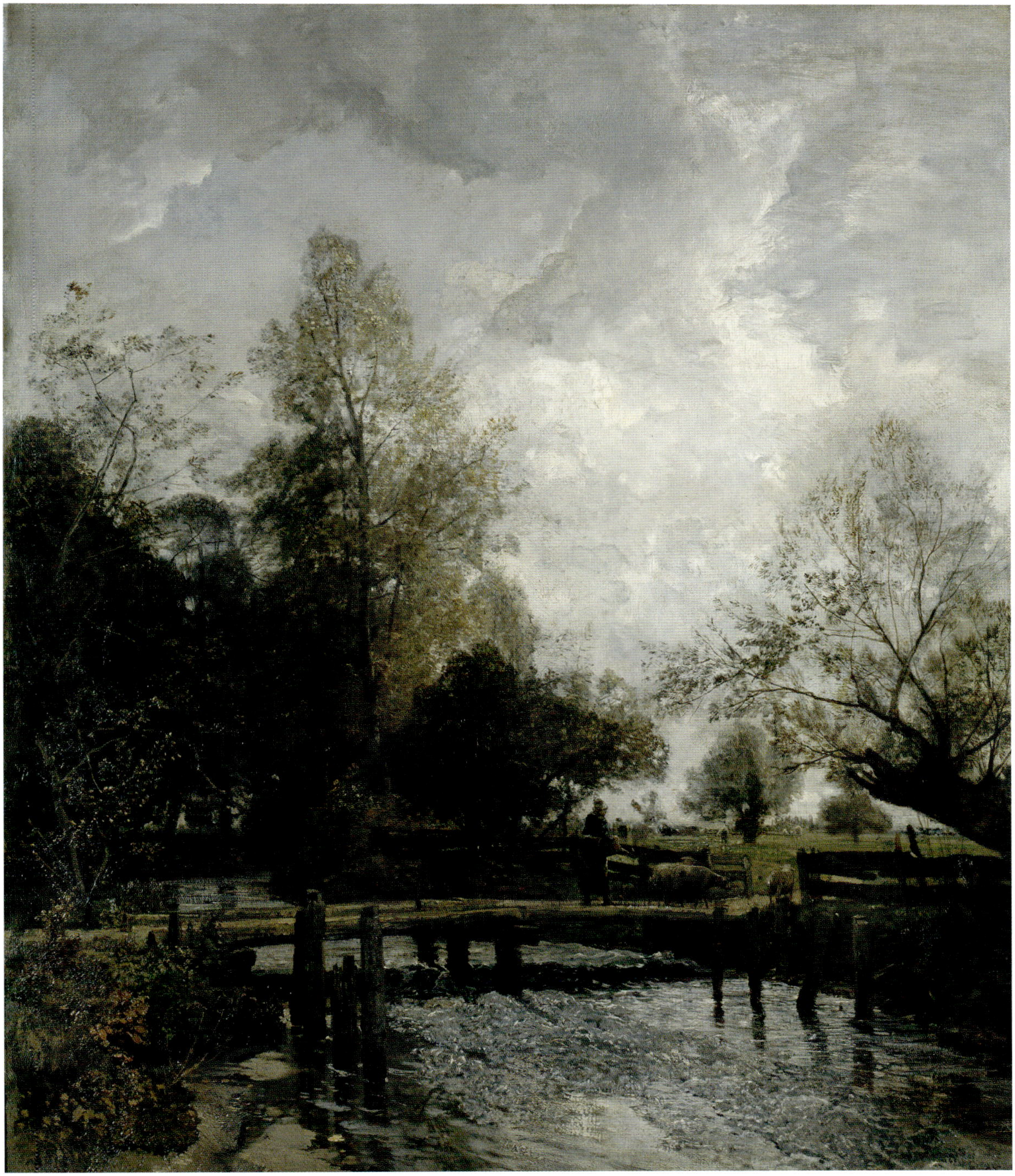

Emil Jakob Schindler, *Bridge near Goisern* (Brücke bei Goisern), 1887,
oil on canvas, 98 x 84 cm, Eisenberger collection, Vienna

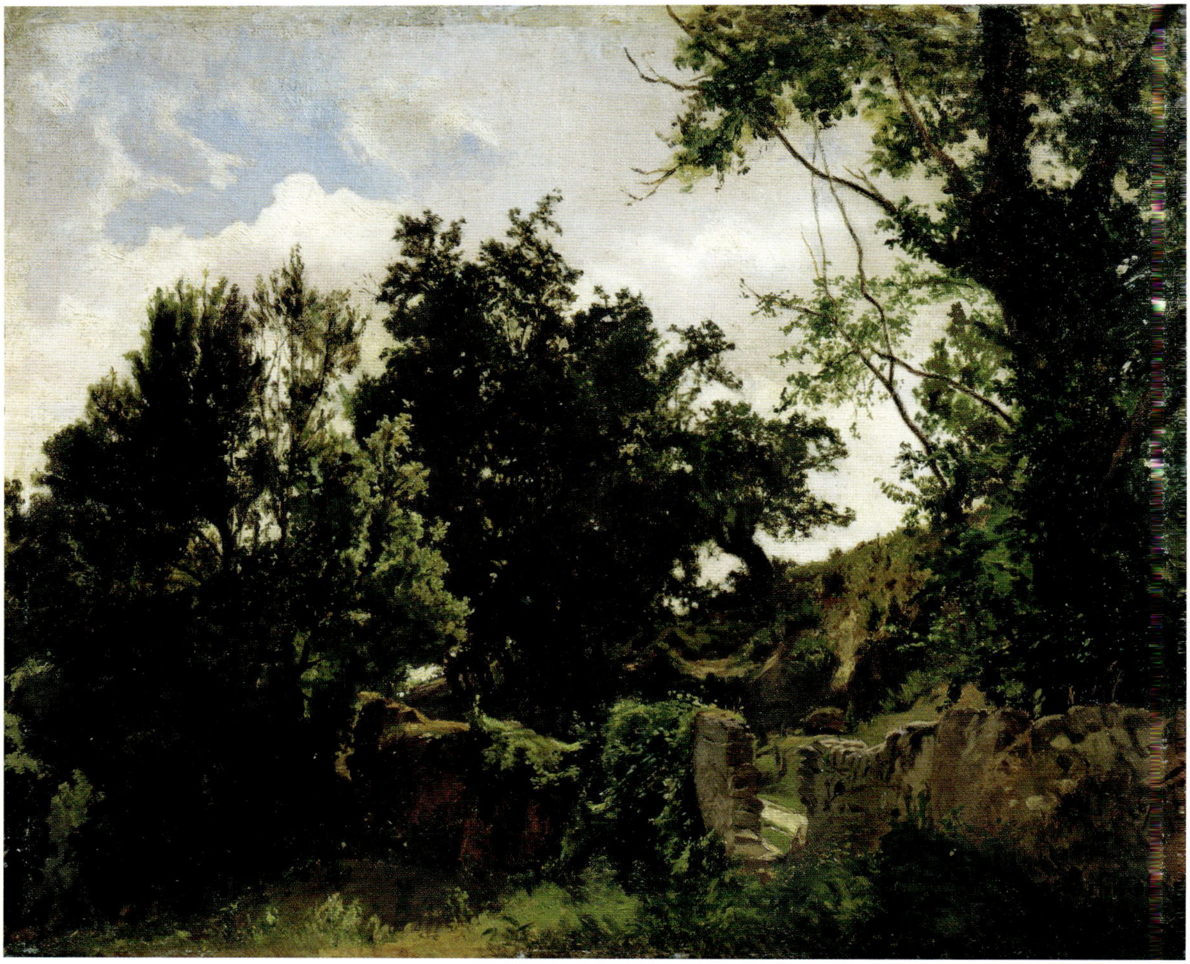

Emil Jakob Schindler, *Castle Wall in Plankenberg* (Schlossmauer in Plankenberg), 1887, oil on canvas on cardboard, 34.5 x 42.5 cm, Belvedere, Vienna

Emil Jakob Schindler, *Meadow in Hacking* (Hackinger Au), 1880, oil on canvas, 90 x 68 cm, Belvedere, Vienna

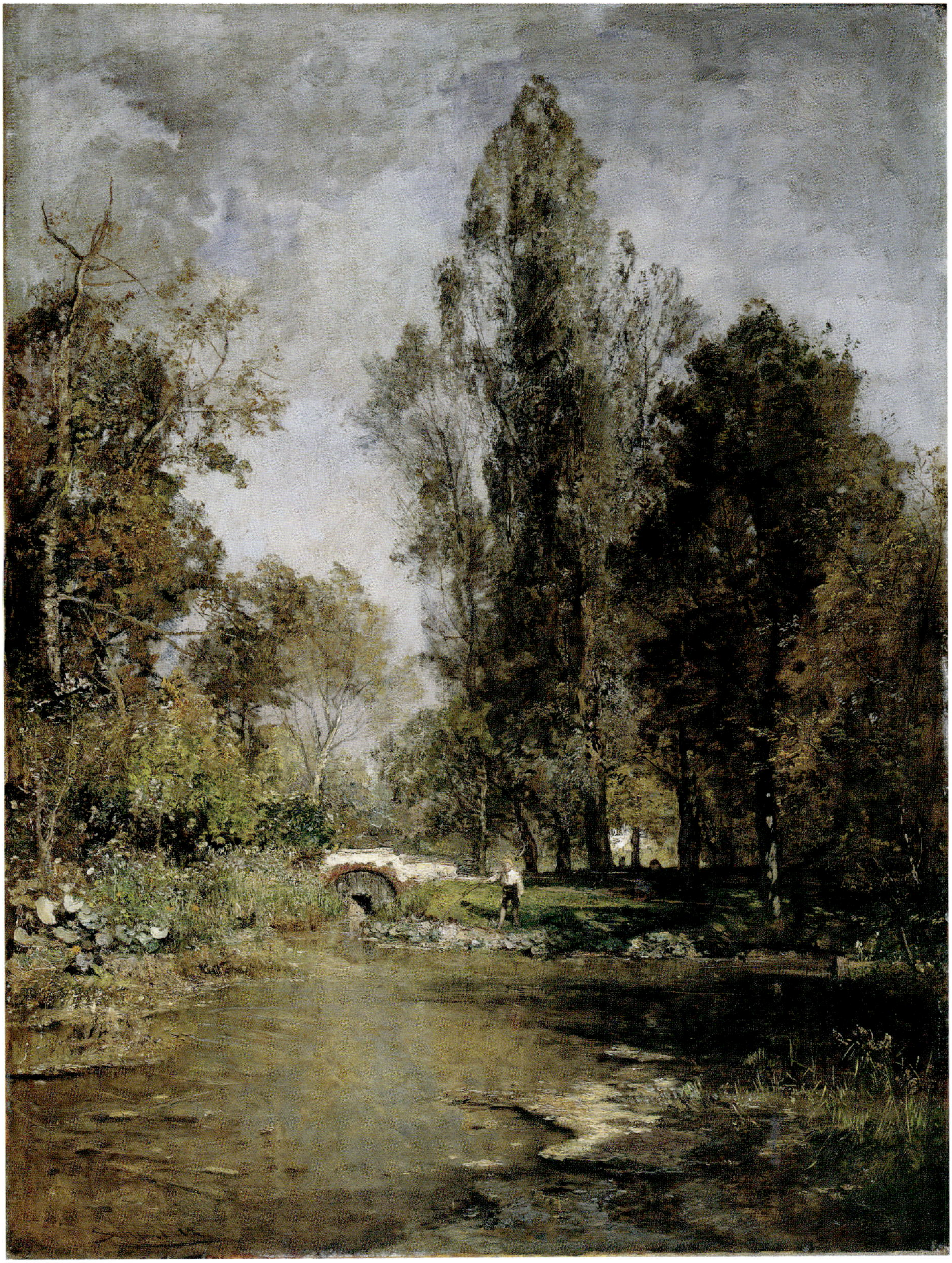

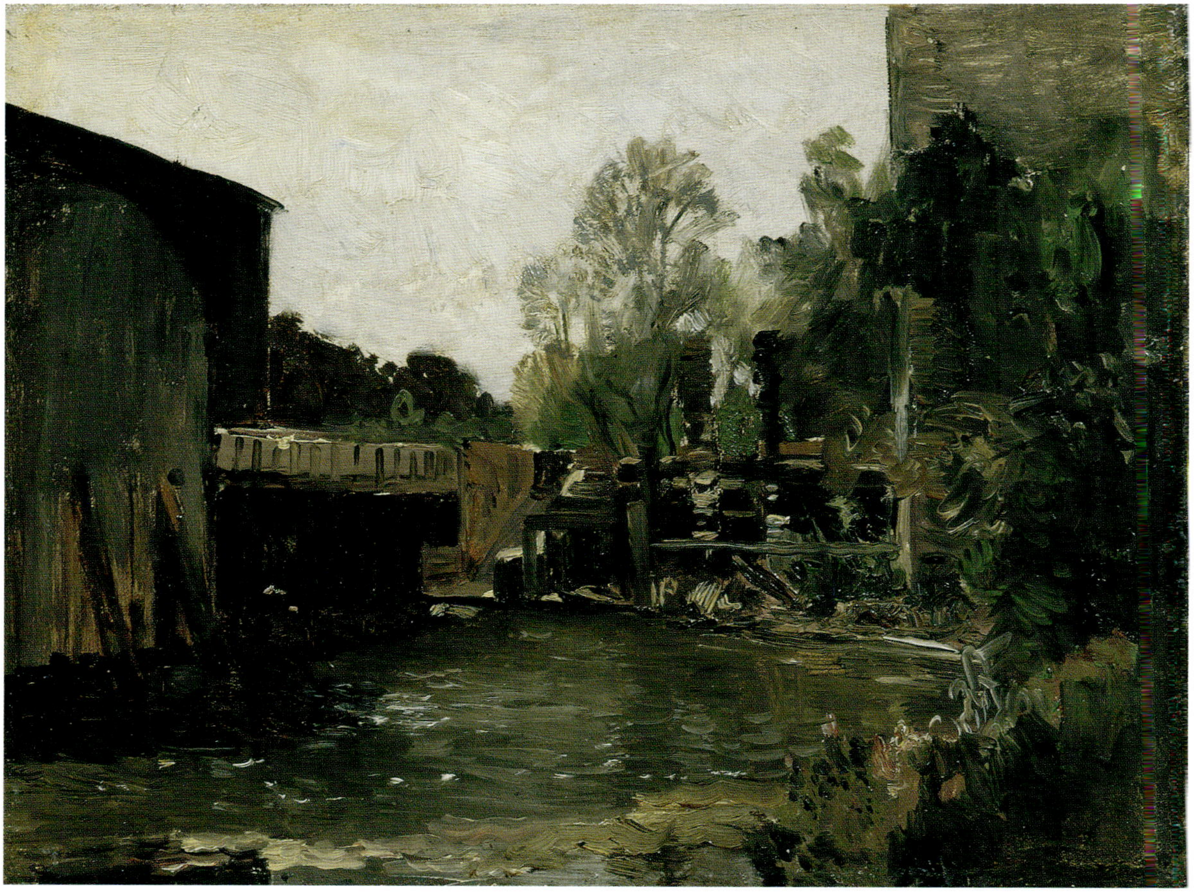

Emil Jakob Schindler *Mill Weir in Plankenberg* (Mühlwehr in Plankenberg), c. 1889/91, oil on canvas, 25 x 34 cm, Belvedere, Vienna

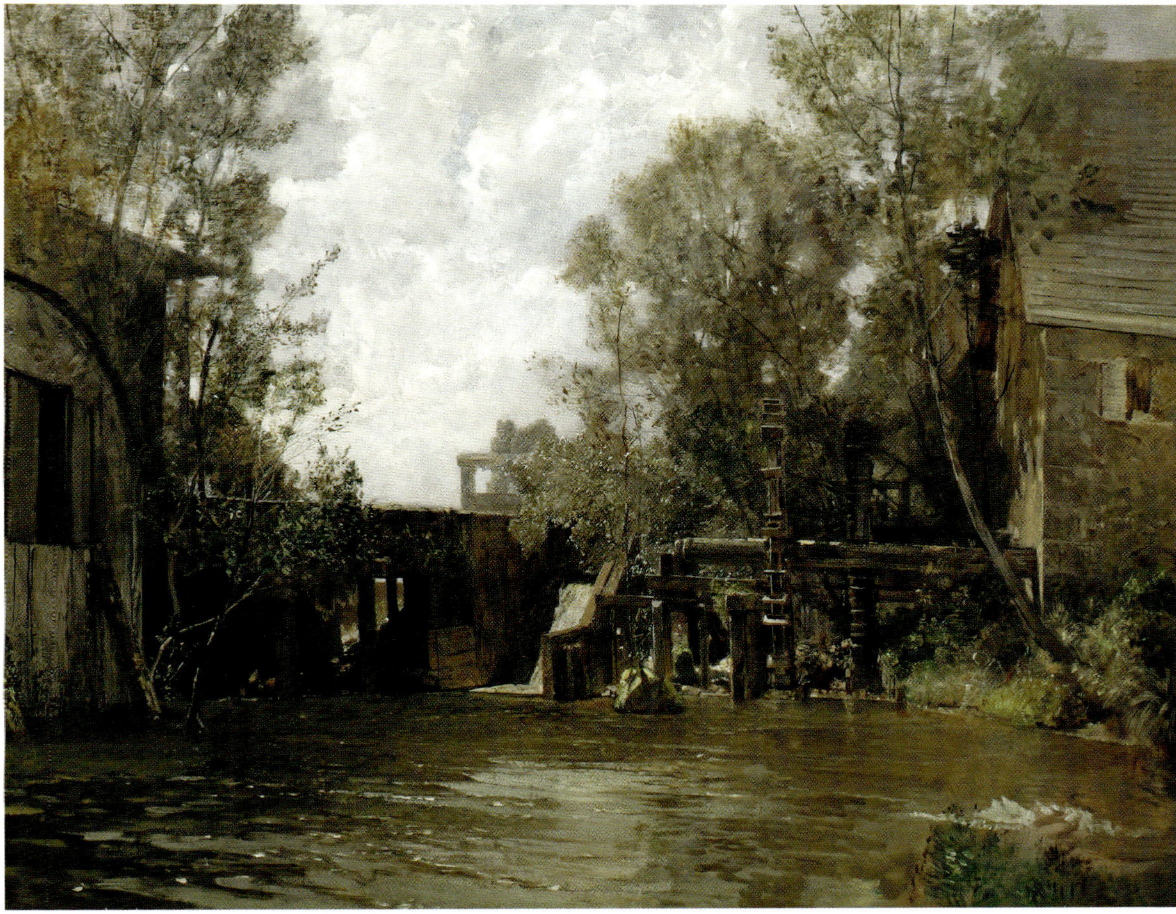

Emil Jakob Schindler, *Mill near Plankenberg* (Mühle bei Plankenberg), 1890, oil on canvas, 95 x 124 cm, Wien Museum

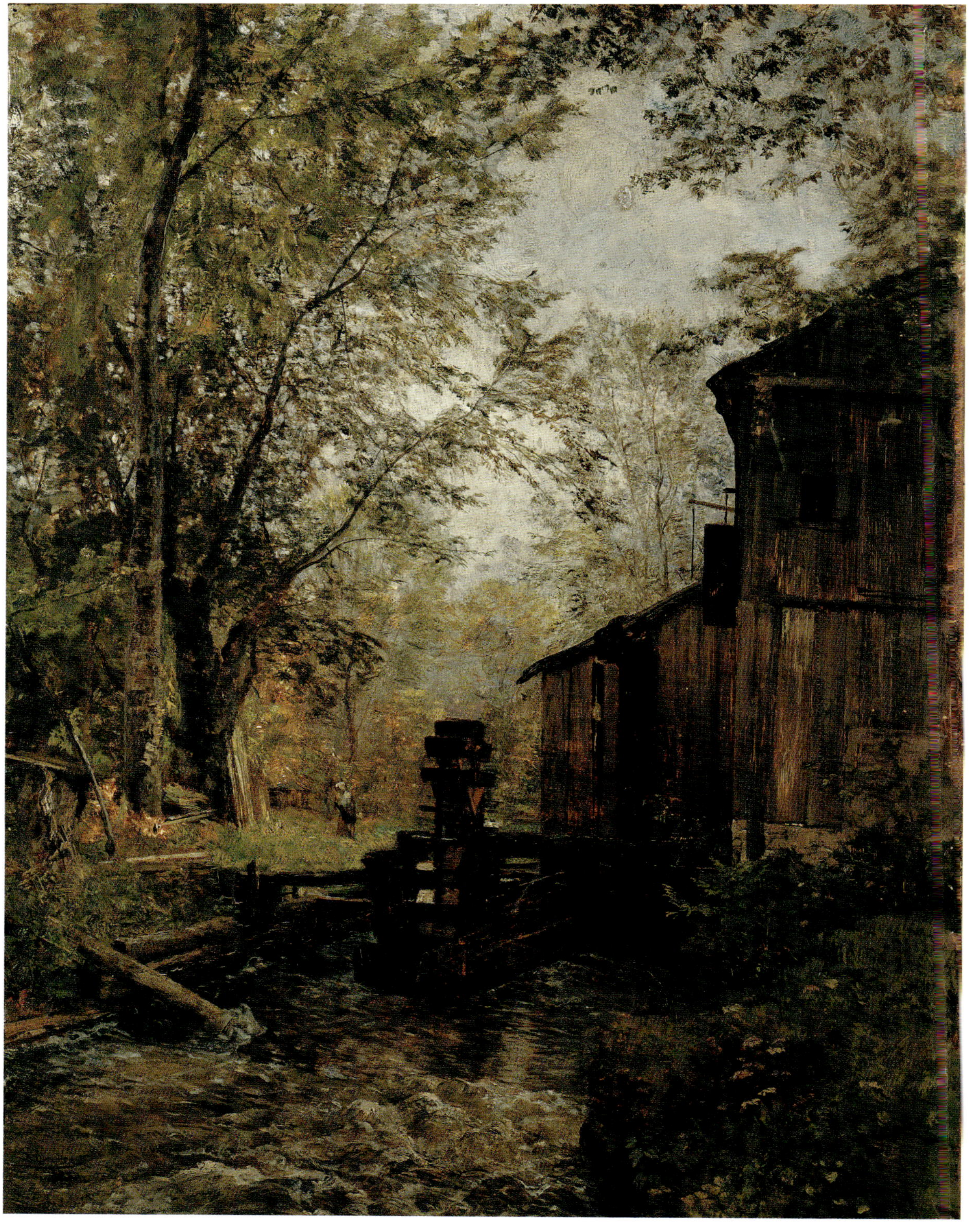

Emil Jakob Schindler, *Gosau Mill near Ischl* (Die Gosaumühle bei Ischl), 1883, oil on wood, 36 x 28 cm, Belvedere, Vienna

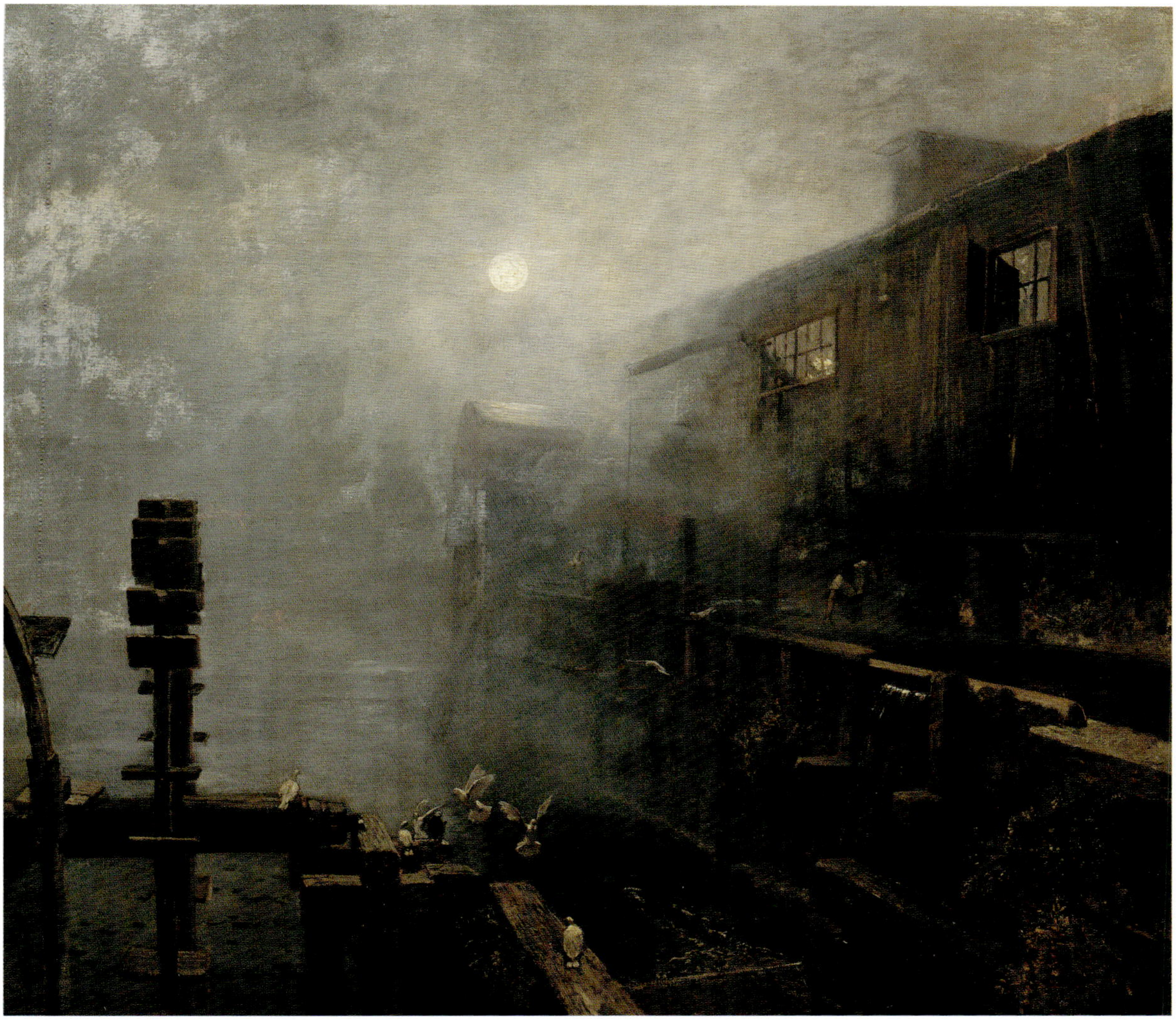

Emil Jakob Schindler, *Sawmill in the Morning Mist* (Sägemühle im Morgennebel), 1886, oil on canvas, 84 x 100 cm, Belvedere, Vienna

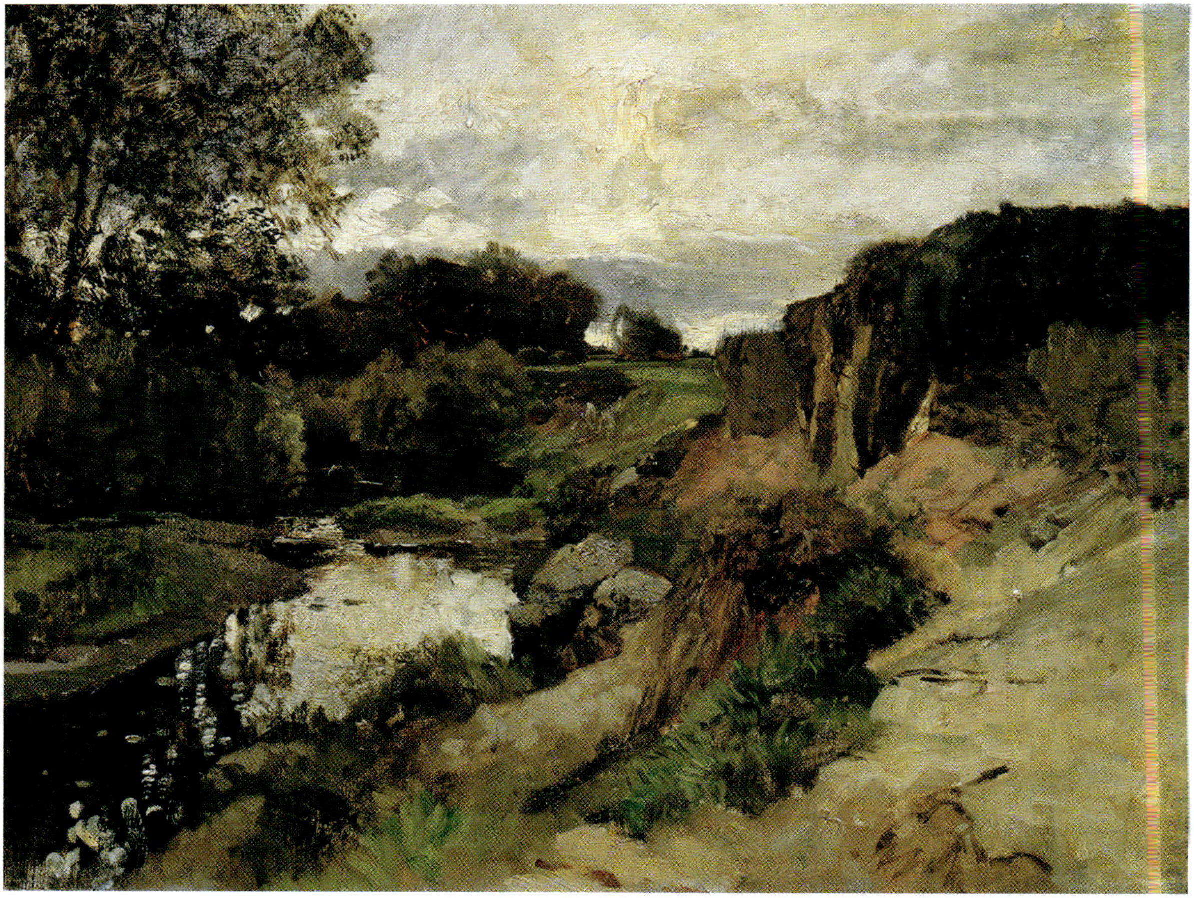

EMIL JAKOB SCHINDLER, *By Tulln Stream near Plankenberg* (Am Tullnbach bei Plankenberg), um 1889/90, oil on canvas, 39 x 54 cm, Belvedere, Vienna

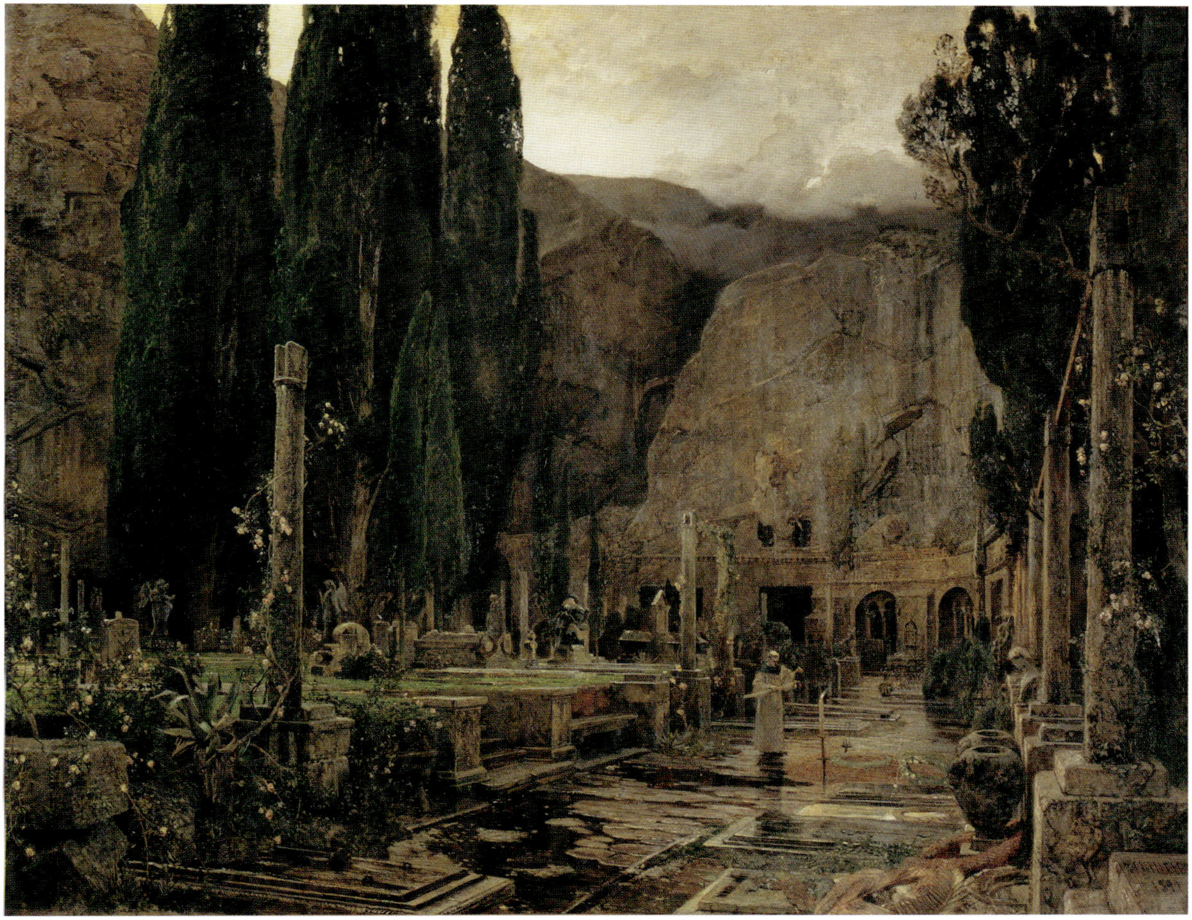

EMIL JAKOB SCHINDLER, *Pax (The Cemetery of Gravosa near Ragusa)* (Pax [Der Friedhof von Gravosa bei Ragusa]), 1891, oil on canvas, 207 x 271 cm, Belvedere, Vienna

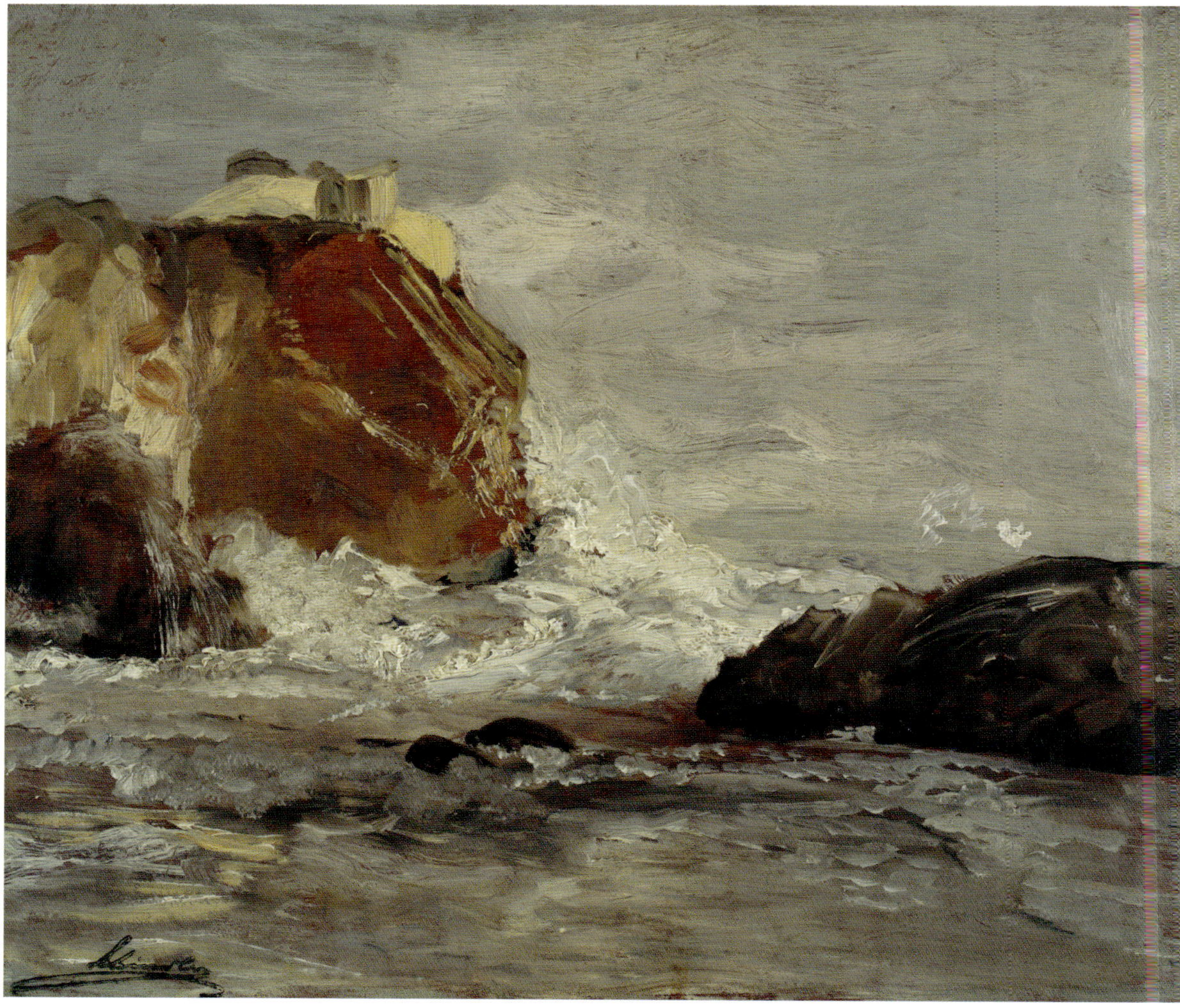

Emil Jakob Schindler, *Surf near Fort Lorenzo in Ragusa* (Meeresbrandung beim Fort Lorenzo in Ragusa), 1887/88, oil on wood, 26 x 32 cm, Wien Museum, Vienna

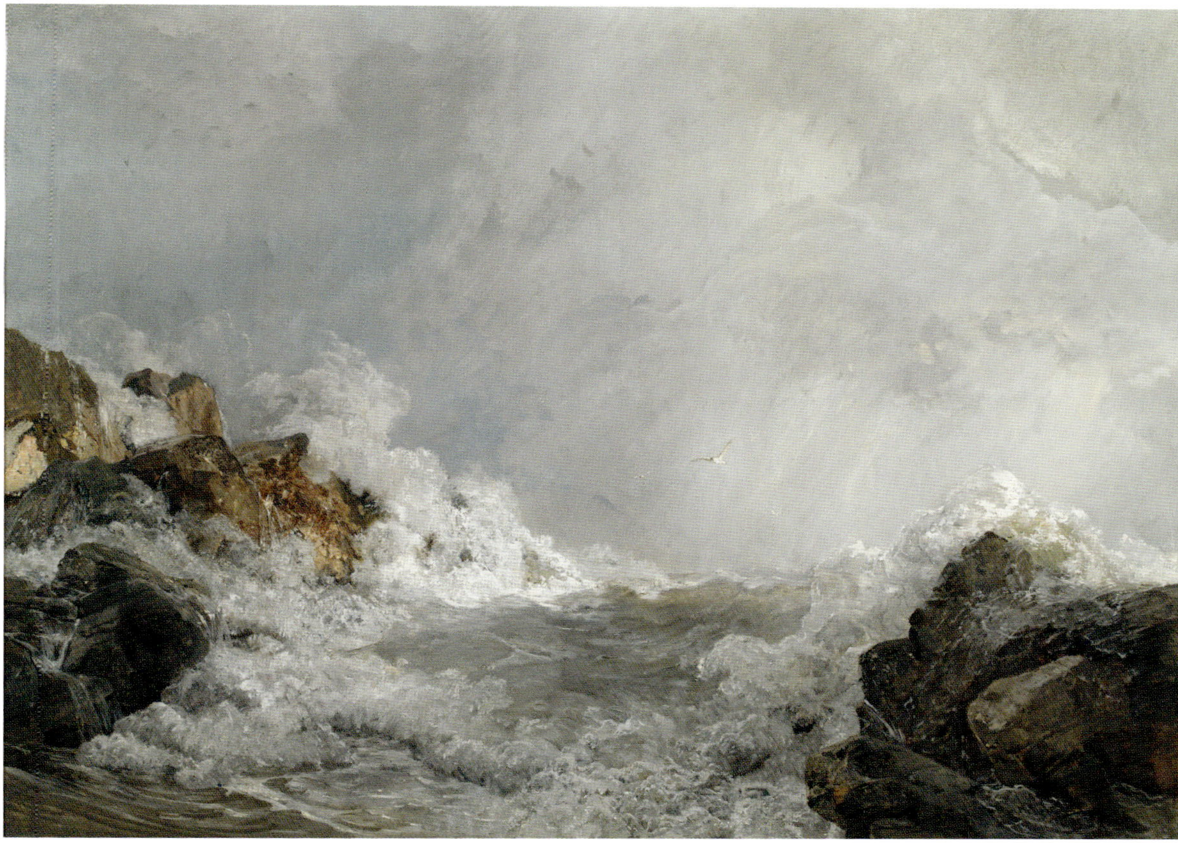

Emil Jakob Schindler, *Surf in the Scirocco near Ragusa* (Brandung bei Scirocco vor Ragusa), 1889,
oil on canvas, 87 x 120 cm, private collection

Next two pages:
Emil Jakob Schindler, *Road by a Wood in Rainy Weather – November Atmosphere*
(Straße an einem Wald bei Regenwetter – Novemberstimmung), c. 1883/85,
oil on canvas, 128 x 97 cm, private collection

Emil Jakob Schindler, *March Atmosphere – Early Spring in the Vienna Woods*
(Märzstimmung – Vorfrühling im Wienerwald), c. 1884, oil on canvas, 130.5 x 100.5 cm, Belvedere, Vienna

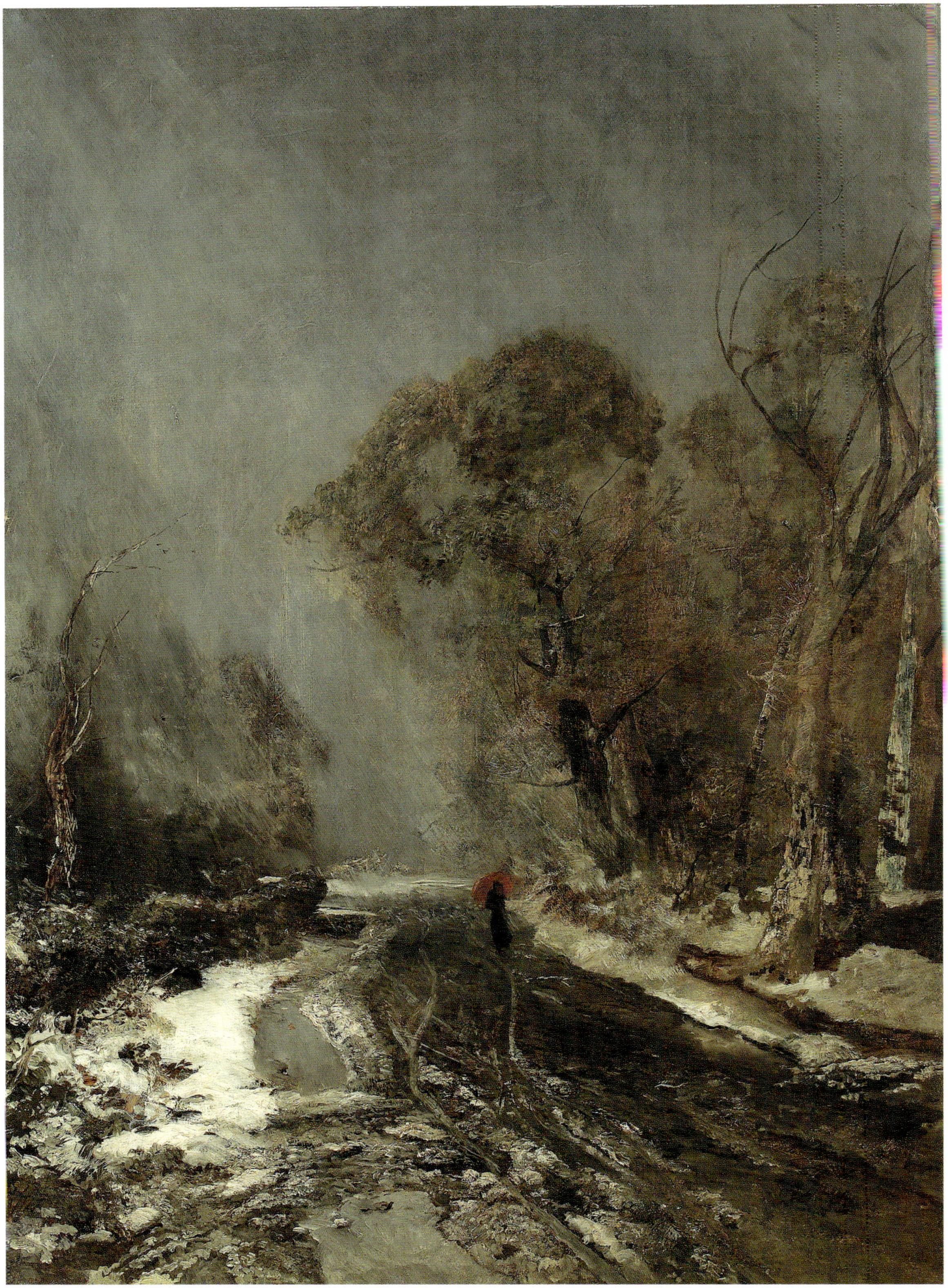

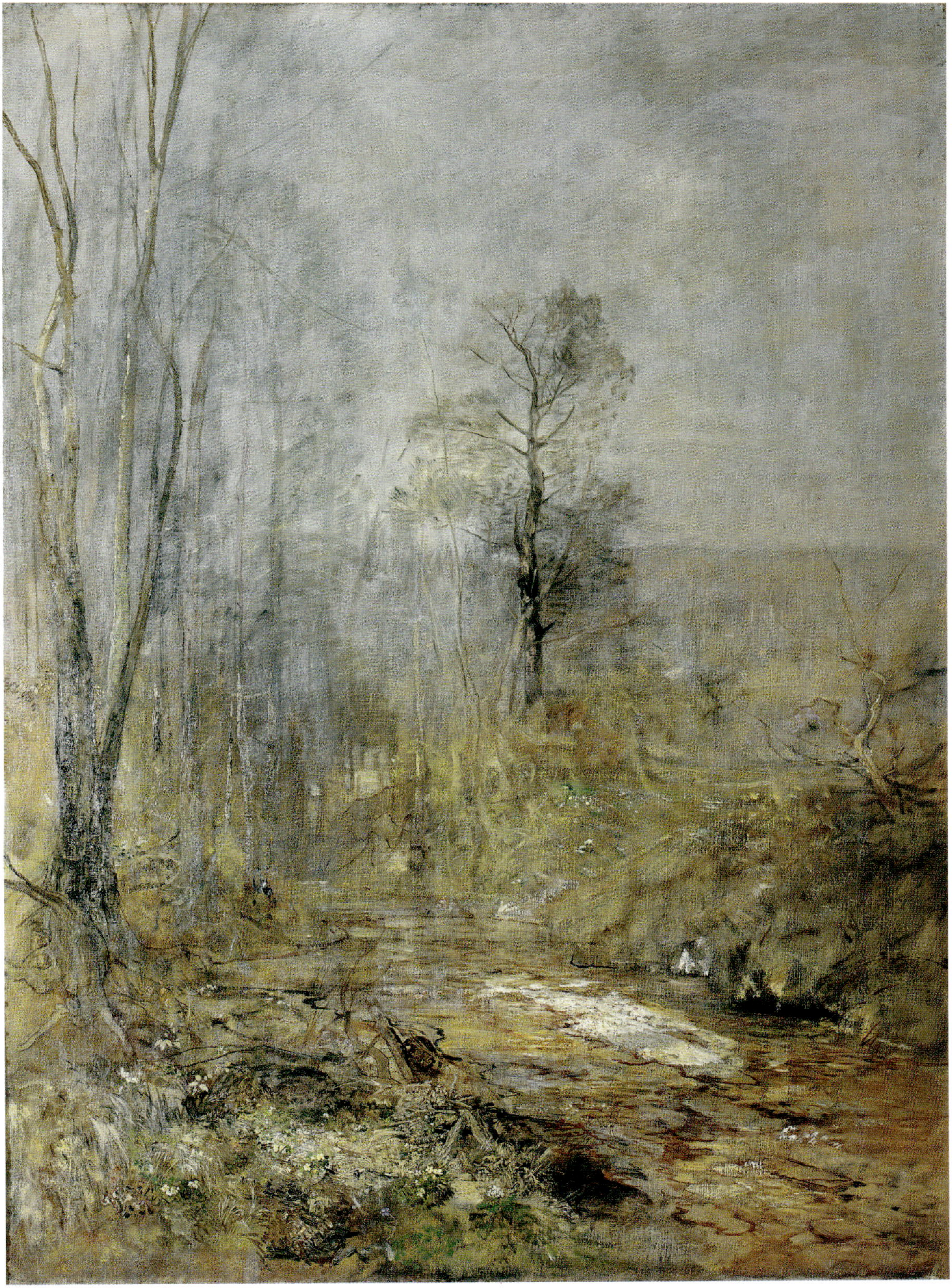

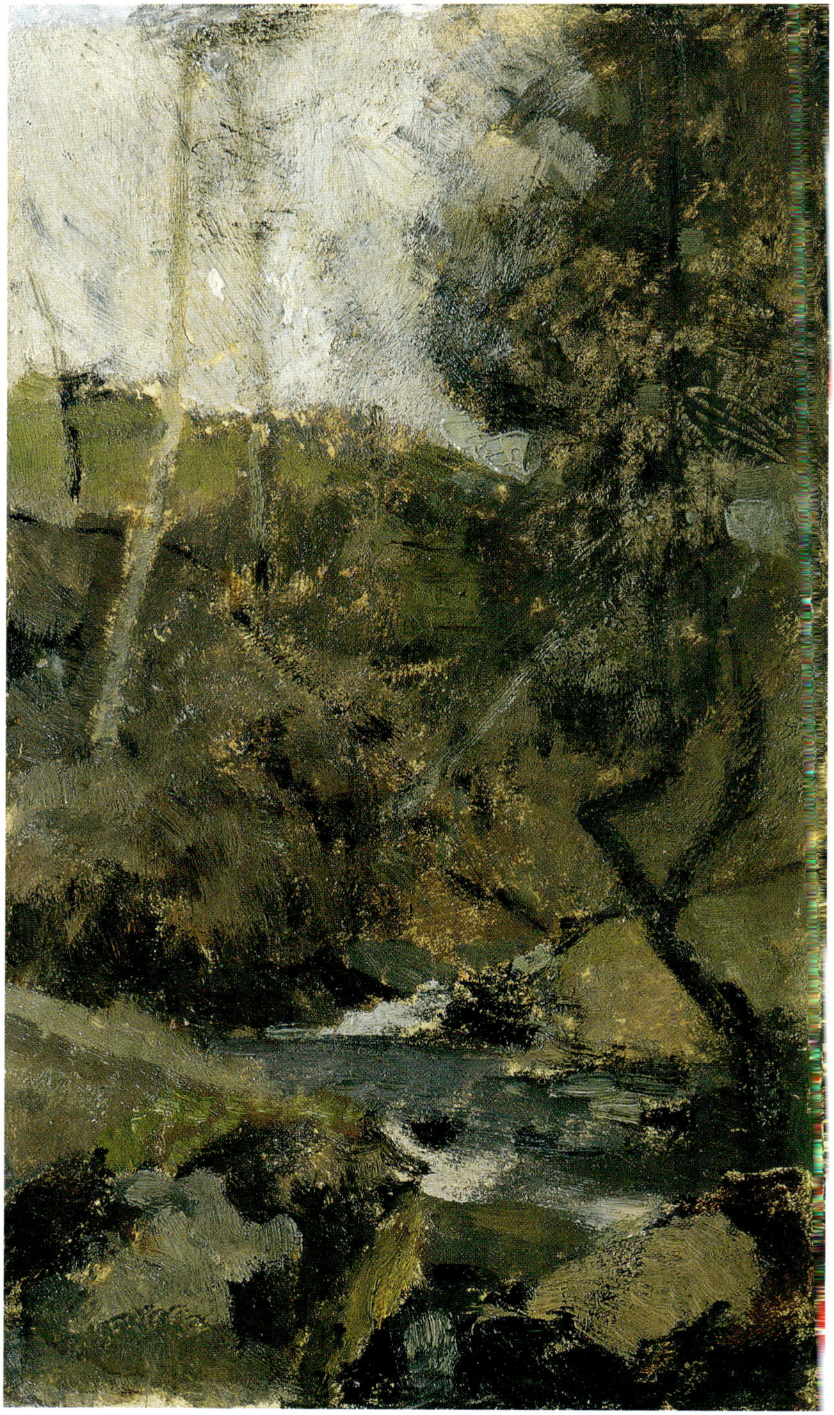

Emil Jakob Schindler, *Stream in the Vienna Woods* (Bach im Wienerwald), c. 1884, oil on wood, 21.5 x 13 cm, Belvedere, Vienna

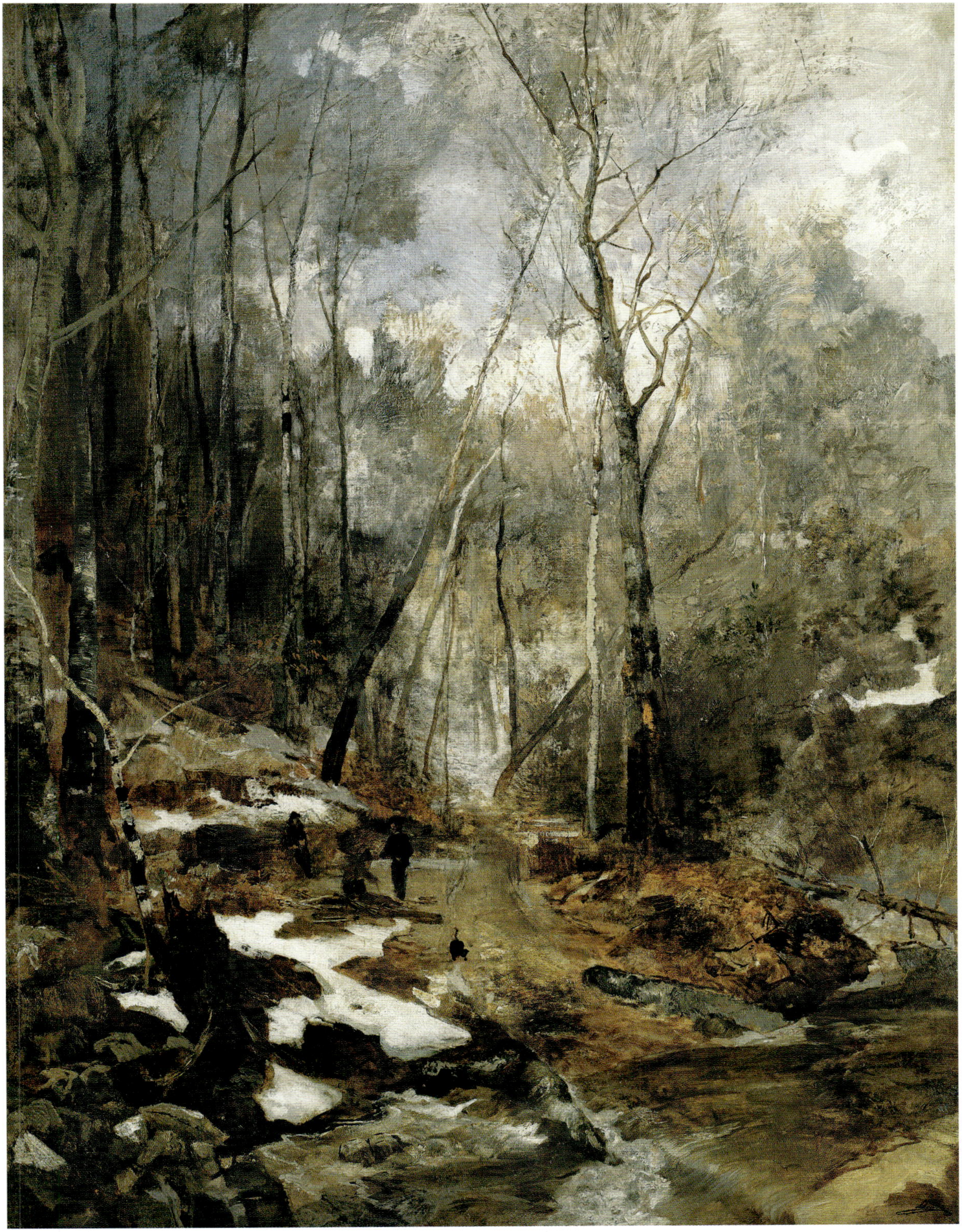

EMIL JAKOB SCHINDLER, *February Atmosphere – Early Spring in the Vienna Woods*
(Februarstimmung – Vorfrühling im Wienerwald), 1884, oil on canvas, 120 x 96 cm, Belvedere, Vienna

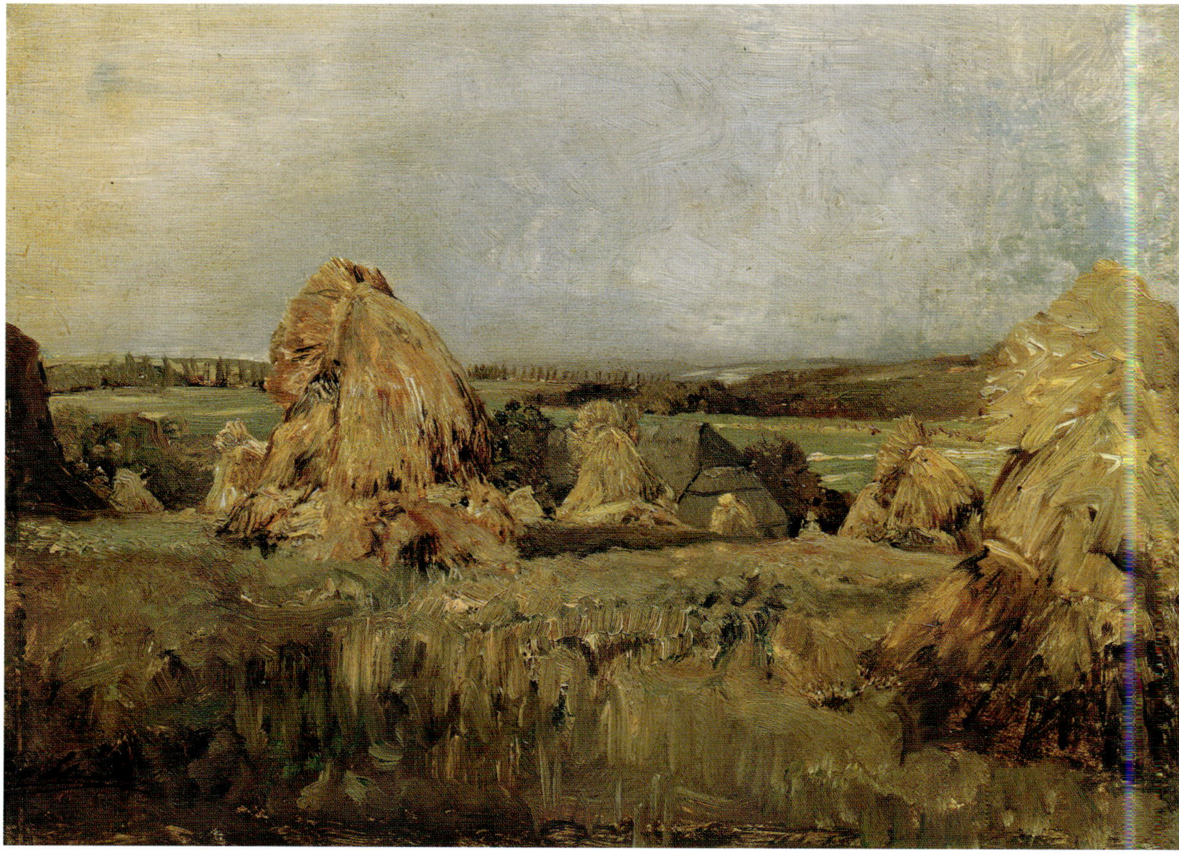

Emil Jakob Schindler, *Harvest Month in Plankenberg* (Erntemonat in Plankenberg), c. 1890, oil on wood, 26.5 x 36 cm, Belvedere, Vienna

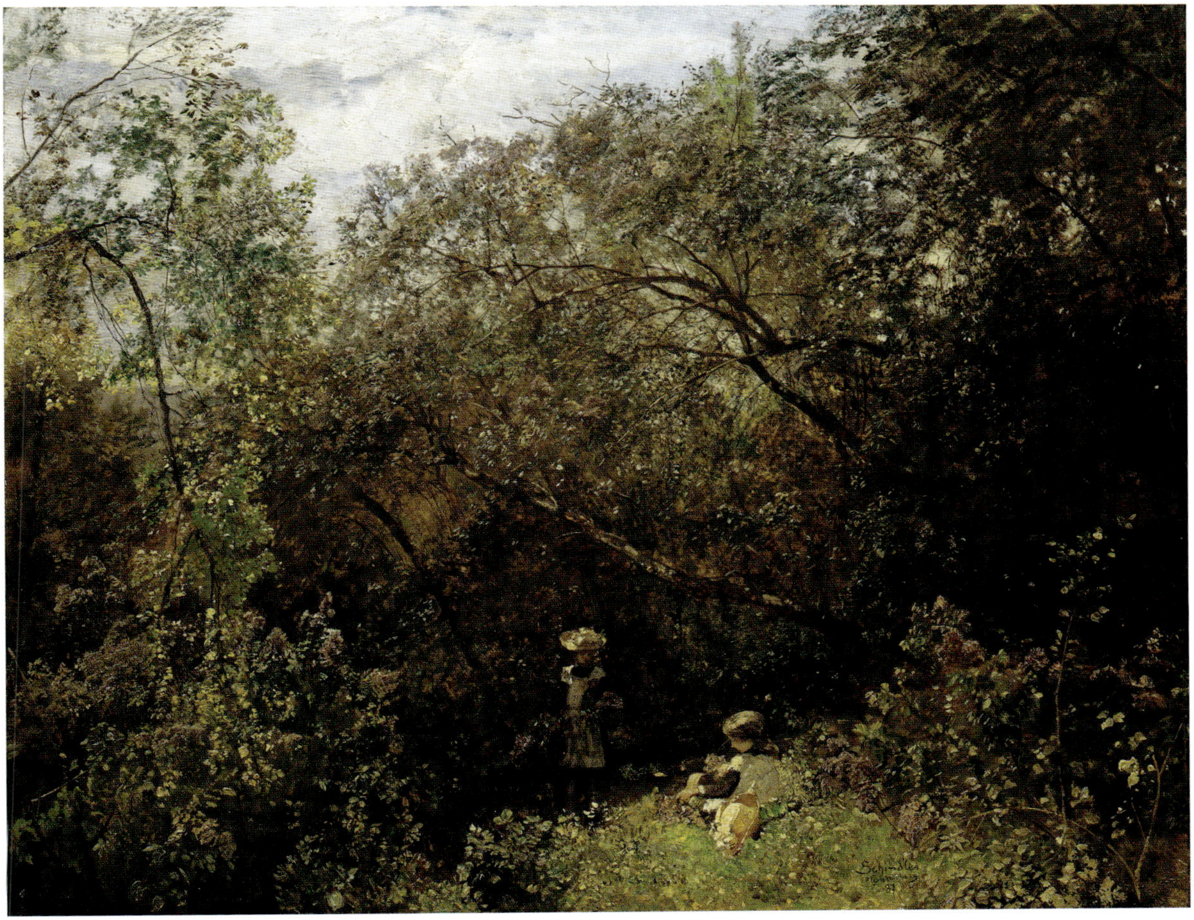

EMIL JAKOB SCHINDLER, *Park Landscape in Plankenberg (Lilac)* (Parklandschaft in Plankenberg [Flieder]), 1887, oil on wood, 49.5 x 66 cm, Belvedere, Vienna

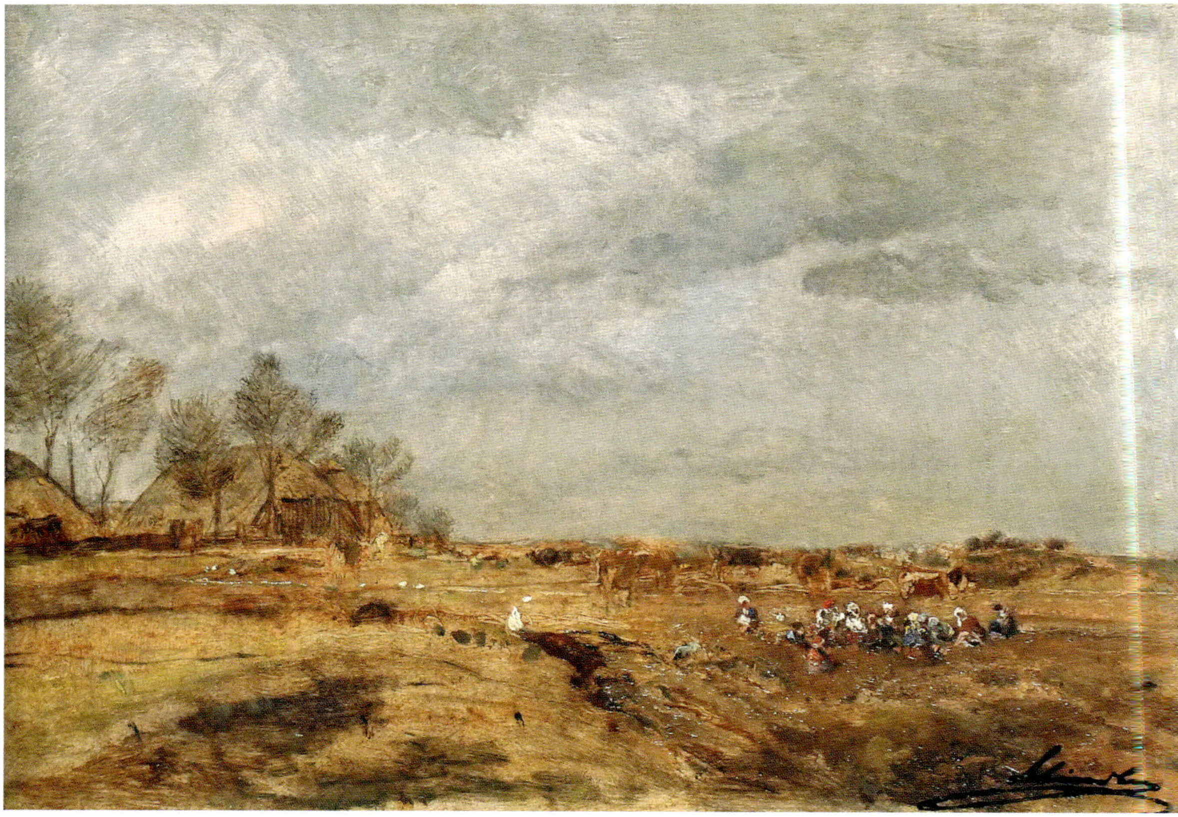

Emil Jakob Schindler, *Potato Harvest* (Die Kartoffelernte), 1891,
oil on wood, 17.9 x 25.9 cm, Kunsthandel Giese & Schweiger, Vienna

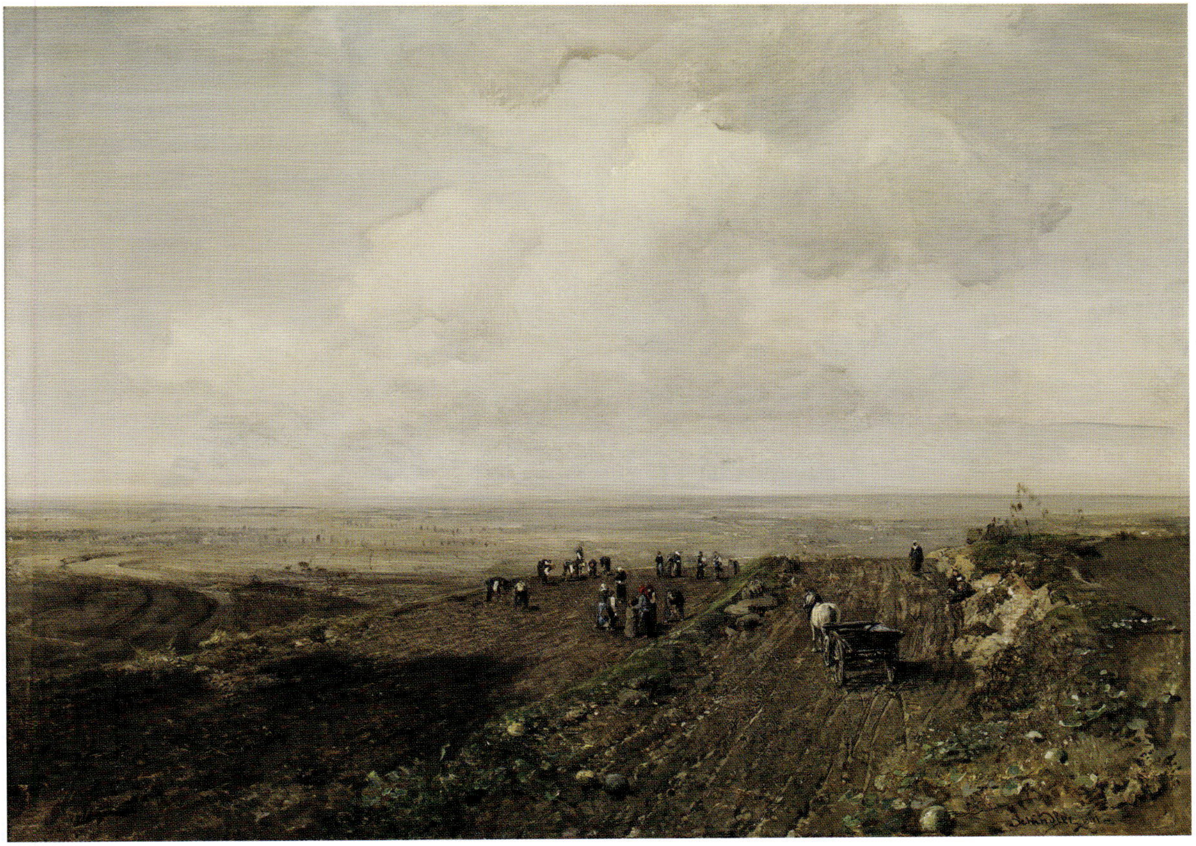

Emil Jakob Schindler, *Potato Harvest* (Die Kartoffelernte), 1891, oil on wood, 42 x 60 cm, private collection

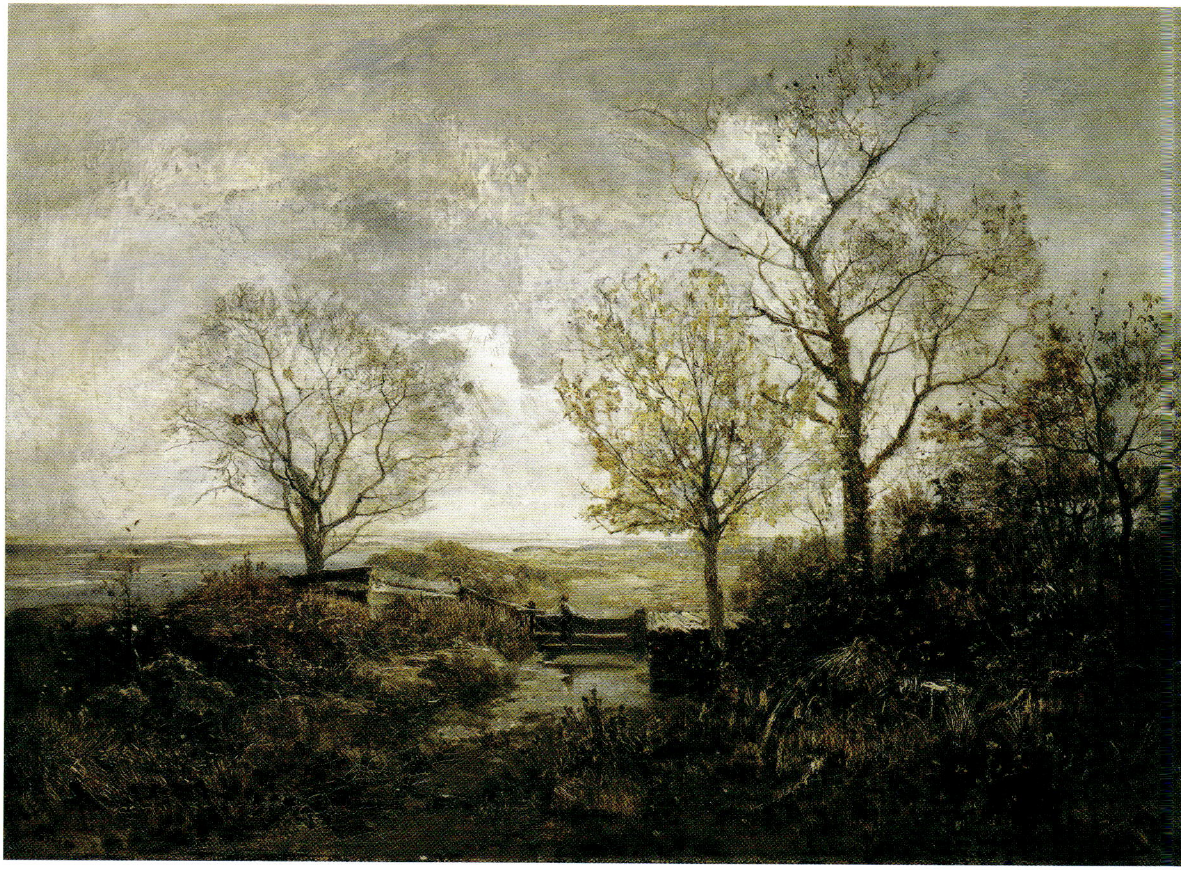

Emil Jakob Schindler, *Autumnal Landscape by a River* (Herbstlandschaft am Fluss), c. 1887/88, oil on canvas, 41 x 56 cm, Belvedere, Vienna

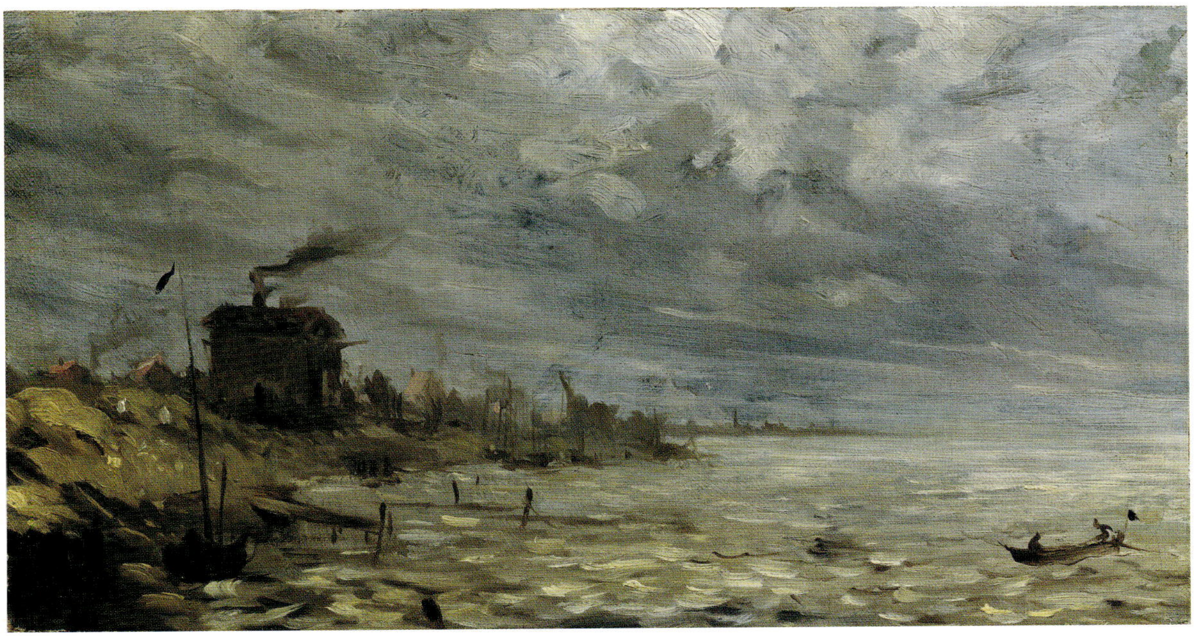

Emil Jakob Schindler, *Coast at Sylt* (Meeresküste auf Sylt), 1892, oil on canvas on wood, 16.5 x 30.5 cm, Belvedere, Vienna

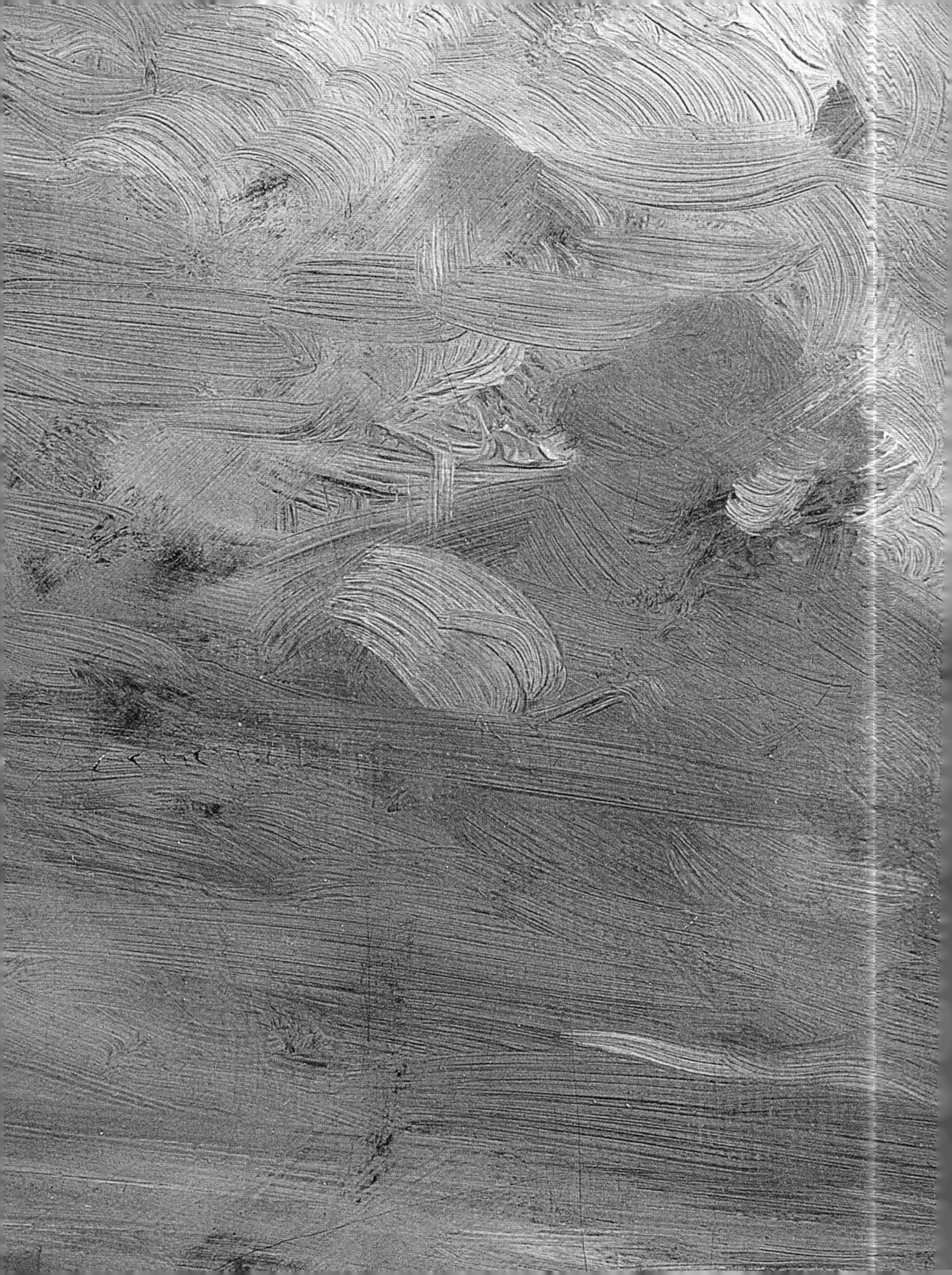

Emil Jakob Schindler in the Belvedere

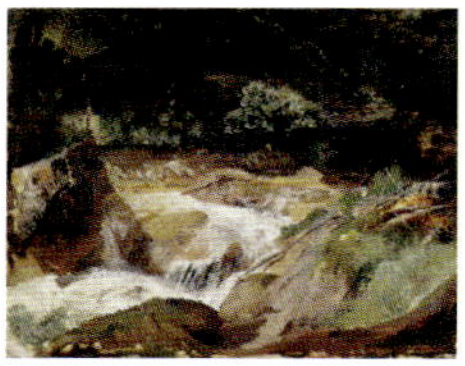

Mountain Stream in the Ramsau (Gebirgsbach in der Ramsau), c. 1868
Oil on paper on cardboard, 26 x 33 cm
Design. on the back: Gebirgs-Bachstudie 25:32 / Papier Nachlass
Belvedere, Vienna, inv. no. 5520
1930 Paul Hamburger, Freudenthal. – 1962 acquisition Galerie Schebesta, Vienna
Fuchs-catalogue raisonné, No. 21

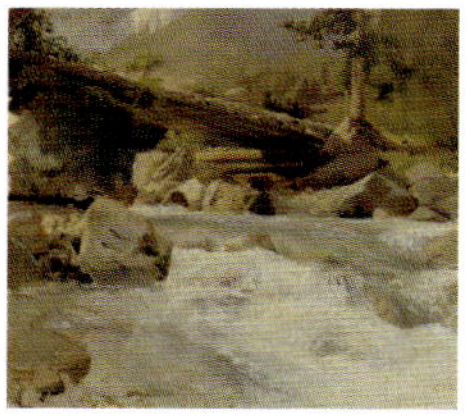

Wood Stream with Footbridge (Stream Study, Motif of the Lake Hintersee) (Waldbach mit Steg) (Bachstudie, Motiv vom Hintersee), c. 1868
Oil on cardboard, 27.5 x 30 cm
Design. bottom left: estate stamp
Belvedere, Vienna, inv. no. Lg 1129, permanent loan from private collection
1892 Schindler estate. – Private collection. – 1962 Kunsthandel Schebesta, Vienna
Fuchs-catalogue raisonné, No. 23

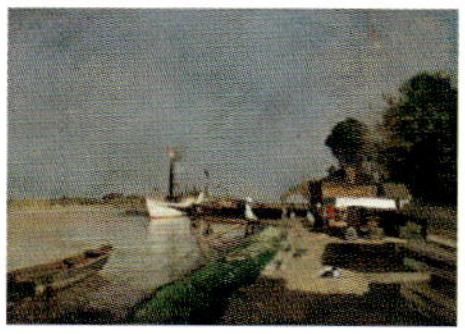

The Steamer Station on the Danube opposite Kaisermühlen (Die Dampfschiffstation an der Donau gegenüber Kaisermühlen), c. 1871/72
Oil on canvas, 55 x 78.5 cm
Design. bottom left: Naturstudie aus dem Prater / gemalt und seinem Freund Dr. J. Scholz […] gewidmet von E. J. Schindler
Belvedere, Vienna, inv. no. 3338
Dr. Josef Scholz, Vienna. – 1936 acquisition private collection, Vienna
Fuchs-catalogue raisonné, No. 89

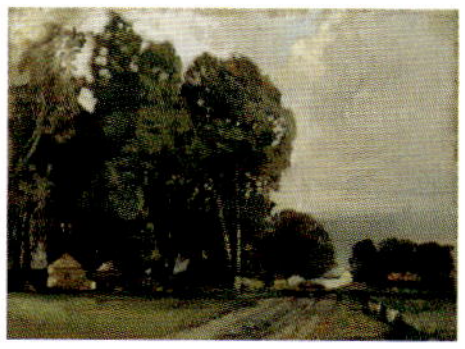

Motif from the Prater – Krieau (Motiv aus dem Prater – Krieau), c. 1873/74
Oil on cardboard on canvas, 27 x 37 cm
Undesignated
Belvedere, Vienna, inv. no. 6553
Alfred Spitzer, Vienna. – 1981 Gift to Hanna Spitzer and Edith Neumann, New York
Fuchs-catalogue raisonné, No. 107

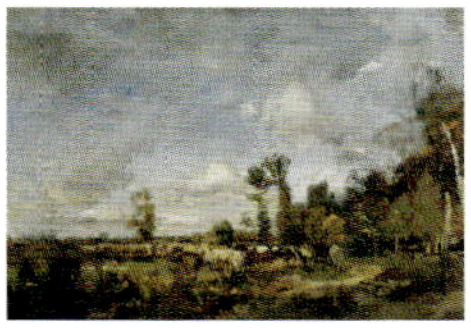

Grazing Cattle in Holland (Weidendes Vieh in Holland), c. 1875
Oil on canvas, 55.5 x 82 cm
Undesignated
Belvedere, Vienna, inv. no. 5973
1973 bequest Ernst Zix, Kaiserslautern
Fuchs-catalogue raisonné, No. 200

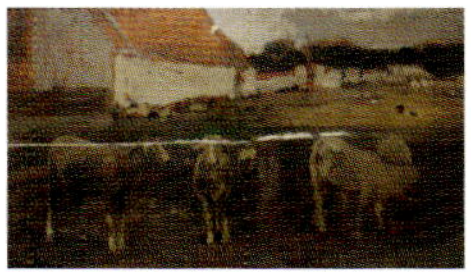

Village Landscape with Sheep (Nature Study from Holland)
(Dorflandschaft mit Schafen [Naturstudie aus Holland]), c. 1875
Oil on wood, 22.5 x 37 cm
Design. bottom left: Schindler (estate stamp)
Belvedere, Vienna, inv. no. 5318
1959 acquisition private collection, Vienna
Fuchs-catalogue raisonné, No. 202

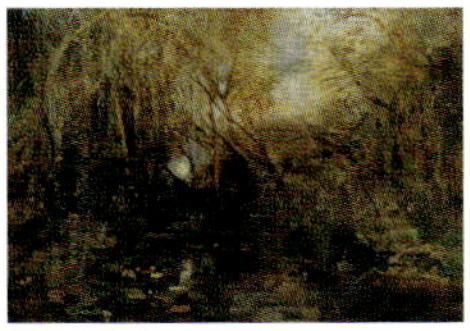

Moonrise in the Prater Meadows (Mondaufgang in der Praterau), c. 1877/78
Oil on canvas, 105.5 x 154.5 cm
Undesignated
Belvedere, Vienna, inv. no. 4010
1945 bequest Carl Moll, Vienna
Fuchs-catalogue raisonné, No. 239

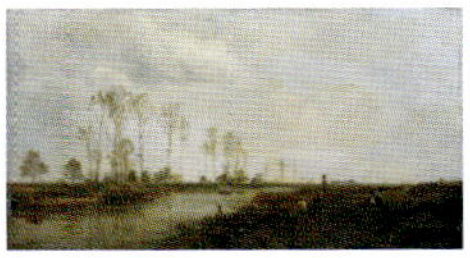

On the Thaya near Lundenburg I (An der Thaya bei Lundenburg I), 1877
Oil on wood, 39.5 x 74 cm
Sig. and dat. bottom left: Schindler 77
Belvedere, Vienna, inv. no. 4586
Until 1904 Emanuel Bratmann collection, Vienna. – Hugo Aubelang (?). – 1931 auction Kende. – 1935 Blanche Mandler, Vienna. – Karl Maget. – 1952 acquired in exchange with the art dealer Leopold Zehetgruber and Franz Schebesta, Vienna
Fuchs-catalogue raisonné, No. 275

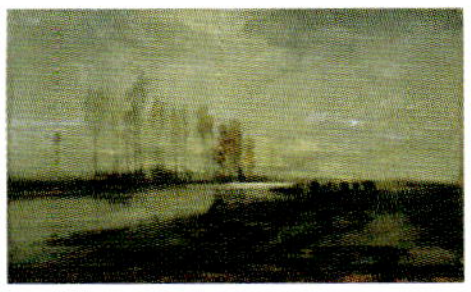

On the Thaya near Lundenburg II (An der Thaya bei Lundenburg II), c. 1877/80
Oil on wood, 47 x 79 cm
Sig. bottom right: Schindler
Belvedere, Vienna, inv. no. 4616
Otto Schulzer. – 1952 acquisition private collection, Vienna
Fuchs-catalogue raisonné, No. 276

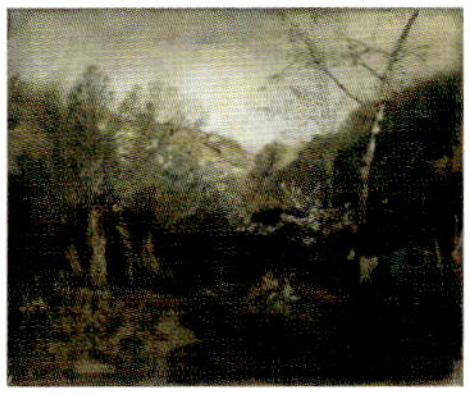

Scene near Haslau on the Danube (Evening Atmosphere, Nature Study) (Partie bei Haslau an der Donau [Abendstimmung, Naturstudie]), c. 1879/80
Oil on canvas, 50.5 x 62 cm
Undesignated
Belvedere, Vienna, inv. no. 5788
1892 Schindler estate. – 1942 private collection Böhm. – 1966 acquisition private collection, Vienna
Fuchs-catalogue raisonné, No. 286

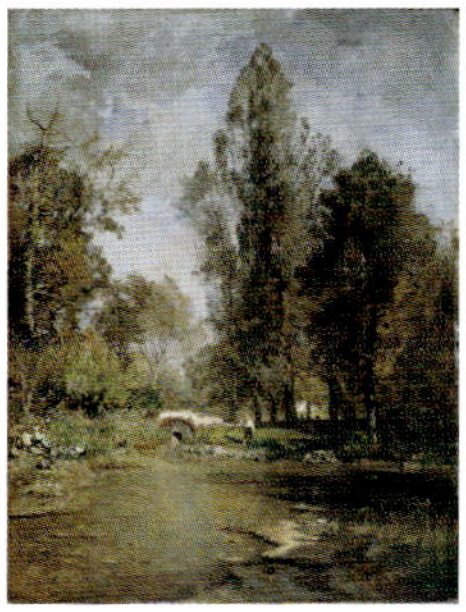

Meadow in Hacking (Hackinger Au), 1880
Oil on canvas, 90 x 68 cm
Sig. bottom left: Schindler
Belvedere, Vienna, inv. no. 4012
1931 Prof. Gustav Jäger, Vienna. – 1945 bequest Carl Moll
Fuchs-catalogue raisonné, No. 330

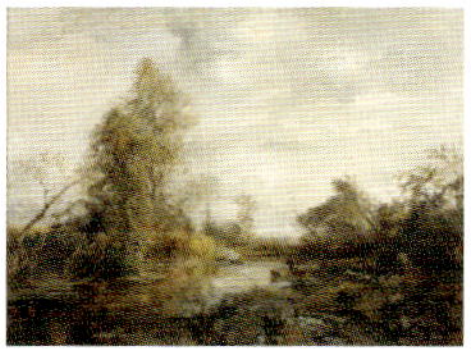

Duck Hunting in the Prater (Entenjagd im Prater), c. 1881
Oil on canvas, 74 x 100 cm
Sig. bottom right: Schindler
Belvedere, Vienna, inv. no. 5423
1892 Anton Dengler, Jedlesee. – 1960 in exchange with Leopold Zehetgruber, London
Fuchs-catalogue raisonné, No. 344

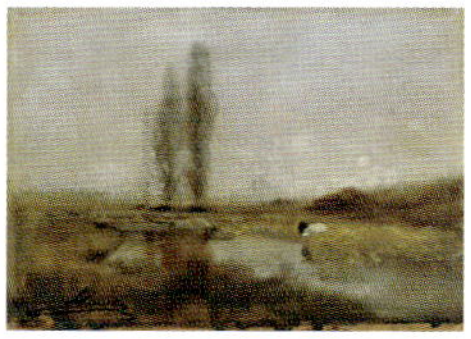

Marshland near Lundenburg (Moorlandschaft bei Lundenburg), c. 1882
Oil on wood, 16.5 x 23 cm
Design. bottom left: Schindler (estate stamp)
Belvedere, Vienna, inv. no. 4295
1892 Schindler estate. – 1948 acquisition private collection, Vienna
Fuchs-catalogue raisonné, No. 358

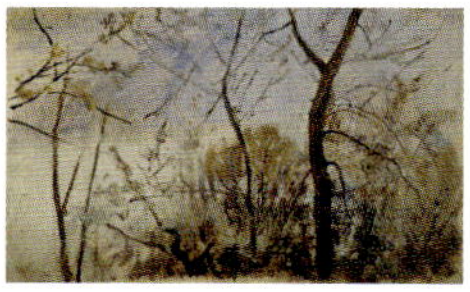

Landscape Study: Spring in Hacking (Landschaftsstudie: Frühling in Hacking), 1882
Oil on wood, 12.5 x 22 cm
Design. bottom left: Schindler (estate stamp)
Design. and dated on the back: Detailstudie. Frühling. Hacking. 1882 / Schindler
Belvedere, Vienna, inv. no. Lg 1128, permanent loan from private collection (2003)
1892 Schindler estate. – 1962 Galerie Schebesta, Vienna. – Private collection
Fuchs-catalogue raisonné, No. 370

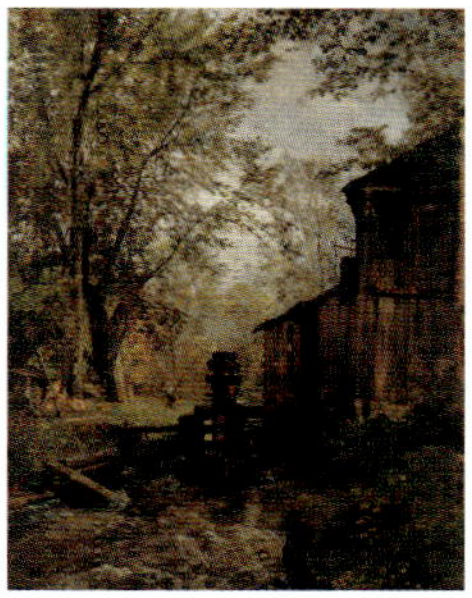

Gosau Mill near Ischl (Die Gosaumühle bei Ischl), 1883
Oil on wood, 36 x 28 cm
Sig. and dat. bottom left: Schindler / 1883
Belvedere, Vienna, inv. no. 335a
1898 bequest Carl Oberleithner, Vienna
Fuchs-catalogue raisonné, No. 388

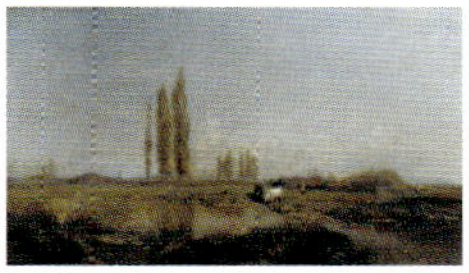

On the Thaya near Lundenburg (An der Thaya bei Lundenburg), c. 1883/84
Oil on wood, 36.5 x 63 cm
Sig. bottom right: Schindler
Belvedere, Vienna, inv. no. 2384
Rudolf Reichert, Vienna. – 1923 acquisition auctioneer C. J. Wawra, Vienna
Fuchs-catalogue raisonné, No. 463

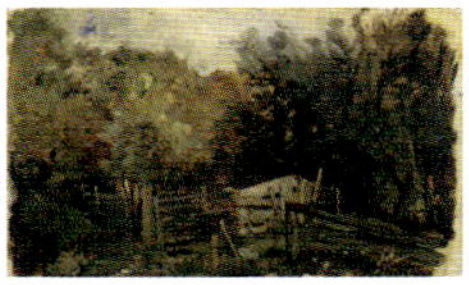

Nature Study from Goisern (Wood Landscape)
(Naturstudie aus Goisern [Waldlandschaft]) c. 1883
Oil on wood, 13 x 21.5 cm
Sig. bottom right: Sch.
Design. on the back: Original sketch (Originalskizze) / by Emil Schindler
Belvedere, Vienna, inv. no. 3667
1939 dedication to Kunstfreund
Fuchs-catalogue raisonné, No. 426

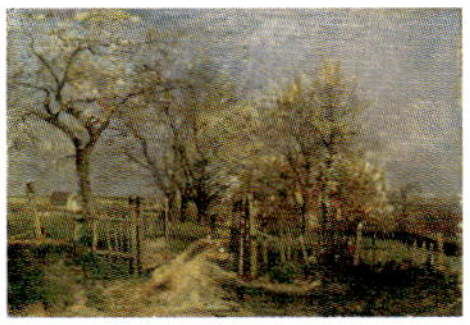

Spring in Hacking (Frühling in Hacking), 1883
Oil on wood, 14 x 21 cm
Sig. and dat. bottom right: Schindler Mai 1883
Belvedere, Vienna, inv. no. 4011
1931 Lili Oppenheimer, Vienna. – 1945 bequest Carl Moll
Fuchs-catalogue raisonné, No. 443

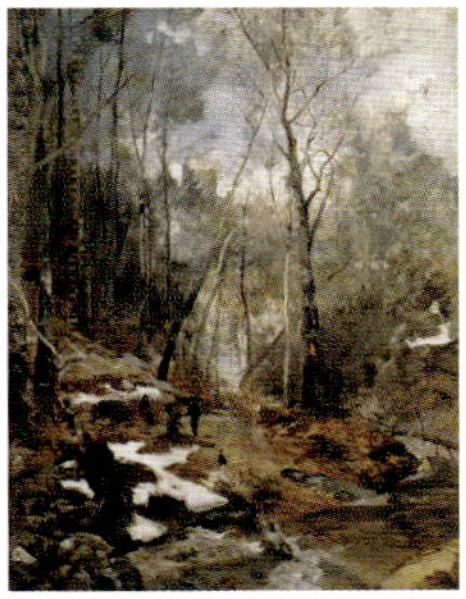

February Atmosphere – Early Spring in the Vienna Woods
(Februarstimmung – Vorfrühling im Wienerwald), 1884
Oil on canvas, 120 x 96 cm
Design. bottom right: Schindler (estate stamp)
Belvedere, Vienna, inv. no. 5228
1892 Schindler estate. – 1927 Gisela Thorn collection, Vienna. – 1931
Dr. Albert Baum. – Private collection, New York. – 1950 Otto Kallir,
New York. – 1957 dedication to Österreichisches Credit-Institut (GiroCredit)
Fuchs-catalogue raisonné, No. 466

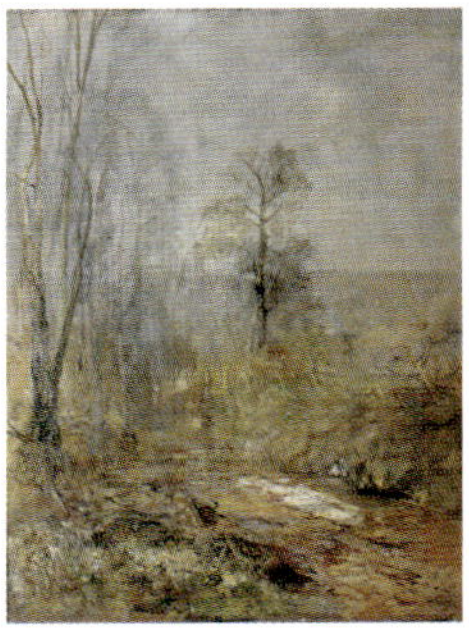

March Atmosphere – Early Spring in the Vienna Woods
(Märzstimmung – Vorfrühling im Wienerwald), c. 1884
Oil on canvas, 130.5 x 100.5 cm
Undesignated
Belvedere, Vienna, inv. no. 4013
1892 Schindler estate. – Private collection. – 1945 bequest Carl Moll
Fuchs-catalogue raisonné, No. 467

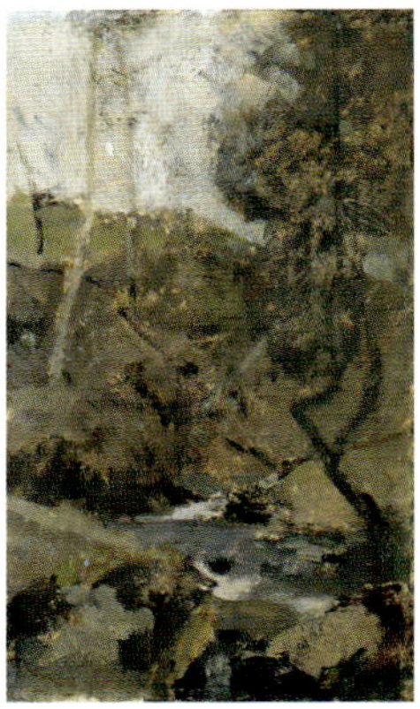

Stream in the Vienna Woods (Bach im Wienerwald), c. 1884
Oil on wood, 21.5 x 13 cm
Design. bottom left: Nachlaß / Schindler (estate stamp)
Belvedere, Vienna, inv. no. 5521
1892 Schindler estate. – Until 1960 Wilhelm Legler. – Alma Mahler-Werfel – Neue Galerie, Vienna. – 1962 acquisition Galerie Schebesta, Vienna
Fuchs-catalogue raisonné, No. 477

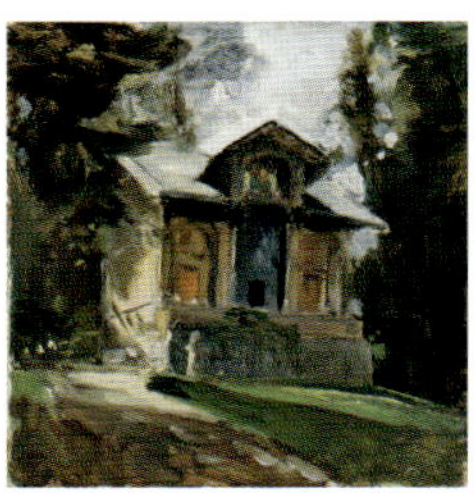

Studio of the Painter Heinrich von Angeli in Reichenau
(Das Atelier des Malers Heinrich von Angeli in der Reichenau), 1884
Oil on wood, 22 x 22 cm
Design.: NACHLASS Schindler / Atelier Angeli (Kleines?) Reichenau / 1884
Belvedere, Vienna, inv. no. 5570
1892 estate Schindler. – 1962 acquisition Galerie Schebesta, Vienna
Fuchs-catalogue raisonné, No. 483

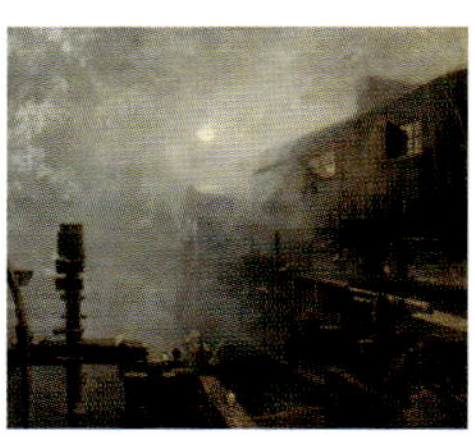

Sawmill in the Morning Mist (Misty Morning, the Beginning of Winter)
(Sägemühle im Morgennebel [Nebliger Morgen, Winteranfang]), 1886
Oil on canvas, 84 x 100 cm
Sig. and dat. bottom left: Schindler 86. Plankenberg
Belvedere, Vienna, inv. no. 381
1892 Jan Wendelstadt, Neubeuern near Rosenheim. – 1900 acquisition art trade Schulte, Berlin
Fuchs-catalogue raisonné, No. 540

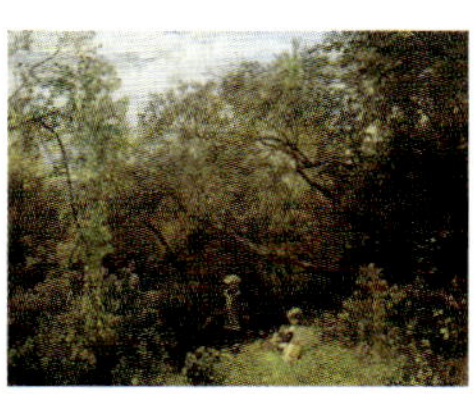

Park Landscape in Plankenberg (Lilac)(Parklandschaft in Plankenberg [Flieder]), 1887
Oil on wood, 49.5 x 66 cm
Sig. and dat. bottom right: Schindler / Plankenberg / 87
Belvedere, Vienna, inv. no. 3815
1892 Rudolf Mosse, Berlin. – 1941 acquired in exchange with private collection, Florence
Fuchs-catalogue raisonné, No. 567

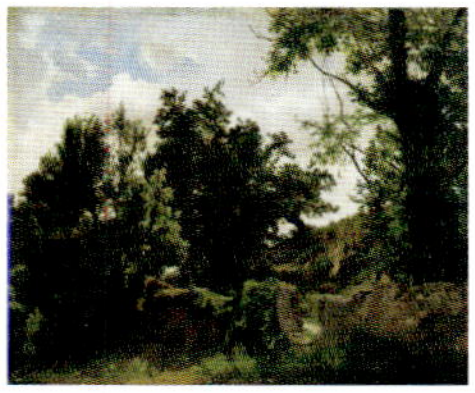

Castle Wall in Plankenberg (Schlossmauer in Plankenberg), 1887
Oil on canvas on cardboard, 34.5 x 42.5 cm
Sig. and dat. bottom right: 26 / 6. 87 / Schindler
Design. on the back: Motiv bei Plankenberg N.Ö. / an der äußeren Schloßmauer
Belvedere, Vienna, inv. no. 4747
1954 acquisition art trade L. T. Neumann, Vienna
Fuchs-catalogue raisonné, No. 608

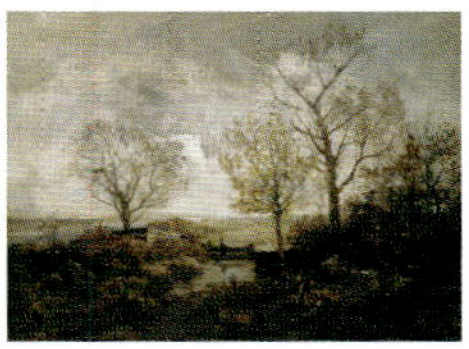

Autumnal Landscape by a River (Herbstlandschaft am Fluss), c. 1887/88
Oil on canvas, 41 x 56 cm
Sig. bottom right: Schindler
Belvedere, Vienna, inv. no. 5087
Otto Weissel Estate, Geneva. – 1956 dedication Maria Weissel, Genf
Fuchs-catalogue raisonné, No. 595

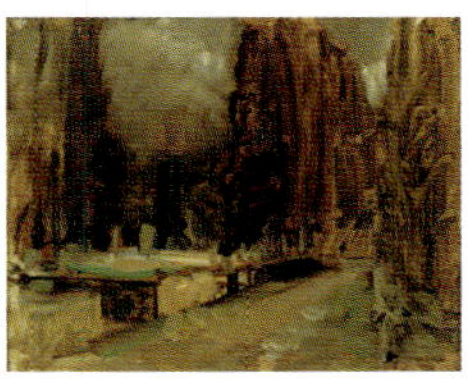

The Cemetery of Gravosa near Ragusa (Study for Pax)
(Der Friedhof von Gravosa bei Ragusa [Studie zu Pax]), 1887/88
Oil on canvas on wood, 26 x 32.5 cm
Design. on the back: Studie zu Pax / J.E. Schindler
Belvedere, Vienna, inv. no. 5568
1942 Carl Moll, Vienna. – Alma Mahler-Werfel. – Neue Galerie, Vienna. – 1963 dedication Theodor Schebesta, Vienna
Fuchs-catalogue raisonné, No. 674

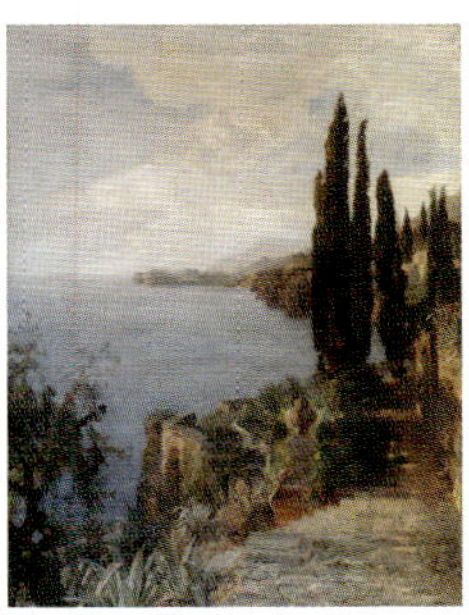

At the Dalmatian Coast near Ragusa
(An der dalmatinischen Küste bei Ragusa), 1888
Oil on canvas, 152 x 120 cm
Sig. and dat. bottom right: Schindler / 88
Belvedere, Vienna, inv. no. 3734
1894 dedication Georg Güterbock, Vienna, to the Imperial Gallery of Paintings. – 1939 acquisition from the Kunsthistorische Museum, Vienna
Fuchs-catalogue raisonné, No. 664

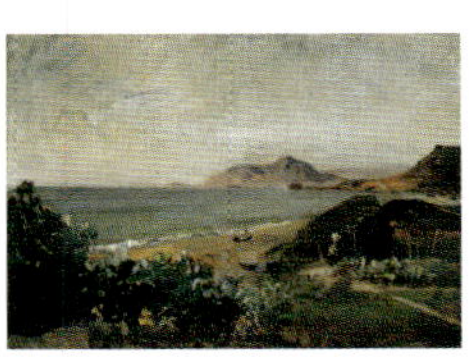

The Ionian Sea near Corfu (Das Ionische Meer bei Korfu), 1888
Oil on canvas, 23 x 33 cm
Design. bottom right: Schindler (estate stamp)
Belvedere, Vienna, inv. no. 4020
1892 Schindler estate. – Anna Moll. – 1945 bequest Carl Moll
Fuchs-catalogue raisonné, No. 669

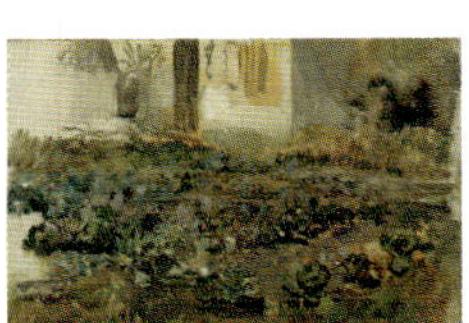

Field of Turnips (Kohlrübenfeld), c. 1888
Oil on canvas, 27 x 38.5 cm
Undesignated
Belvedere, Vienna, inv. no. 5438
1961 acquisition from private collection, Oberwaltersdorf
Fuchs-catalogue raisonné, No. 685

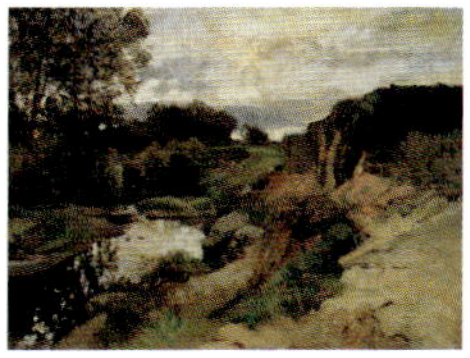

By Tulln Stream near Plankenberg (Am Tullnbach bei Plankenberg), c. 1889/90
Oil on canvas, 39 x 54 cm
Undesignated
Belvedere, Vienna, inv. no. 4018
1892 Schindler estate. – 1945 bequest Carl Moll
Fuchs-catalogue raisonné, No. 720

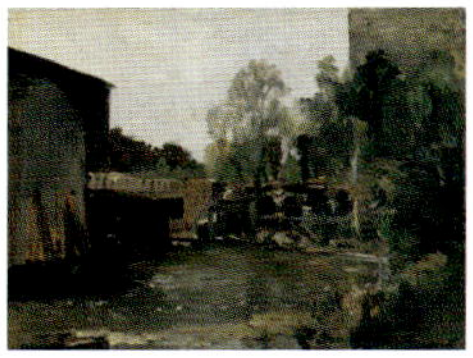

Mill Weir in Plankenberg (Mühlwehr in Plankenberg), c. 1889/91
Oil on canvas, 25 x 34 cm
Design. on the back: Bestätigung, dass ein Bild / Mühle in Plankenberg NÖ /
im Jahre 89 von J.Schindler / gemalt worden ist / Maler Carl Moll
Belvedere, Vienna, inv. no. 2440
1923 acquisition Kunsthandel Artaria & Co., Vienna
Fuchs-catalogue raisonné, No. 749

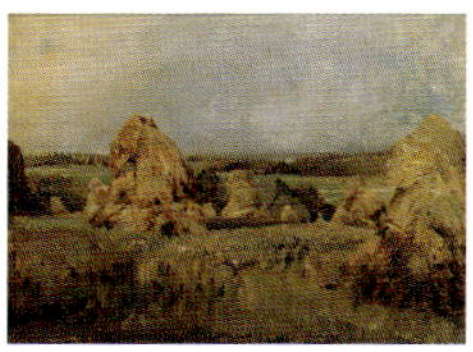

Harvest Month in Plankenberg (Erntemonat in Plankenberg), c. 1890
Oil on wood, 26.5 x 36 cm
Design. bottom left: Schindler (estate stamp)
Belvedere, Vienna, inv. no. 3655
1892 Schindler estate. – 1939 acquisition Carl Moll, Vienna
Fuchs-catalogue raisonné, No. 742

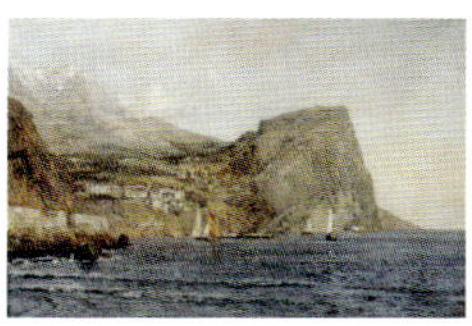

Coast Landscape in Dalmatia (Küstenlandschaft in Dalmatien), 1890
Oil on wood, 71 x 106 cm
Sig. and dat. bottom right: Schindler / 90
Belvedere, Vienna, inv. no. 5971
1973 bequest Ernst Zix, Kaiserslautern
Fuchs-catalogue raisonné, No. 732

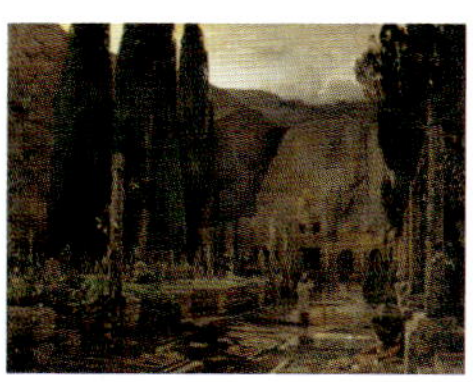

Pax (The Cemetery of Gravosa near Ragusa)
(Pax [Der Friedhof von Gravosa bei Ragusa]), 1891
Oil on canvas, 207 x 271 cm
Sig. and dat. bottom right: SCHINDLER / 1891
Belvedere, Vienna, inv. no. 2548
1892 acquisition estate auction for the Imperial Painting Gallery. –
1921 acquisition from the Kunsthistorische Museum, Vienna
Fuchs-catalogue raisonné, No. 778

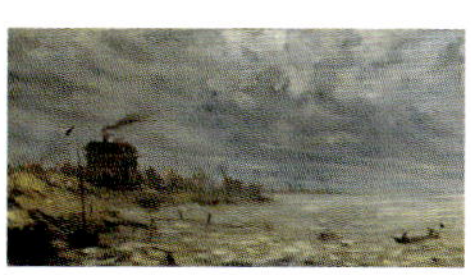

Coast at Sylt (Meeresküste von Sylt), 1892
Oil on canvas on wood, 16.5 x 30.5 cm
Undesignated
Belvedere, Vienna, inv. no. 4796
1955 acquisition Dorotheum, Vienna
Fuchs-catalogue raisonné, No. 786

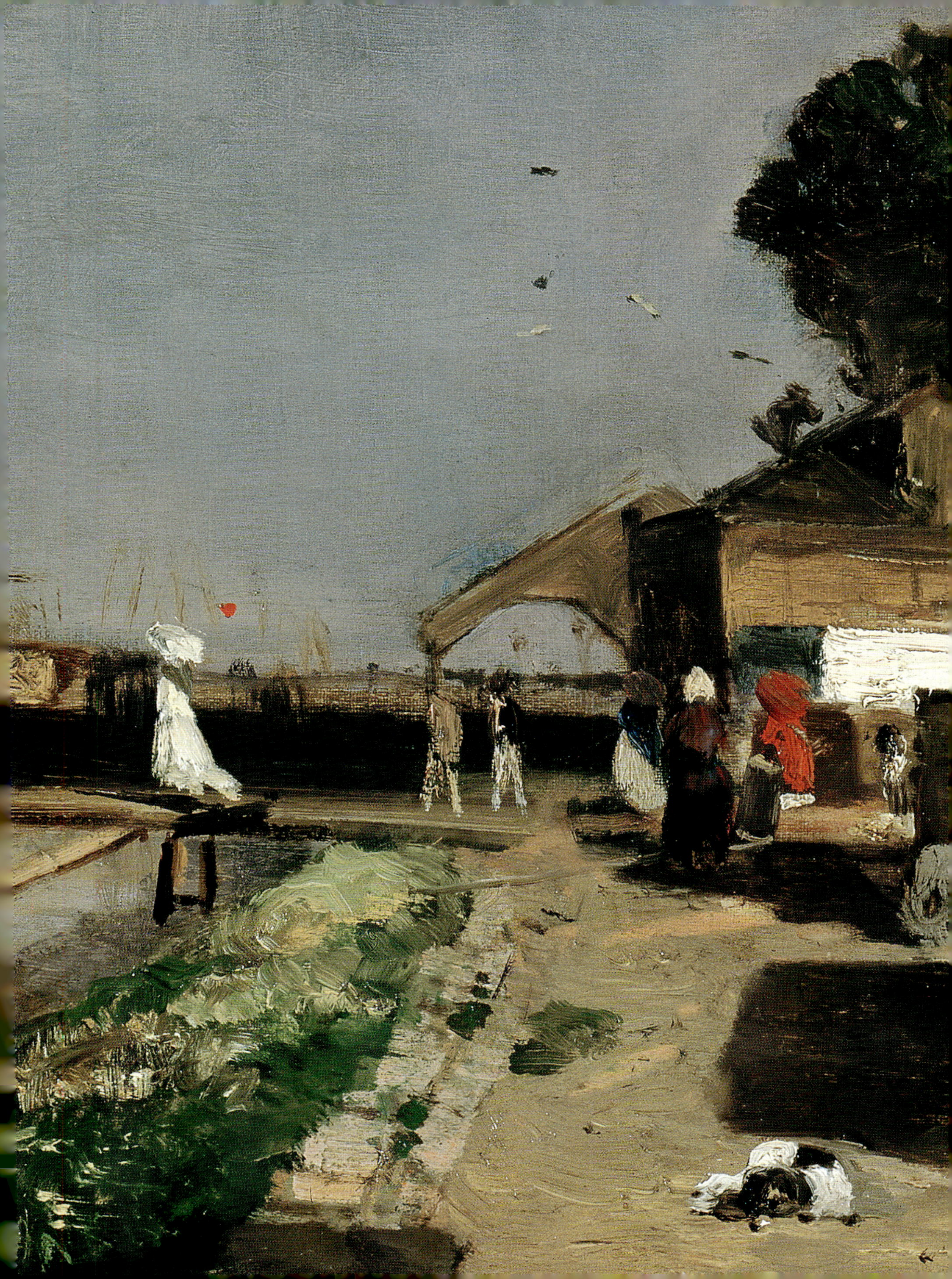

Emil Jakob Schindler – Biography*

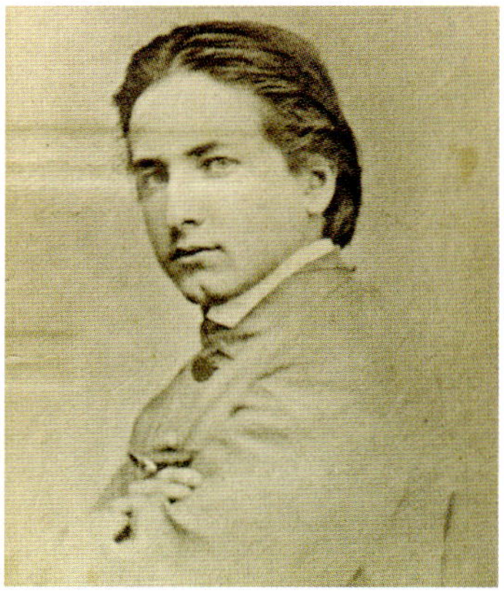

Fig.1.
ANONYMOUS
Emil Jakob Schindler, c. 1862
Van Pelt-Dietrich Library,
University of Pennsylvania

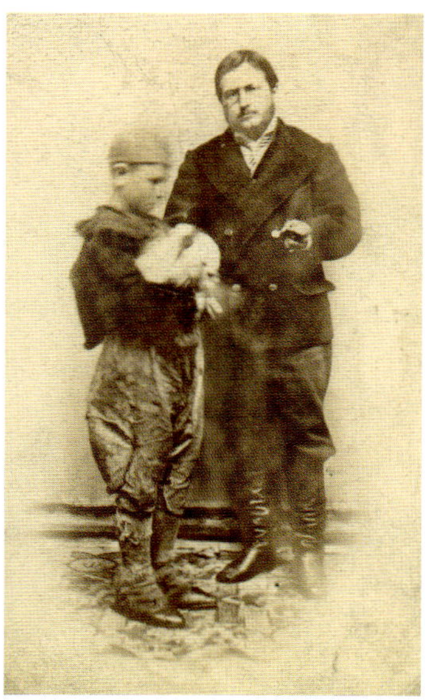

Fig.2.
ANONYMOUS
Emil Jakob Schindler with a Farmboy, c. 1875
Van Pelt-Dietrich Library,
University of Pennsylvania

April 27, 1842 Emil Jakob Schindler is born as the son of a partner in a trading company, Jakob Schindler, and his wife Maria Schindler, née Penz, in Leopoldstadt in Vienna.

1846 Death of his father. Schindler's mother marries the imperial army captain Eduard Nepalleck.

1849 Birth of his stepsister Alexandrine Nepalleck.

1860 Joins Albert Zimmermann's class at the Imperial Academy of Fine Arts in Vienna. At the beginning of his studies Schindler lives in Perchtoldsdorf. His fellow students are Rudolf Ribarz, Robert Russ, Eugen Jettel and László Paál.

1861 Participation in the first study excursion headed by Albert Zimmermann, which takes him among other places to Salzburg.

1863 Stay in the Ramsau.

1865 Schindler paints on Lake Chiemsee. Awarding of the "Füger'sche Prize medal" at the Imperial Academy of Fine Arts in Vienna. Awarding of the Koch-scholarship worth 210 guilders. Study trip to Spital am Pyhrn.

1866 Mid-June to early August: study residency in Golling in the Ramsau. Schindler paints the Mühlental near Prien with the Lake Chiemsee.

1868 Schindler leaves the Academy. Exhibition of the municipal architect Bösch's collection in the Vienna Künstlerhaus (House of Artists) with works by Charles-François Daubigny, Jules Dupré and Théodore Rousseau.

1869 Schindler joins the Wiener Künstlergenossenschaft (Vienna Artists' Association).

1870/71 Stays in the surrounding of Kaisermühlen, in the Prater and near Fischamend.

1872 Stays in Maria Ellend and in Fischamend. Schindler works here with his colleagues Eugen Jettel, Julius Victor Berger, Franz Rumpler, Eduard Charlemont and Tina Blau.
The art trader and auctioneer Georg Plach auctions Friedrich Jakob Gsell's collection.

1873 Study trip to Venice, further stay in Fischamend.

1874 Journey to Italy and Dalmatia. The artist produces wood engravings for the *Wiener Illustrierte Zeitung* (newspaper) with Dalmatian landscapes on which Schindler writes brief comments. Schindler rents the "Pavillon des Amateurs" (amateur pavilion) of the Vienna World Exhibition. Death of his stepfather. During this period Marie Parmentier and Luise Begas-Parmentier take lessons from Schindler.

1875 Schindler shares a studio with Tina Blau and travels with her to Holland. In the 1870s, he has a close relationship with Hans Makart, who allows Schindler to work in his small studio in Gußhausstraße.

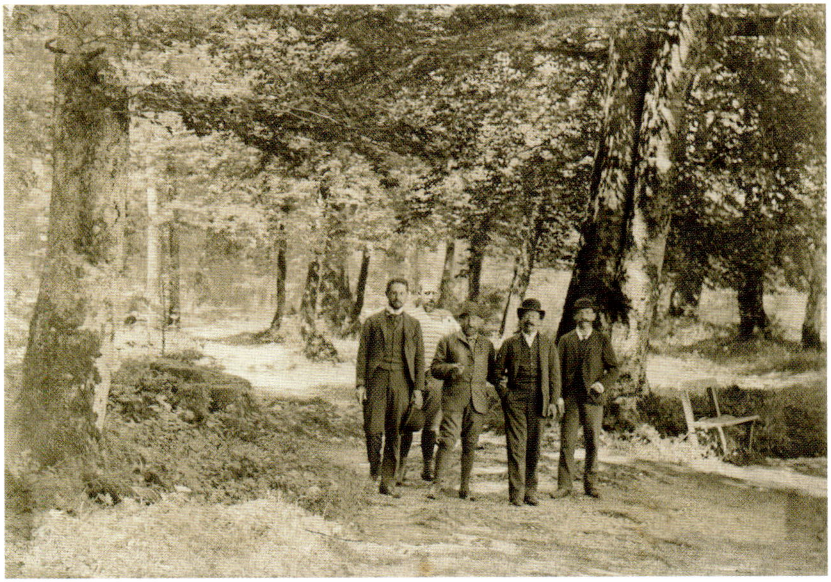

Fig.3.
ANONYMOUS
Carl Moll, Emil Jakob Schindler and Others in Plankenberg Park, undated
Van Pelt-Dietrich Library,
University of Pennsylvania

1878 "Karl-Ludwig-Medal" for the painting *Moonrise in the Prater Meadows.* Schindler gets to know the Hamburg singer Anna Bergen, whom he marries in 1879. He hands over his Prater studio to Tina Blau.
The young couple move from Vienna to Haslau.
Pictures painted in Weißenkirchen.

1879 August: birth of daughter Alma.

1880 May: stay in Paris.
December: stay in Venice.

1881 April: award of the "Reichel-Prize".
August to September: stay on the island of Borkum.
August: birth of daughter Margarete.
Schindler takes on Carl Moll, Maria Egner and Olga Wisinger-Florian as students. In spring Schindler often travels with them to southern Moravia, to Stillfried, Dürnkrut and Lundenburg-Themenau (Břeclav-Poštorná), during the summer and autumn months he stays with them in Goisern.

1882 April to May: study residency in Lundenburg (Břeclav) and Eisgrub (Lednice) with Carl Moll and Olga Wisinger-Florian.
Summer and autumn: stay in Goisern.

1883 May to June: stay in Lundenburg (Břeclav).
July to October: stay in Goisern.

1884 Study trip to Lundenburg (Břeclav).
Summer and autumn: stay in Goisern.
Schindler rents Plankenberg Castle.

1884/85 Stay in Venice.

1885 Schindler presents a small retrospective with 14 works at the annual exhibition in the Vienna Künstlerhaus.
He is invited to cooperate on the Kronprinzenwerk [i.e. encyclopedia of the Austro-Hungarian Empire].
Plankenberg Castle becomes his permanent residence.

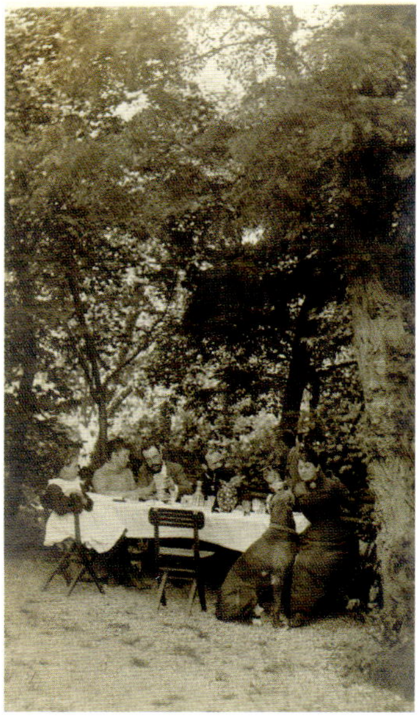

Fig.4.
ANONYMOUS
Emil Jakob Schindler with Anna Schindler, Carl Moll and Others in the Garden of Plankenberg, c. 1885/90
Van Pelt-Dietrich Library,
University of Pennsylvania

1887 Study trip to Dalmatia and Istria with his whole family accompanied by Carl Moll. Here, the traveling company is visited by among others Nikolaus Dumba. Winter stay in Ragusa (Dubrovnik) and Corfu (Kérkyra).

1888 April: return to Vienna.
Summer stay in Vienna.
Schindler becomes honorary member of the Imperial Academy of Fine Arts in Vienna.

1889 Friendship and exchange of letters with Archduke Johann Nepomuk Salvator (Johann Orth).
Journey to Berlin accompanied by Carl Moll. Adolf Menzel welcomes Schindler and Moll as friends.
Participation in the design of the Naturhistorische Museum (Museum of Natural History) in Vienna with four decorative paintings.

1890 Journey to Fiume (Rijeka).

1891 Gold Medal for the painting *Pax* on the International Art Exhibition in Berlin.

1892 Schindler exhibits 16 works on the 21st annual exhibition in the Vienna Künstlerhaus.
Gold Medal for the painting *Pax* at the annual exhibition in Munich.
Schindler dies on August 9 during a vacation in Westerland on the island of Sylt.

* Compiled on the basis of Elisabeth Kamenicek's dissertation.

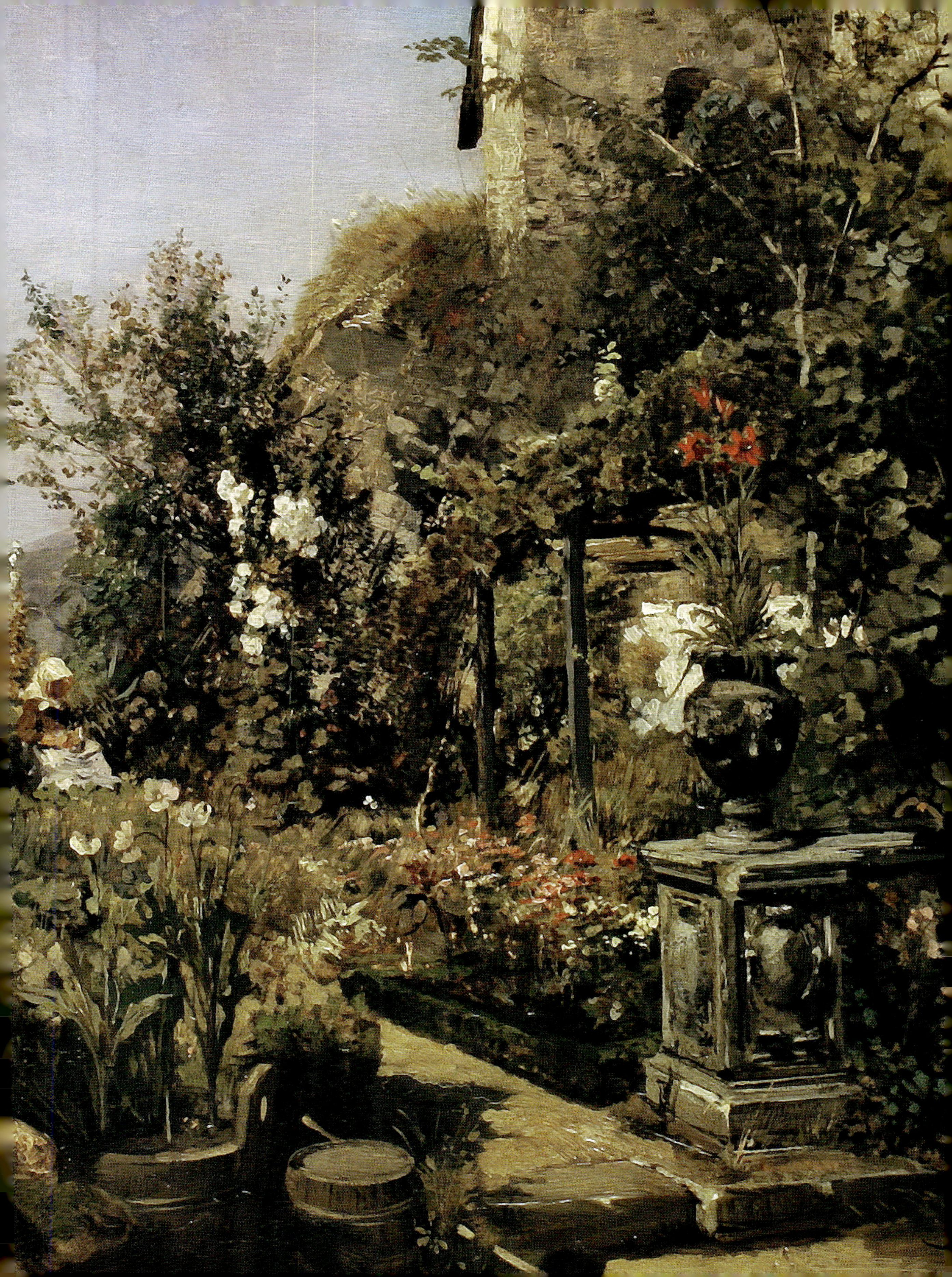

Authors

Stephanie Auer

The art historian Stephanie Auer has been a curatorial assistant at the Belvedere since 2007. She wrote her diploma thesis on Federico García Lorca's work as visual artist. As well as multi-talented artists, the main focus of her research covers Austrian and middle-European painting of the second half of the 19th and 20th century.

Markus Fellinger

Markus Fellinger has worked for the Belvedere since December 2010. Initially as assistant he participated in the compilation of catalogues raisonnés by Josef Danhauser and Hans Makart in the Research Center. Since August 2011 he has been a curatorial assistant at the Belvedere for art around the turn of the 20th century.

Agnes Husslein-Arco

Agnes Husslein-Arco, director of the Belvedere in Vienna since 2007, is an art historian and curator of numerous exhibitions on classical, modern and contemporary art. She is also an author and editor of academic publications. She opened the Vienna office of Sotheby's in 1981 and directed its operations through 2000. In 1988 she additionally assumed directorship of the company's branches in Budapest and Prague. In the 1990s, Husslein-Arco was director of European art at the Solomon R. Guggenheim Museum in New York. From 2001 to 2003 she directed the Rupertinum in Salzburg and from 2003 to 2005 was founding director of the Museum der Moderne Salzburg. From 2002 to 2004 she organized the establishment of the Museum Moderner Kunst Kärnten in Klagenfurt at Lake Wörthersee.

Elisabeth Edith Kamenicek
Elisabeth Edith Kamenicek studied art history, history and philosophy at the Paris-Lodron University of Salzburg. She wrote her doctoral thesis on Emil Jakob Schindler and is a curator with national and international exhibition projects. Her achievements include numerous research projects on art mediation in Austria and on the life, work and practice of Ludwig Wittgenstein. She is currently working on a research project on the Wittgenstein-Stonborough estate in the Austrian National Library in Vienna. An accompanying publication is in preparation.

Alexander Klee
Since 2010 the art historian Alexander Klee has been the Belvedere's curator for the second half of the 19th century and the beginning of the 20th century. He is a founding member of the Adolf Hölzel-Foundation in Stuttgart and compiles Adolf Hölzel's catalogue raisonné. With numerous publications on Hölzel, Georg Karl Pfahler and artists of the Classical Modernism period, his research emphasis is in the 19th and 20th century.

Andrea Winklbauer
The art historian Andrea Winklbauer is curator for visual art in the Jewish Museum Vienna. She has curated and worked among other things on exhibitions for the Jewish Museum Vienna, Kunstforum Wien, Kunsthaus Mürzzuschlag, Forum Frohner and the Kunsthalle Krems. Winklbauer is an author of texts for the *Neue Zürcher Zeitung*, *Eikon*, *Springerin*, *Dérive* and for numerous publications on art and cultural history.

Imprint

This catalogue is published on the occasion of the exhibition
Emil Jakob Schindler
Poetic Realism
from September 27, 2012 to January 13, 2013 in the Belvedere, Vienna.

Director: Agnes Husslein-Arco
Curator: Alexander Klee
Curatorial assistant: Markus Fellinger

Österreichische Galerie Belvedere
Prinz Eugen Straße 27
1030 Vienna

Publication
Editors: Agnes Husslein-Arco, Alexander Klee
Publication management: Eva Lahnsteiner
Image editor: Melanie Tiller
Translator: Dörte Eliass
English copy-editor: David Westacott
Graphic design and setting: Peter Baldinger
Lithography: Pixelstorm, Vienna
Printed and bound: Printer Trento Srl.

Printed in Italy

Published by:
Hirmer Verlag GmbH
Nymphenburger Straße 84
80636 Munich

Bibliographic information published by the Deutsche Nationalbibliothek
The Deutsche Nationalbibliothek lists this publication in the Deutsche Nationalbibliografie; detailed bibliographic data are available in the Internet at http://www.dnb.de.

ISBN: 978-3-7774-2032-5

www.hirmerverlag.de

Picture Credits:

© Albertina, Vienna: pp. 44, 45 – © Belvedere, Vienna: p. 119 – © bpk / Bayerische Staatsgemäldesammlungen: p. 65 – © Dorotheum Vienna, auction catalog April 1, 2009: p. 24; auction catalog June 2, 2010: pp. 38, 39; auction catalog April 12, 2011: p. 43 – © Kunsthandel Giese & Schweiger, Vienna: p. 100 – © Kunsthalle zu Kiel, photo: Martin Frommhagen: p. 11 – © Niederösterreichisches Landesmuseum, photo: Peter Böttcher: p. 17; photo: Christoph Fuchs: pp. 26, 74, 76, 77, 84; photo: Martin Vavra: p. 85 – © Museum of Fine Arts Budapest, 2012: p. 18 – © National Gallery in Prague 2012: p. 28 – © Oberösterreichische Landesmuseen: p. 123 – © ÖNB /Herberth: p. 50 – © ÖNB: pp. 29, 30, 31, 51, 53, 55, 57, 63, 64 – © Rheinisches Bildarchiv Köln, rba_d018866: p. 29 (fig. 5) – © StadtMuseum, Bonn www.bonn.de/stadtmuseum: p. 15 – © photo: Christian Schindler (Pixelstorm): pp. 79, 99, 107 – © photo: Galerie Martin Suppan, Vienna: pp. 66, 71 – © The Paintings Gallery of the Academy of Fine Arts Vienna: p. 19 – © Van Pelt-Dietrich Library, University of Pennsylvania: pp. 120, 121, 122 – © Wien Museum: pp. 27, 63, 93, 98 – © Wienbibliothek im Rathaus: pp. 7, 30, 31.

Cover picture: Emil Jakob Schindler, *The Steamer Station on the Danube opposite Kaisermühlen* (Die Dampfschiffstation an der Donau gegenüber Kaisermühlen) (detail), c. 1871/1872, Belvedere, Vienna
Front endpapers: Emil Jakob Schindler, *The Water Mills on the Danube, preliminary drawing for the Kronprinzenwerk* (Die Schiffsmühlen am Donaustrom, Vorzeichnung zum Kronprinzenwerk), before 1886, ÖNB, Vienna, Picture Archive and Graphic Collection
Rear endpapers: Ernst Krottendorfer, *Water Mills in Vienna* (Schiffsmühlen in Wien), c. 1920, ÖNB, Vienna, Picture Archive

The editor would like to express her sincere gratitude to Antal P. de Bekessy, whose generous assistance in the context of the Friends of the Belvedere has made this English version of the book possible.

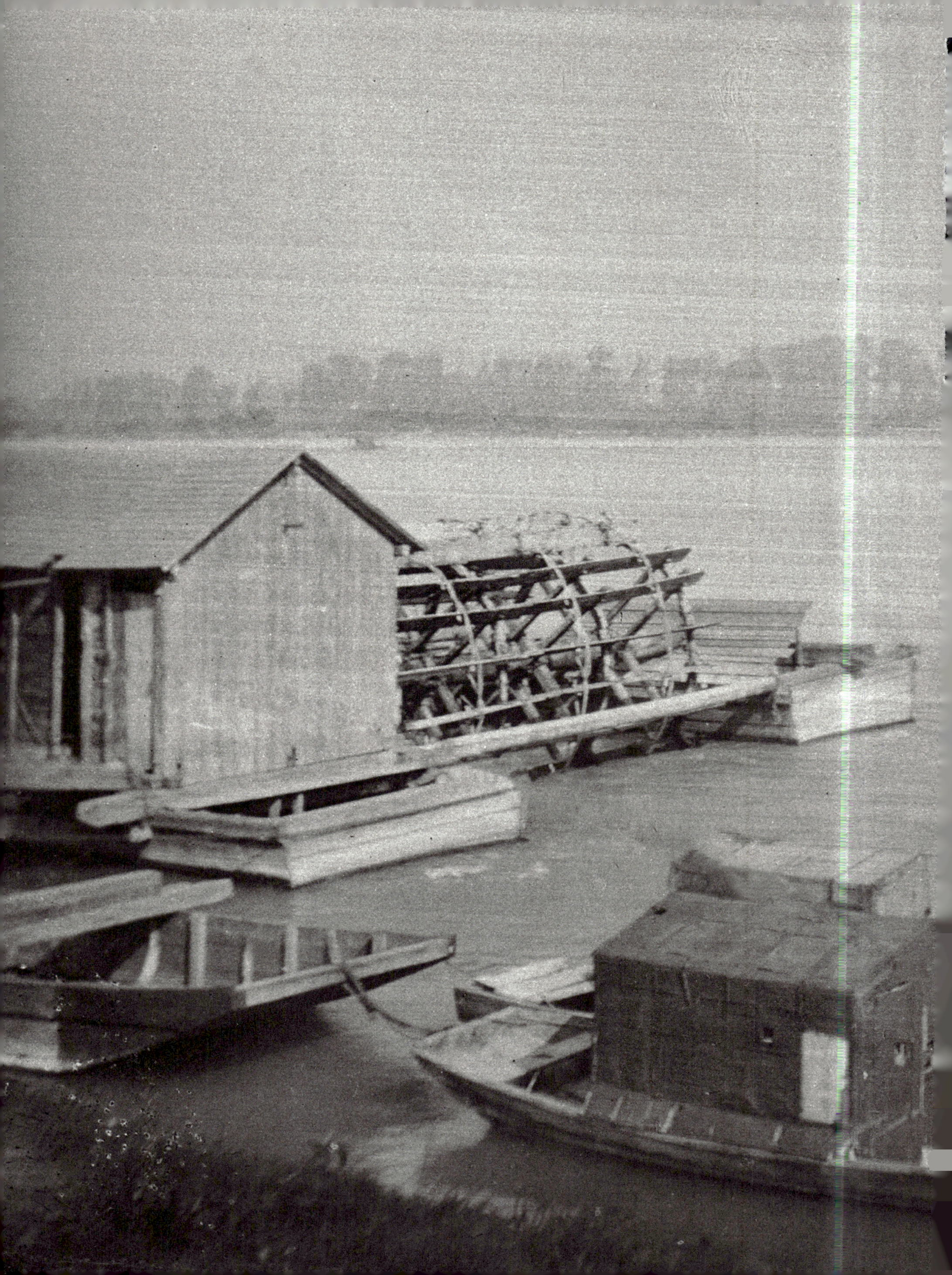